D1104649

THE INDUSTRIAL ARCHAEOLOGY OF
THE ISLE OF MAN

THE INDUSTRIAL ARCHAEOLOGY
OF THE BRITISH ISLES
Series Editor: E. R. R. GREEN

Derbyshire, by Frank Nixon
The East Midlands, by David M. Smith
Galloway (South-west Scotland), by Ian Donnachie
Hertfordshire, by W. Branch Johnson
The Isle of Man, by L. S. Garrad, T. A. Bawden, J. K. Qualtrough, W. J. Scatchard
The Lake Counties, by J. D. Marshall and M. Davies-Shiel
Lancashire, by Owen Ashmore
The Peak District, by Helen Harris
Scotland, by John Butt
Southern England (second edition, revised), by Kenneth Hudson

ASSOCIATED VOLUMES

The Bristol Region, by R. A. Buchanan and Neil Cossons
Dartmoor, by Helen Harris
Gloucestershire Woollen Mills, by Jennifer Tann
Stone Blocks and Iron Rails, by Bertram Baxter
The Tamar Valley (second impression, revised), by Frank Booker
Techniques of Industrial Archaeology, by J. P. M. Pannell

OTHER INDUSTRIAL HISTORY

The British Iron and Steel Industry, by W. K. V. Gale
The Early Factory Masters, by Stanley D. Chapman
The Engineering Industry of the North of Ireland, by W. E. Coe
The History of Water Power in Ulster, by H. D. Gribbon

All these books are in uniform format

The Industrial Archaeology of
THE ISLE OF MAN

L. S. GARRAD, BA, PhD, AMA, FRGS
with T. A. BAWDEN
J. K. QUALTROUGH, FSA Scot
and W. J. SCATCHARD

DAVID & CHARLES : NEWTON ABBOT

ISBN 7153 5440 X

Set in Imprint, 11pt 2pt leaded
and printed in Great Britain by
Latimer Trend & Company Limited Plymouth
for David & Charles (Publishers) Limited
South Devon House Newton Abbot Devon

Contents

6   *Contents*

List of Illustrations

PLATES

PAGE

Illustrations by courtesy of The Manx Museum and The National Trust unless otherwise stated

IN TEXT

SECTION ONE

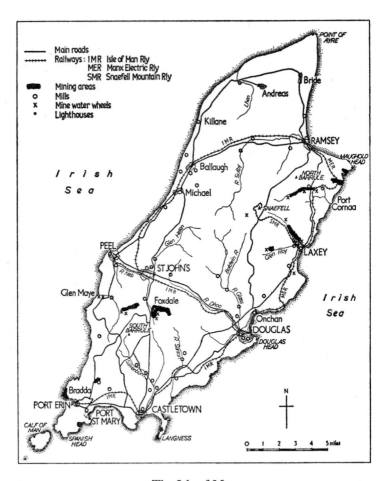

The Isle of Man

CHAPTER ONE

The Isle of Man

THE Isle of Man, standing in the Irish Sea almost midway between England, Scotland, Wales and Ireland, is some 35 miles long by 10 broad. Its central hills run north-east/south-west from Maughold Head to the Calf of Man, the islet situated off the southern tip of the main island. Most of the rocks belong to the heavily mineralised Manx slate series, which have been much affected by tectonic movement. There are limestone exposures round Castletown, some red sandstone at Peel and small granitic areas at the Dhoon, Foxdale and Oatlands, Santon. The northern plain, fringed by a raised beach covered in sand and known as the Ayres, is composed entirely of glacial deposits and is consequently deficient in building stone.

It would seem likely that the Cumberland coalfields extend beneath Man but attempts to locate coal have been fruitless. The Island—the capital 'I' is the common Manx usage and will be used throughout for the sake of clarity—was almost completely devoid of woodland at the beginning of the historic period and, consequently, the main local fuel was peat. This was one reason for the development of water power and had a considerable adverse effect on the development of the Manx mines, which were forced to export their ores for processing. Coal, mainly from the Whitehaven district, was imported into Man from a comparatively early date.

Some 60 per cent of Man lies more than 250ft above sea level, though only Snaefell is technically a mountain, by 34ft. However, the way in which the hills rise out of the sea makes them appear higher. The Isle of Man has superb coastal scenery, with cliffs along much of its length—even those cut in the glacial deposits attaining a height of some 200ft near Cranstal. There are some sheltered bays but most required considerable harbour works to make them adequate refuges for large craft. The few main rivers and many small streams show a great and rapid variation in flow between drought and spate. The more important include the Sulby (which reaches the sea at Ramsey), the Neb (which drains half the central valley towards Peel), the Dhoo and the Glass (which join near Douglas), and the Silverburn (on which is situated the ancient capital, Castletown). The climate is western: wet, often with strong westerly winds, high humidity and an annual temperature range without extremes of heat or cold. Because of the abrupt topography the rainfall range within the Island exceeds 30in. However, most of the streams rise in the wetter areas and this, together with the steepness of their courses, made it possible to use even the smallest as a source of water power. Between Peel and Douglas the hills are cut by a wide boggy valley and there are other areas of waterlogged fen, notably the Curraghs in Ballaugh parish. This combination of waterlogged valleys and rugged hills meant that it was usually easier to travel by sea; so the main settlements are on the coast, usually where an area of raised beach at the head of a more or less sheltered bay provided a good site.

The earliest evidence of human habitation in Man dates only from the Mesolithic Period. After this successive waves of settlers made the Island their home. Although the Romans in Britain were aware of the existence of the Island (they apparently called it Mona, a name also used for Anglesey) and may indeed have visited it, since their fleet used Chester, they did not apparently invade or settle it. The inhabitants at that time were Celts, who were soon converted to Christianity by missionaries from the Celtic Church. The Norsemen are first recorded as having sailed southward into the Irish Sea in the year 798 and during the ensuing century became a constant menace to the safety of the people of the Isle of Man. They found many suitable landing places and soon the good agricultural land lured them to settle. The first 200 years of increasing Norse dominance in Man are known mainly from archaeological evidence but after 1079 historical records, though scanty, provide an outline of political events.

It would appear from the *Chronicon Manninae* that refugees from the Norse army defeated at the battle of Stamford Bridge in 1066 came to the Isle of Man under the leadership of Godred Crovan. His antecedents and precise claims are obscure but he successfully made himself King of Mann and the Isles—most of the western isles of Scotland, but to the Norsemen the *Sudrejr*, or Southern Isles, (hence the title, Bishop of *Sodor* and Man). Having established his kingdom he seems to have formalised the existing civil divisions and lawgiving system of the Island. Like Godred Crovan's their origins are uncertain. However, it is apparent that Tynwald, the oldest parliament in the world with an unbroken tradition and the most remarkable instance of the tenacity with which Manxmen have striven to retain the features of their national life, is essentially a Norse institution. For some 800 years there have been twenty-four *Keys*, the elected members of the Manx Parliament.

The Kings of Man soon lost control of the western isles and many centuries have elapsed since their eight Keysmen steered their galleys south each summer to attend the King's court at Tynwald. However, their places were kept open so the Keys still number twenty-four. The annual parliamentary assembly was also a feature of life in other areas where the Vikings settled, such as Iceland. The meeting was held on midsummer day in the open air at the *Thing-vollr*, or assembly field. From the accounts in the sagas it is clear that such assemblies dispensed justice as well as proclaiming law, and that they were preceded by a religious ceremony which included the marking out of the assembly ground within which a truce was declared. The modern Tynwald (the name derives from *Thing-vollr*) is still preceded by a service in the adjacent church—which probably replaced an earlier sacred site—and the court is still 'fenced' in ancient form.

The main electoral divisions are called *Sheadings* and probably originated from the units which provided ships for insular defence. Some adjustments have been made in respect of the towns but most of the original names are still used. Each sheading is divided into parishes; again there have been slight boundary changes but most of the ancient names survive. Throughout this book this administrative parish will be used to indicate the location of places which, because of duplication of names, might otherwise be unclear—eg Ballagawne, *Rushen*.

The Division of Sheadings into Parishes

Sheading of:	*Parishes*	
AYRE	Bride, Andreas and Lezayre	
MICHAEL	Jurby, Ballaugh and Michael	NORTHSIDE
GARFF	Maughold and Lonan	
GLENFABA	German, Patrick and Marown	
MIDDLE	Braddan, Onchan[1] and Santan[2]	SOUTHSIDE
RUSHEN	Rushen, Arbory and Malew	

[1] Conchan was the older spelling.
[2] Santon is gaining currency.

For a century and a half after the eclipse of the Norse kingdom control of the Island passed to and fro between the rulers of Scotland and England and the lords they nominated. England finally gained possession but the Island retained its independence in that it was a lordship of the crown and never a part of what became the United Kingdom. Thus, Queen Elizabeth's title is properly 'Lord of Mann'. In 1405 the Island and its regalities were granted by Henry IV to Sir John Stanley. For the next 360 years his family, who became Earls of Derby, and their successors in the female line, the Dukes of Atholl, held the Island—first as kings and later as lords.

During the Stanley régime Manx trade was regulated in a somewhat primitive manner, though perhaps one suited to so small an island. No goods could be imported or exported without the Lord's permission. Customs duties were levied on all imports and exports by Tynwald until 1737, when those on exports were suspended. Originally the master of an incoming ship had to attend in person before the Governor to indicate the nature of his cargo and supply the latest news. The Receivers of Castle Rushen and Peel Castle, the chief fortresses, had first choice of goods. After their needs were met the remainder of the cargo was disposed of by the 'four merchants' whose duty it was to bargain on behalf of the lord and people of

Man. Because of the near subsistence economy exports were controlled to such an extent that between 1660 and 1700 the duties on both exports and imports combined produced less than £100 annually.

Manxmen, among their other characteristics, have a marked aptitude for seafaring, but their trading was hampered by restrictions imposed by the governments of neighbouring countries. Normal trade with England was practically impossible because the Navigation Acts prohibited imports except in British bottoms and after 1689 the English tariff was so high that trading was unprofitable. It is, therefore, not surprising that towards the end of the seventeenth century smuggling became tempting. Wines and spirits, tea, tobacco and other goods liable to heavy British duty could be bought abroad—for example, George Moore of Ballamoar, Patrick, purchased tea in Gothenburg and Rotterdam, as well as directly from Cawnpore—with the added advantage that such purchases were outside the control of the English monopolies, and landed in Man on payment of only a small duty. They could then be freely re-exported from Man but landed secretly to defraud the British customs.

The British government had no desire to be continually deprived of one of its main sources of revenue, and so it threatened to raise Manx duties to match those of Britain. It even sent undercover agents to watch over its interests in Man. The British Parliament also went so far as to pass an Act prohibiting the import of foreign goods into Man for re-export to Britain. The validity of this Act was extremely doubtful but the two sides reached an agreement that a similar Act would be passed in Man in return for the British government's withdrawing duties on Manx-produced goods. As this agreement was not kept, Tynwald did not feel bound to honour its part. The situation was resolved in favour of the British government when the Duke of Atholl sold the regalities of the Isle of Man back to the Crown—the *Revestment Act* of 1765.

The smuggling period had produced considerable local prosperity but the benefits of the Revestment to the Island were initially conspicuous by their absence. Man came directly under the Crown, usually represented by someone who wrote letters, reminiscent of those of Pliny the Younger to his emperor, over every trivial decision. Matters were not improved by the appointment of the fourth Duke of Atholl as Governor in 1793, since his nepotism led to friction which ended only with his death in 1830. Subsequently, only a lieutenant-governor has been appointed to represent the Crown. The economy slowly recovered from the Revestment and there was an outburst of industrial development based on water power. The improved conditions at the beginning of the nineteenth century resulted in a very low cost of living.

The modern constitutional relationship between the Isle of Man and the United Kingdom may be said to date from 1866. In that year two important Acts were passed, one in the British parliament and the other by the Manx legislature. The Isle of Man Customs, Harbours and Public Purposes Act separated the Manx revenue from that of the United Kingdom and gave Tynwald a limited measure of control over insular expenditure. These provisions made finance available for the first time in many years for carrying out public works and, in particular, much-needed harbour improvements. The Act passed by the Manx government was the much-sought-after House of Keys Election Act, which transformed it from a self-elected body into one elected by popular franchise. Since 1866 the constitutional relationship has evolved as a progressive handing over to Tynwald of control of insular revenues and the more general aspects of executive government. Recently, the Royal Commission on the Constitution has taken evidence in the Isle of Man and a joint working party on the constitutional relations was set up in 1967.

The Manx legislature at present consists of the lieutenant-governor appointed by the Crown, the Legislative Council and the House of Keys, the whole assembly when sitting together being known as the Tynwald Court. The Legislative Council consists of the Lord Bishop of Sodor and Man, His Honour the First Deemster and Clerk of the Rolls (one of the Island's High Court judges), Her

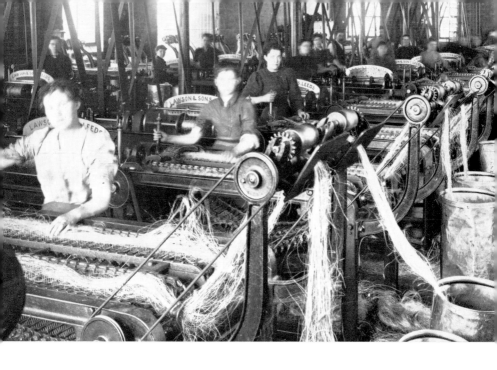

Page 17　(above) *The interior of Quiggin's ropeworks, Douglas, c 1900;* (below) *an export order for Quiggins, about 1910*

Page 18 (above) *The opening of the 'Lady Isabella', 1854. The title of the original print was:*
'The Opening of the Great Water Wheel at the Mines Laxey Glen, Isle of Man, Sept. 1854
Captain R. Rowe, Manager'; (below) the washing floors of the Great Laxey Mining Company Ltd

Majesty's Attorney-General (all being Crown appointments) and seven persons elected by the House of Keys. The House of Keys has retained its original composition of twenty-four members elected for a term of five years by universal popular suffrage. An Act of Tynwald does not become law (though it may come into effect) until it has been promulgated at the unique ceremony held each year on 5 July at Tynwald Hill. Here a short summary of each of the new laws for the year is read aloud to the assembled people, in Manx and English. Despite all efforts at erosion Tynwald has managed to retain a considerable degree of independence—the first legal commercial radio station in the British Isles, Manx Radio, was established in the Island.

The presence of immigrants attracted by the low cost of living of the early nineteenth century augmented the growth of a middle class whose presence encouraged the development of new amenities and services. Although the lack of coal made industries based on steam power uneconomic, the development of the mines kept the economy healthy until the end of the century. This was helped by the growth of the tourist trade, which continued to expand until 1914. Between the wars there was considerable depression, since even the tourist trade was adversely affected by the recession in British industry. But the situation has now greatly improved. The Manx government's low taxation policy (under which there is no death duty, surtax, capital gains tax or selective employment tax, and income tax is low and mortgages are relatively cheap) has attracted many new residents as well as demonstrating the Island's independence. Industry is becoming more diversified, with exports ranging from tweed to ejector seats and rustic furniture to shaving brushes. Local needs are also being met locally and this light industry is providing more skilled jobs. The numbers employed directly in the fishery are low but shell-fish are now going to European and American as well as English markets. The result is that the Manx today enjoy a standard of living comparable with the affluent and industrialised countries of the world, in an extremely pleasant setting, without any loss of the

B

benefits of the welfare state enjoyed by people in the United Kingdom.

The Deemster's Oath

By this book and by the Holy contents thereof and by the wonderful works that God hath miraculously wrought in Heaven above and in the Earth beneath in Six days and Seven nights:

I do swear that I will without respect of favour or friendship, love or gain, consanguinity or affinity, envy or malice, Execute the Laws of this Isle Justly, betwixt Our Sovereign Lady the Queen and Her Subjects within this Isle, and betwixt party and party as indifferently as the Herring backbone doth lie in the midst of the fish

So Help me God
and by the Contents of this Book

CHAPTER TWO

The Sea

SHIPS AND SHIPBUILDING

SINCE Man is an island, shipbuilding must have been of importance from the earliest times. The earliest vessels likely to have been Manx-built of which any trace remains are those buried with their Viking owners. The first ship burial to be excavated in the British Isles was that at Knoc y Doonee. Like the boat from Balladoole this was probably about 9m long and 3m wide, clinker-built, with about five strakes on each side, but only the iron clench nails survived. Although a shortage of good locally grown timber was already making itself felt it is likely that ships were built in Man throughout the Norse period and later, but documentary evidence does not appear before the seventeenth century. One Manx-built vessel which proved as durable as the accounts of her building is the *Peggy* of Castletown. Built for George Quayle in 1789 she is still preserved in her contemporary boathouse at the Nautical Museum, Castletown.

Before the nineteenth century it was the Manx custom to build quite sizeable boats wherever convenient even if this was inland and required a complicated overland journey for the launch. Shipbuilding, therefore, received a considerable stimulus when the Bath Yard was re-established in Douglas in 1826. Six years later another yard opened in Ramsey, followed by a third, in Peel, in 1833. Not all the yards were well sited: at Peel, Watson's had to launch under the bridge at the head of the harbour and Corris's to manoeuvre boats down a main street. The Bath Yard marked its first year by launching the *Columbine* of 200 tons, the first vessel of this size to be built in Man. The new yards flourished because they had the considerable advantage that duty on imported timber was lower than in the United Kingdom, and their success was such as to cause the British government to raise the duty eventually. This action was prevented initially by very strong Manx protest, was again considered in 1845 and finally enforced in 1866.

On 17 April 1835 the *Orleana* of 650 tons was launched from the Bath Yard. Four years later the *Manks Advertiser* reported:

> 26 Feb 1839
> We observe that accounts have been received at Liverpool of the progress of the Orleana, the first of the line of packet-ships which has lately been established between Liverpool and South Australia. On the 12th of October, eight days after leaving port, she passed close to the Island of Madeira, in order to give the passengers a view of that beautiful spot. The captain states that he has a very agreeable party in the cabin, who are highly pleased with the progress of the vessel; while the weather has been so fine that they had not yet had a reef in their topsails. The Orleana was built in the Bath Ship Building Yard in this town, under the supervision of Mr Winram, and we understand several emigrants from this island are on board of her. . . .

The yard continued to flourish, one of its most notable vessels being the *King Orry*, launched in 1841 and built for the Isle of Man Steam Packet Company. The builder's half-model is preserved in the Manx Museum. When the brig *Handley*, of 250 tons, was launched in 1831 the yard was said to employ upwards of eighty men permanently, an indication of its continuing prosperity. However, shipbuilding economics finally forced its closure and the site has been obliterated.

There were several other Douglas yards. These included one near the site of Quiggin's Lake works, where Robert Oates launched vessels such as 'the new lifeboat built locally', which went to the rescue of the crew of the sloop *Eclipse* of Glasgow in 1830. John Moore & Company had a small yard adjoining the Howe brewery (later the Preserved Potato works, see map, p. 151) and Williamson's built vessels on the Tongue, where they had to be launched broadside. In 1882 the Douglas boatbuilders were listed in the *Directory* as William Curphey of 20 Bridge Road, Cain & Corlett of 47 Atholl Street and Qualtrough & Company of Castletown Road.

The last firm had a distinguished career. Among other vessels of note it built seven for the Australia run at the time of the gold rush. These included the *Yarra-Yarra*, whose tiller, carved with an elegant ropework pattern, is displayed in the Nautical Museum, the *Emu* and the *Gold Seeker*. William Qualtrough sailed the last out himself—the journey taking six months—and she was employed in the coasting trade in Australia. Her hull was used as a houseboat in the Bristol channel until about 1965 and her figurehead, depicting a moustached and smocked prospector, is now preserved in the Manx Museum, Douglas. However, by 1900:

> Owing to the gradual falling off in the fishing and coasting trade of Douglas, boat building has lately much decreased in the port. The only boat-builder of the place happens to be a descendant and successor of the oldest firm in Douglas—that of Qualtrough and Company, on Douglas Bridge. It may be within the remembrance of some old natives of Douglas that the place on which the boat-yard stands was formerly an apple orchard. It was at this place that almost the whole of the sailing, fishing and rowing boats of Douglas were built. Nickeys and nobbies are still turned out to order, but the bulk of the output seems to be small sailing craft and row boats, with a large admixture of repairs to all kinds of vessels, yachts and fishing vessels.

The decline of the fishing fleet continued—larger vessels already required more sophisticated yards—and the building of traditional wooden craft ceased.

During the prosperous period the amount of work was considerable and it was done quickly. In 1846 four smacks and a lugger were building in Port St Mary in April and a schooner, two luggers and two smacks in Peel in May. A nickie could be built in twenty-eight days. To supply the wood for this building boom fast vessels, such as the *Nora*, made the round trip to Arendal in Norway in three to four weeks. Manx-built vessels traded all over the world, as surviving accounts show. Moreover, they gained such a reputation for swiftness that in the mid-nineteenth century many were chartered for the developing Liverpool fruit trade.

There were two major yards in Peel of which photographic records exist. Graves's built the *Vixen*, the log of whose memorable voyage to

Australia survives, together with sea chests and items of the crews' clothing. The yard stood on a site subsequently occupied by Watterson's smithy and Quirk's coalyard on the right bank of the harbour. The other Peel yard was Tom Watson's—on the banks of the Neb above the harbour bridge. Its only mechanical aid was a water-powered saw but it continued working until 1930 and the last two Manx-built schooners were launched from this yard. The *Phoebe*, built in 1891, was rammed and sunk by a cross-channel steamer in 1900 and the larger *Griqualand West*, launched in 1894, was wrecked in the Bristol Channel in 1898. As has been mentioned there was great difficulty in launching large vessels. The channel under the bridge had to be deepened by divers and the hull ballasted with everything available. This often included the local schoolchildren, who had the great advantage that they were easily off-loaded or moved about to alter the trim!

The Ramsey yard is the only one of which substantial remains survive, despite a period of use as a salt works. Summarising its history—Taggart & Co, a local firm, ran it from 1832 to 1837; it was closed temporarily in June 1837 and was then apparently bought by Chas Humberston & Co of Newcastle, who advertised it for resale in December; Gibson & Co of Newcastle bought and intended to reopen 'the Shipbuilding premises at Ramsey formerly those of J. Taggart & Co' early in 1839. The *Manks Advertiser* had some waspish comments on their chances of success:

> Much eulogium has been passed by our radical contemporaries upon the gentlemen who have taken the Ship-yard at Ramsey—we are told that they intend to lay down a steamer for the trade between that port and Liverpool, and to offer her to the inhabitants in shares, and if not taken they will 'reserve her for themselves'. We certainly wish it may succeed, but several meetings have heretofore taken place on the subject, we have our doubts. Fifty new cottages are also, according to the statement of our contemporaries, to be built for the accommodation of the workmen, and a new patent slip is to be added to the concern.

Despite this the yard prospered for many years, employing at least 250 men and 'building ships of wood or iron to 2000 tons burden'.

By 1870, 300–400 men were employed and it was one of the most progressive small yards in the British Isles. Among its famous products was the *Euterpe*, subsequently renamed the *Star of India* and now preserved at the San Diego Maritime Museum, California, USA. She was used as an emigrant ship, making eighteen round trips in twenty-five years, and was one of four three-masted barques built by the yard. The others were the *Euridica*, *Erato* and *Ramsey*. The last is believed to have been the first 'iron tank-ship' ever built. The demand for larger ships, however, finally forced this adventurous firm to close. It reopened in the 1960s for building and refitting small, often specialised, craft but despite very heavy expenditure in government subsidies it has hardly paid its way. The only other firms now working in Man are producing non-traditional pleasure craft in modern manmade materials such as fibreglass.

There were also shipbuilders at Castletown and Port St Mary, mainly members of the Qualtrough family. Qualtrough's timber yard at Castletown occupies part of Cooil & Qualtrough's original site, while Huntersfold now uses Joseph Qualtrough's solidly built limestone warehouse at Port St Mary. At various times there were several other firms: at Ramsey in 1882 there were Aldreth Bros, Shore; Collins Bros, King Street; John Dodds, Quay; and Ed Looney, Maughold Street. There were also at least two other yards at Port St Mary which, like those at Peel, specialised in fishing boats. A very great deal of documentary evidence and a considerable number of builder's models and half-models survive but the full history of Manx shipbuilding and shipowning has yet to be written.

THE ANCILLARY TRADES OF THE SHIPBUILDERS

In 1883 it was estimated that 2,870 men and boys depended on the Manx fisheries for their livelihood and a further 700 were engaged in related trades such as fish processing and sail, net and rope manufacture. These people had an estimated 13,000 dependants, so a total of nearly a quarter of the population lived off the fisheries. When it is realised that the ancillary textile trades also supplied the needs of trading, passenger and pleasure craft, visiting vessels and a large export market their importance is easier to see.

Sailmaking

Sailmaking was the most difficult of the textile trades to mechanise and in the Isle of Man it was only the production of materials that was much affected. Douglas, Peel, Castletown, Ramsey and Port St Mary all had firms whose necessarily large premises often survive. Clucas of Port St Mary started about 1858 and specialised in suits of sails for fishing boats. To give some idea of the quantity of material handled, a nickie—a Manx type of fishing boat—usually had a big foresail with some 200 running yd, a second foresail of 170 yd, a trisail of 120 yd, and so on up to a total of seven or eight. Each of these had to be cut and joined from narrow widths (the canvas produced at Tromode was normally only 24in wide) and equipped with ropes, etc. Usually fishing boats had cotton sails and the larger schooners flax. Sails were often tanned for increased durability. The production of sailcloth is described in the section on textiles (p 172) but it is worth mentioning that in 1852 '. . . the owners of the mammoth steam ship GREAT BRITAIN have intimated their intention of supplying that vessel with Manx canvas . . .'. The Tromode factory is also said to have had a naval contract, presumably for unbleached canvas.

Net Factories and Ropewalks

The large quantities of nets required by the Manx fisheries were originally made at home by the fishermen's families. The earliest indication of an attempt to mechanise net production is found in a letter from Peter Heywood to the Duke of Atholl dated 8 Oct 1786 (AP 122 4th—11):

. . . a young man, a native of the Isle of a Mechanical Turn has . . . brought to a considerable state of perfection a machine or loom for making fishing nets . . . It will make 52 knots of every mesh at one stroke which is done in something less than half a minute, the reason why the machine is so long in performing the operation is owing to some seconds employed in adjusting the threads . . . He calculates that he will make with the machine as much Herring net in one day as 30 men . . .

This first machine was not powered and a mesh wider than 104 knots could not be made. However, inventors elsewhere were more successful and several net factories were set up. Nets were made at the Tromode mills, 1852–66, but the machinery was then sold to a Peel firm. William Knox's Douglas engineering works has been credited with introducing the first netmaking machinery, which totally superseded the old slow hand process, but William Corrin, who founded the first factory in Peel, is said to have imported his from Scotland. His works lay between Michael Street and Factory Lane, to which it gave its name. Some forty people were employed. The net weavers stood in front of the looms which had wooden drums and large pedals (see p 72). Each operation of the pedal produced a row of mesh. When the required length was complete it was taken off the loom and finished by outworkers in their homes. This entailed reinforcing the edges and attaching fittings for the ropes and floats. The finished net was then taken to the bark house—which might be independent. After repeated dippings in the preservatives and dryings it was taken to the large net loft where the ropes, etc, were attached.

There were two more Peel factories: J. Joughin's and T. C. S. Moore's. Nets were made at Port St Mary by Qualtrough's—building SC 209674—and Castletown. Here J. Qualtrough & Co had their looms (one of which is preserved in the Nautical Museum, Castletown) in 27 Hope Street, and their bark pits, the slabs of which still survive beneath the lawn at 22 and 22a. All the factories closed by the beginning of World War II, Corrin's machinery and key workers being shipped back to Lanark.

Very large amounts of rope of varying thicknesses were required in fitting out even a modest sailing vessel and there must have been ropemaking establishments from an early date. Originally these must have been the characteristic long 'ropewalks' which are shown on the 25in OS map at Douglas (SC 375765 and Quiggin's SC 377753), Peel (SC 241837), Port St Mary (SC 210672), Ramsey (SC 450946) and Castletown (SC 265675 and SC 270678). Buildings survive only at Quiggin's (established 1821) in Douglas, now mainly a builder's merchant and timber supplier's yard. The illustration on p 17 shows an export order and the main floor after machines had been installed; other floors were used for preparing the fibres and laying the coils.

List of Ropemakers

James Bowman	Big Street, Peel, 1843
Hugh Brown	Quay, Ramsey, 1843–6
Quayle Cannell	Quay, Ramsey, 1846–57
Henry Corlett	Strand Street, Douglas, 1824
Andrew Craughan (or Croughan)	Flax dresser, rope and twine manufacturer, 1824–43. Margaret Craughan, 1846
Thomas Dinwoody	College Green, Castletown, 1846—probably the walk behind site of Bay House, SC 270678
Thomas Fargher	Castletown 1846
Graves' shipyard	Peel, dates unknown
William Harrison	Arbory Street, Castletown, 1824
William Jordan & Co	Lezayre Street, 1843; Bourne Place, 1857; Ramsey
John Moore & Co	Bridge Street, 1837–46; Ramsey
Quiggin & Co	Lake Works, Douglas, 1821 to twentieth century
Thomas Rimmer	Peel, 1843
Evan Shimmin	10 Castle Street, Douglas, 1843
Thomas Taubman	Peel, 1824
John Teare	Quay, Peel, 1846–57
Robert Teare	Lezayre Street, Ramsey, 1846

HARBOURS

Much documentary evidence survives concerning Manx harbours, but for brevity we are here concerned mainly with extant features. For convenient reference the installations of each harbour—including movable but not fixed bridges, and warehouses—will be dealt with together.

Castletown harbour must have been of importance from an early date since the town was the place of residence of the Lord of Mann, or his governor, and the insular capital. It was rather small and Derbyhaven, a little further along the coast, was also used early; indeed there is some indication that the Vikings dragged boats overland between Castletown Bay and Derbyhaven. The history of the development of Castletown is of the improving of the natural quays provided by the rocks on either side of the Silverburn and the provision of shelter by means of harbour walls. The first light was established in 1765—Derbyhaven apparently had a light as early as 1650—but this burnt all night only during the herring season.

The first protection for the harbour mouth at Castletown was afforded by a stone breakwater, with berths along its inner face, erected 1844–5 at a cost of £2,685. This was extended by a further 30yd in 1849 and a light inscribed 'V R 1849' was erected on its seaward end. The light's fine-cut limestone ashlars are now masked by many coats of paint. It is 32ft above high-water mark and its original red light was visible 8 miles out to sea. The earliest movable bridge across the harbour, on the line now occupied by the footbridge, was erected in 1795. In 1886 an iron swing-bridge, designed and built by the Patent Shaft & Axletree Co Ltd of Wednesbury, carried a new road across the harbour between the brewery site and the bottom of the Bank. This had a 16ft carriageway, was 60ft long and cost a mere £1,000; it has recently been demolished. In 1903 a swing-footbridge was erected across the mouth of the river, its plate proclaiming it to be the work of Andrew Hardy & Sons, London & Derby. This bridge is in fair repair and is frequently repainted: with a sensitivity commended by Ian Nairn, the colour chosen is not 'standard green' but pale blue-green.

The town had a lifeboat from 1856 to 1922 and its record boards are preserved in the Gate House of Castle Rushen. The limestone boathouse now used as an office by the container service still survives as does the slipway in the outer harbour. Many of the older buildings along the right quay are likely to be demolished, a fate that has already overtaken those backing on to the outer harbour and the large umber warehouse on the left or Irish quay. Noteworthy buildings include a four-storey warehouse with Poyllvaish marble lintels, and the 1912 Steam Packet office in limestone with moulded red-brick details. The Customs are now housed in a building which probably dates, like the nearby Castle Arms (or 'Glue Pot') pub, from the seventeenth century; at one time this was the garrison library. The Rocket Station, also in limestone, stands at the top of Parliament Lane, and group photographs of the nineteenth-century Castletown Volunteer Rocket Brigade still exist. There is a smaller pier on the right bank of the river which has been used more since a large crane was erected (on a vast concrete support) to load and unload the container ships. Although coal for the gasworks—which has now ceased to make gas— is no longer required, domestic fuel still comes in through the port. Timber boats also call fairly often and a very considerable container traffic has been developed. The containers are now moved within the Island by road, and not, as initially, on the steam railway.

Derbyhaven was defended by at least two batteries in the seventeenth century, an indication of its importance then. The British government erected a sea mark on Langness in the form of a tower of limestone, SC 285657, in 1811. The limestone island breakwater was built in 1842–3 at a cost of £3,524 but plans for further development were not carried out and the haven is now little used except by small pleasure craft. The buildings along its shore include the old customs house and somewhat ruinous remains of herring houses, probably dating from 1771.

Douglas, now the insular capital, is served by a complex of piers that enable the regular passenger boats to discharge at all states of the tide. The most northerly, the Victoria pier, was opened in 1872, lengthened by 400ft in 1887 and has since been further improved. It was the first Manx harbour work in which the then newly discovered Portland cement was used. Its outer casing is of dressed limestone. Passengers using this pier pass through the new Sea

Terminal, whose cast concrete structure is enlivened by panels of blue ceramic tiles and whose elegant spire surmounting the fluted roof provides a fitting end to the sweep of the promenades. It is pleasant to see a modern interpretation of Victorian seaside Gothic fantasy, particularly in a utilitarian building.

The newest pier, one of the few public works named for Edward VIII, was opened in May 1936. Its starting point was the stump of the old Red Pier, built of sandstone from Annan in Scotland (1793–1801). Shelter from the south-east is provided by the Battery Pier, with a light at its tip, whose outer 280ft consist entirely of solid blocks, now reinforced by steel tie-rods. There is a monument to the founder of the RNLI, Sir William Hillary, at its base and the present lifeboat house stands on stilts just to the east; an earlier lifeboat house may be seen in the nearby Harbour Board yard.

The inner harbour is tidal. Its North Quay was faced with dry-stone walling of local slate on a foundation of native rock, and the South Quay, carried over softer ground on a raft of timber, was faced with Port St Mary limestone and filled with slate rubble. But recent repairs have obliterated most traces of the original facing and there have been some alterations of line, notably at the Double Corner. Further quayage is provided by the Tongue, erected on a former gravel bank on the left of the river. The survival of the timber stops, which served to prevent the paddle boxes of the old paddlers from lodging on the quay, is notable although some were demolished in 1971.

A swing-bridge, 76ft long, was erected to cross the harbour just above the Steam Packet Co's offices in 1894. It is now closed to vehicles. Warehouses survive precariously on the North Quay and traces of the 'Red Herring Houses' marked on Peter Fannin's map of 1769 still exist on the site of the National Coal Board's yard, now a fish-packer's works, and elsewhere on the South Quay. Noteworthy buildings include the present Steam Packet warehouse, with a roof supported on iron columns, and a new office block with attractive blue mosaic panels. The lifeboat house, already mentioned, is an undistinguished structure. The town had its first boat in 1824, and a second operated from 1874–96. There was a curious brainchild of the wife of the founder of the service. Lady Hillary had a limestone mock castle, the Tower of Refuge, erected in 1834 on Conister Rock, so that sailors wrecked on this hazard could shelter until they could be reached from the shore. The RNLI flag is still flown from this structure in summer.

The harbour at Laxey was not acquired by the Isle of Man Harbour Commissioners until 1890. The works consist of two small limestone-faced piers, which suffice to shelter small vessels, and typically Manx 'pepperpot' lights mark their ends. The large warehouse owned by the mines company is now used as a pipe factory.

Peel is the principal port of the Manx herring fishery, and the history of its harbour is, as elsewhere, a succession of improvements. St Patrick's Isle was joined to the mainland and a breakwater constructed north-east from the islet to shelter the harbour mouth. The lifeboat house (lifeboat established 1828) is at the base of this breakwater. The sides of the harbour are faced and the line of the right bank is extended to give further shelter. The usual pepperpots mark their ends. Most of the northern quay buildings were once used as warehouses, shipyards, net factories and for similar marine purposes—not forgetting the pubs—but most have now been much altered into, among other things, the Vikings' long hall, a garage and a coal yard. Kippering survives as a Peel industry, with automated gutting machines replacing the herring lassies, and salting fish remains important. Boats are now built in fibreglass instead of timber.

Port Erin was a site selected for a grandiose development of the type beloved in the nineteenth century; but as with the transatlantic harbour off the end of Brean Down (near Weston-super-Mare in Somerset) only a line of tumbled blocks marks the site of the ill-fated breakwater destroyed in 1881. The harbour is now protected by a short breakwater of cut limestone, with a light at its tip. (There is a second, leading, light on the shore.) The lifeboat house stands on iron columns to seaward (the lifeboat was not established until 1883) and there is also a short concrete jetty usable at low tide. The only other facilities are a line of stores for ships' gear built under the raised roadway. Mention must be made, however, of the Liverpool University Marine Biological Station, which has done important work on the Manx fisheries and, more recently, on the development of fish farming.

Port St Mary had the advantage of some natural shelter from the prevailing wind and this was enhanced by two main piers, built of cut limestone. The foundation of the Alfred Pier was laid on 31 January 1882 by the Duke of Edinburgh and it was not completed until 1886. It is alleged that the original bollards of the old pier were cannon found off the Chasms by the Laird of Melgin in 1664, and one apparent survivor is near the hexagonal light tower. Cannon were used also in this way at Douglas and the specimen presented to the Manx Museum may well be of seventeenth-century date. As usual the ends of the piers are marked by lights. Although the harbour dries out completely at low tide—the lifeboat, established in 1896, remains permanently at anchor for this reason—it is a popular centre for pleasure craft and has a developing shellfish industry. Most of its warehouses have been converted to other purposes.

The location of the Ramsey harbour has changed with that of the river mouth, which is now protected by two stone piers, with lights. The South Pier was started in 1790 and extended to 570ft in 1874–6, and the North Pier, costing £2,570, was erected between March 1842 and late November 1868. The tidal harbour is crossed by an iron swing-bridge painted pink and maroon, built by the Cleveland Bridge and Engineering Co Ltd of Darlington in 1892 at a cost of £2,325. The banks of the river were faced for a considerable distance as are those of the gore between the old and new river mouths, where the shipyard is situated. A lifeboat, housed outside the south pier, has been stationed here since 1829. There are several handsome warehouses and a notable survival of ships' chandlers. The latest plan is to provide a 'floating harbour' for small craft. The main landing place for passengers was the long iron Queen's Pier, opened on 22 July 1886 at a cost of £45,000. Its railway is a fine example of Victorian practicality. Although this pier was still used occasionally by Steam Packet vessels until 1970, the structure is said to be in a poor state and the cost of repairs prohibitive.

LIGHTHOUSES

The Calf of Man has one of the finest series of lighthouses in the British Isles. The first documentary evidence of the existence of lights on the islet is Richard Wilson's survey of 1771 but it has been suggested by D. B. Hague (personal communication) that the ruins usually called Bushel's house may in fact be the remains of a late medieval beacon tower. This would indicate that Wilson's castellated towers are rather more than a cartographer's convention, though no trace survives beyond a pile of stones on Caigher. In 1818 the twin lights designed by Robert Stevenson came into operation. Plans and sections of these survive but the structures themselves become yearly more dilapidated and the handsome keepers' houses attached to each are virtually ruinous.

These lights were superseded in 1875 by Chicken Rock. Work on this isolated rock light was started in 1869, the tower being of Dalbeattie granite from Scotland. Each ring of stones was cut, fitted and marked in Port St Mary before being dispatched by boat to the site. The lower 32ft 8in of the tower is solid. The keepers' families lived in houses in Port St Mary erected after 1887. Following a disastrous fire in 1960 the light and fog signal became automatic. In 1966 work started on a new light sited between the two existing on the Calf and this is now in operation having been opened on 24 July 1968 by the lieutenant-governor. Its 2 million candlepower light is visible for 23 miles.

The Calf was farmed until recently and both the farmers and the Commissioners for Northern Lights (who are responsible for those of

Page 35   *An ornamental panel, made of Laxey ores to celebrate Queen Victoria's Jubilee—a fine example of a 'miner's grotto'*

Page 36　*Old Foxdale:* (above) *a typical waterwheel as used for pumping and winding;* (below) *miners gathered on the washing floors in 1899. Compare ducts with those excavated a[t] Beckwith's mine, p 54*

the Isle of Man) have improved the natural harbours. On the Sound, which separates the Calf from the main island, there is Cow Harbour —with a limestone boathouse and a concreted slipway. Its name derives from the fact that cattle used to be swum across at this point. Grant's harbour and Cary's harbour—with elaborate stone break-water and dry dock—are to the east of Cow. South harbour, on the other side of the islet, is better sheltered from the prevailing wind. Its concrete jetty has recently been lengthened and a mark placed on the rocks, but the stone-built storehouse is a survivor from the nine-teenth century, if not earlier. The final seamark in this area is the concrete and iron structure on Thousla rock in the Sound.

The lighthouse at Langness, with three attached keepers' houses, was built in 1880. Like most other Manx lighthouses and adjacent buildings, it is kept well whitewashed, the lanterns being painted yellow-buff and black. Douglas probably had a light at an early period. The light on the old Red Pier was damaged in 1787 and ulti-mately replaced by a lantern with argand lamps and reflectors. The first light on Douglas Head was erected by the Isle of Man Harbour Commissioners (under II Geo 3 c 52) around 1832–3 and was 104ft above high-water mark and allegedly visible from Blackpool Tower. It was transferred to the Commissioners for Northern Lights on 1 August 1859 and was rebuilt in its present form in 1892.

Maughold Head is the most recent of Manx lights apart from that on the Calf. The keepers' houses are on the cliff above the door of the tower to which 129 steps descend. The Point of Ayre, like the Calf lights, was built only three years after the Commissioners for Nor-thern Lights were empowered to erect lights in Man. Its tower, 103ft above high-water mark, is striped in red (now fluorescent) and white. It was also a Stevenson design and Robert sacked the Inspector of Works when he personally inspected the works during building. The keepers' houses stand in the same enclosure and the fog signal plus a subsidiary light are situated slightly to the north-east. Originally it was fitted with argand lamps with a 2ft reflector, the light so pro-duced being visible for 18 miles. Since the main shipping channel to

c

Liverpool passes east of the Island there was less need of lights on its west coast. However, the Milner tower at Port Erin and Corrin's tower at Peel serve as seamarks. Despite its small size the Isle of Man has an unusually interesting group of lights, most of which are easily accessible for study, being open at the discretion of the principal keepers during some daylight hours.

CHAPTER THREE

Service Industries

TRANSPORT

Roads

THE many miles of roads in the Island, allegedly over 2,000, are largely the product of the late nineteenth century. About 1763 the Duke of Atholl brought a Scot, James Hamilton, over to build roads. Two years later he was made 'supervisor-general' by the Committee of Tynwald which had been appointed to consider the improvement and maintenance of highways. Nevertheless, the roads remained dangerous for horsemen in winter and for carriages even in summer, and in 1811 there were still only three carriage roads—from Douglas to Castletown, from Douglas to Peel and from Castletown to Ramsey by way of Ballacraine. They were usually built of broken slate, which soon becomes a viscous clay, and small quarries for road metal may still be seen near many roads—beside the hill on the old Castletown–Douglas road just south of the Port Grenaugh turning, for example. In the south limestone was used and the roads were consequently better. Otherwise they remained mere bridle paths, like that still surviving between Eary Cushlin and Dalby. They were seldom more than a few feet wide and were confined between high earth 'hedges', while their gradients, as on the approaches to Old Laxey village, were very steep. Turnpike trusts did not operate in Man and there were no toll roads.

The fine straights coming down from Creg ny Baa replaced the meanders of the old road about 1865, and nearly halved the distance to be travelled. About the same time the Disafforesting Commissioners constructed several roads over the mountains, but their schemes never reached full fruition because the money ran out. The Isle of Man Mining Co established a network of straight, if narrow, roads about Foxdale to facilitate the work in the many mines and trials. (The miners themselves created an even more complex system of footpaths.) As the roads improved, road metal could be moved more easily and so the surfaces became more uniform. There have been many quarries for road metal, those used more recently being mainly on igneous outcrops (Oatlands, Dhoon, Poortown) or on intrusive veins of harder rock in the Manx slate series (Crosby Quarry). Gradually more and more tracks were surfaced and main roads widened and the whole of the Mountain Circuit, over which the TT races are run, became a first-class road. Successive editions of the OS 1in map show how the system has developed until virtually all public roads are negotiable in a modern car.

River Crossings

The old roads generally crossed streams by means of fords, the only sizeable early bridge being that about 200yd upstream from Rushen Abbey, the *Monks' Bridge*, SC 280705. Until about 1730 such local traffic as did not move by sea progressed by foot or horseback, so the lack of bridges was of little concern to the inhabitants. A Bridges Act then provided that

> . . . a Bridge first be built over the River of Sulby,[1] in the Parish of Kirk Christ Lezayre . . . and in the second place another Bridge shall be built over the River called the Great River, in the Parish of Kirk German, between St John's Chappel and Peeltown[2]. . . and a third bridge shall be built over that River between Kirk Malew and Kirk St Anne upon the Highway between Castletown and Douglas[3]. . . and a fourth Bridge over that River between Ramsey and Kirk Bride and Kirk Andreas[4]. . . and a fifth Bridge over that River near Peeltown, between Kirk German and Kirk Patrick.[5]

Some of these bridges remain, though they have been widened, strengthened and altered. Other noteworthy bridges are Hamilton, Lower Foxdale, SC 277792, Campbell, SC 302760, the old Fairy

[1] Sulby bridge, SC 392948.   [2] Ballaleece, SC 273820.   [3] Mullin y Quinney, SC 300711.   [4] Ramsey 'stone bridge', SC 448947.   [5] Glenfaba, SC 242830.

bridge near Kewaigue, SC 345742 and the Atholl bridge across the Silverburn, SC 273715. The economical but attractive 'mining company style' of bridge survives in several places round Foxdale, for example, near the wheelcase behind the brickworks, SC 283778. The Stone bridge across the top of Douglas Harbour, SC 378752, is a recent construction (opened 1937) but some traces of its eighteenth-century predecessor can be seen a little way upstream (see map, p 150). The Quarterbridge, SC 365762, and the Alexandra bridge at Castletown, SC 267679, are also worthy of mention. Movable bridges are described with the harbours they serve.

Railways and Tramways

This part of the Manx transport system has been dealt with by other authors both intensively and extensively and only a brief summary will be given here. The deficiencies of the insular road system had early led to agitation for railways to be built. In 1872 Tynwald passed an Act authorising the establishment of the Isle of Man Railway Co. Its first 11½ miles of track, from Douglas to Peel, was opened in 1873 and just over a year later its second line, from Douglas to Port Erin, started working. This was an attempt to derive benefit from the new harbour facilities at Port Erin but the destruction of the new breakwater negated this. However, it is this stretch of line, 15¼ miles long, which is still operating as the Isle of Man Victorian Steam Railway. In 1877 the citizens of Ramsey formed the Manx Northern Railway Co to connect their town to Douglas because the finances of the original company were insufficient. The link was via Kirk Michael to St Johns. The Manx 'standard gauge' for railways is 3ft.

The traffic from the Foxdale mines seemed a likely source of non-seasonal revenue, so in 1883 the Foxdale Railway Company was set up. It likewise joined the 'main line' at St Johns and was operated by the MNR. Unfortunately the cost of running it was such that this company was forced in 1904 to amalgamate with the IMR. Nevertheless, it continued working for some time, among its oddities being the suggestion that it should run a special train to enable a supply teacher from Douglas to reach the school at Foxdale. Its line is now ruinous, though the handsome viaduct near the St John's nurseries and the station at Foxdale survive virtually intact.

The steam railway has several handsome red-brick stations, eg Port Soderick, Port St Mary and Port Erin. That at Douglas—rebuilt in 1903—has some claim to be among the finest on any narrow-gauge system in the British Isles and is considerably larger than either of the Athens termini. Again of smooth-surfaced red brick, its main building houses the ticket office and waiting room. An adjoining building, more or less at right-angles, provided office space and a licensed refreshment room. There are two glass-roofed island platforms, each with space for two average trains. The spacious carriage sheds, locomotive sheds and works, coal stores and warehouses run along the river side of the tracks for some distance. The pedestrian entrance to the station is beneath an arch, flanked by towers with gilded cupolas, and down a wide flight of steps to the forecourt. All the red-brick stations have moulded details and most have some flamboyant but anonymous ironwork which has successfully survived two wars.

Castletown station, like the bulk of the bridges on the southern section of the line, is built of locally quarried limestone. Peel was perhaps the least interesting of the stations but it had magnificent sanitary fittings, the handbasins and closets having matching fluted pedestals. It has now been sold. The Ramsey line required the building of two spectacular viaducts at Glen Mooar and Glen Wyllin. Both have three spans carried on stone piers. Those of the first, of latticed steel, were renewed in 1919, and those of the second were replaced by plate girders in 1915. The small stations on this stretch are usually built of Peel sandstone and include living accommodation. They have gradually been sold as the line falls into ever greater disrepair, and it seems extremely unlikely that this line, or the Foxdale branch, can ever be reopened.

The Douglas Horse Tramway, also 3ft gauge, runs the length of the Promenade from the Sea Terminal to Derby Castle; it was opened in 1876 and from 1894 to 1902 was run by the Isle of Man Tramways and Electric Power Company. This company also ran the Manx Electric Railway, which was started in 1893 with 2½ miles of single track from Derby Castle to Groudle Glen; by stages this reached Laxey (with a double track in 1894) and finally Ramsey (1899), a total distance of 17 miles. In 1896 the company also built a cable tramway in Douglas which closed on 19 August 1929 and has left virtually no trace. The company also acquired the Snaefell Mountain Railway, which was built in 1895, and rises from Laxey to the summit of Snaefell, 2,034ft, over 5 miles of 3ft 6in track with a special centre rail of *Fell* type to enable its cars to remain on the track. This attraction and the horse trams now operate only in the season but cars to Ramsey run along the delightful scenic coast route throughout the year. In the winter closed cars are used but when the weather is suitable open 'toast rack' trailers appear.

The original Ramsey station has gone, to be replaced by a modern bungalow-style building. There are no major structures on the line, though most halts are provided with small wooden shelters, with a rather larger one at Laxey, and the Summit Hotel on Snaefell is a classic example of railway architecture. There is a tendency to the picturesque in the design of the small buildings, both the Derby Castle booking office and the booths at Laxey having 'rustic' branches nailed on as ornament. Despite its tendency to collapse, the Bulgham Bay stretch of the line is a great engineering feat. Although the Electric Railway tends to be thought of as a tourist attraction it serves a very real need, with the great advantage that its cars can run even when snow on the steeper hills brings buses to a halt.

The Douglas Southern Electric Tramway from Douglas to Port Soderick was constructed in 1895 to a 4ft 8½in gauge, but closed in 1939 and never reopened. Its route is now followed by the Marine Drive, but some traces of the considerable engineering works for its bridges can still be seen as well as the tollhouse at the Douglas end.

The beds of the two cliff railways at its termini, Douglas Head and Port Soderick, can also be seen. About a mile of 2ft gauge track laid along the north side of Groudle Glen as a tourist attraction was opened on 20 July 1896, and it seems to have been one of the earliest miniature railways. Unfortunately its surviving engine, *Polar Bear*, finally failed and the line has been abandoned to vandals. The now obsolescent Ramsey Pier has a 3ft gauge track along its 2,300ft length, opened in 1886. This was once man-hauled but a petrol locomotive took over in 1937 and continued to function each summer after the war.

In addition to the busy line served by the *Ant* and the *Bee* at the Laxey mines there were several temporary tramways. These included that erected along Peel Hill in connection with harbour improvements and the 7ft gauge spur used at Port Erin during the building of the ill-fated breakwater. Part of the route used for the West Baldwin Reservoir Railway can still be traced. It is hoped that ultimately the relics of the Manx railways will be gathered together in an insular transport museum but hopes of establishing a permanent home for this seem to be receding.

Airports

Always a progressive place the Isle of Man had several attempts to set up a service in the early days of air travel. Originally the service operated from a grass strip, grandiloquently called Hall Caine Field, after the Manx writer, near Ramsey. Flights occasionally also started from Douglas Beach. The flat well-drained southern plain and the north provided a choice of sites, and airports were developed at Jurby and Ronaldsway—near Castletown. There was a third wartime field near Andreas. After the war it was decided to develop Ronaldsway as the main civil airport (though Jurby has markedly less fog) and it has been steadily improved, the largest plane currently using it being the BAC 111. Its functional concrete and girder passenger building and control tower are now being linked to provide more modern facilities. Despite its climatic disadvantages it appears likely that it will continue to be the Island's major civil airport, though Jurby, now relinquished by the RAF, is maintained for emergency use.

SERVICES

Water

Although the Isle of Man is relatively small its water supplies used to be provided by a number of companies. The first enabling Act, relating to Douglas, was passed in 1834, followed by Castletown in 1837, Ramsey in 1839, Port Erin in 1885 and Rushen in 1886. Of the companies formed Douglas alone survives, the rest having been amalgamated under government auspices. The earliest reservoirs were in Summer Hill Glen, Douglas, and the upper survives as a source of water for street-washing and watering the Villa Marina and Promenade gardens. The Clypse reservoir, which holds 20 million gallons, was completed about 1878. The clay used for waterproofing is alleged to have been dug from behind the Shore Hotel, Gansey, where the large flooded pit may still be traced despite recent dumping. Like the nearby Kerrowdhoo, opened in 1893 and holding 50 million gallons, the Clypse is 40ft deep.

With the growth of the tourist industry further supplies were required. The 300 million gallon, 70ft maximum depth Baldwin reservoir was constructed by damming the Baldwin river some $2\frac{1}{2}$ miles from its source. The work was carried out in the period 1900–5 by the Douglas water undertaking itself. An interesting 3ft gauge railway used to carry the building materials and traces of it may still be seen. The clay for the dam came from Ballacreetch farm, SC 373793, and the sandstone from a specially opened quarry near Peel. This reservoir can supply half a million gallons a day in the driest conditions, rising to 2·35 million gallons in the season.

The connection from the Baldwin reservoir was at first a 12in main which was supplemented by a 15in main in 1926–7. The installation of the Deacon system of waste-water metering in 1910 resulted in such saving that no further major reservoirs were required. In November 1909, the waste was such that 2 million gallons a day were being supplied—as compared to the 1½ million normally used by a much enlarged area fifty years later. Direct labour was again employed for various refinements such as roofing the Ballaquayle service reservoir, constructing that at Glencrutchery and, most important, installing the filter plant in 1934. One feature of interest at the latter is the presence of a Pelton wheel as a power source for chlorination, though it can only be used when levels are high.

Outside the Douglas area there are a number of small reservoirs situated high up on smallish streams: Michael, SC 335892; Glen Rushen (in the old slate quarry), SC 246782; and the 11 million gallon Bloc Eary, SC 900389, for example. The main supplies for the south come from Cringle, SC 253745 (31 million gallon), and for the north from Ballure, SC 454929 (23 million gallon). In recent droughts the Douglas company's reservoirs have supplied the south and there is considerable agitation to unite the water undertakings in order to spread supply and demand. Supplies of water for industrial purposes are poor. The Peel power station has a small supply in the quarry across the river, for example, but this could not provide any surplus for other purposes. If any large-scale user of water wished for some reason to set up a factory in the Island it would be necessary to build a new reservoir, and indeed a further dam on one of the Sulby tributaries was suggested in connection with the erection of an oil refinery on the Ayres. Fortunately for conservationists this came to nothing.

Sewage

The enabling Acts for Castletown, Douglas, Peel and Ramsey were passed in 1852 and main sewers were subsequently laid in these

areas. Since most of the towns lie on the coast the sewers discharge
into the sea. There are small inland installations having filter beds
fitted with rotating arms, such as Foxdale, SC 279787. No elaborate
works or pumps were required and nothing of outstanding interest
has been located.

Gas

The towns used to be supplied by five separate companies—
Douglas in 1836; Castletown, Peel and Ramsey in 1857 and Port St
Mary in 1898. Gradually these companies have been merged and the
works modernised, the generation of coal gas having ceased in 1971.
Castletown is now a mere storage depot linked to Port St Mary by
a pipeline laid along the railway track. The works were all small and
simple. A brief description of Castletown is included as an illustration of the type and origin of the equipment—now being demolished.
Its final firing was filmed and it is hoped to make this a permanent
record.

Castletown Gasworks. The works are constructed of local limestone
and comprised a main building housing the retorts and purifying
equipment and, facing this across a yard, the pump house and office/
house for the manager. There was underground storage for creosote
waste and two gasometers of which that nearest the road—demolished
1971—probably dated from about 1860. A single bed of six horizontal
retorts (R. J. Dempster Ltd, Makers, Manchester) was in use at a
time, being replaced about every five years. They were supplied,
initially in tubs on 2ft gauge metal rails and later by barrow from
coal heaps at the end of the building. The coal was imported through
Castletown harbour in small coasting vessels and had to be unloaded
into carts (later lorries) since there was no direct link from the quay
to the works. The purifying equipment was mostly supplied by
Drake Ltd—also described as 'Drake Ltd, Contractor, Hanley' and
'Drake of Hanley and Alport' on various items. The station meter

by J. S. Braddock of Oldham was the original until 1970. Most of the company's records are now in the Manx Museum.

Electricity

Electricity was supplied to the public from 1923 by Douglas Corporation's generating station on the North Quay, SC 378754, of which the building, in local limestone, survives. At present the Douglas and Onchan area is supplied from Pulrose station, opened 1928 though most of the structure dates from 1935, and the rest of the Island from Peel station, opened in 1950, and Ramsey station, opened in 1960. All now use oil for generating. Many local firms had private generators, and the Manx Electric Railway also made available a limited supply to the public, but apart from an iron MER plaque on the sluice gates of the mill in the lower Laxey valley, which was a generating station, no traces of the early period survive. As with the other services the plant and distribution system is simple and there are no major engineering feats or great lines of metal pylons.

CHAPTER FOUR

Extractive Industries

QUARRIES

MANX quarries were primarily for building materials and road metal, though the production of lime for agricultural use has increased in importance during the last 150 years. Most quarries had a short life and frequently were opened only to obtain stone for a specific building or stretch of road. The dominant rocks belong to the Manx slate series, which, because of the tectonic pressures to which they were subjected, yield inferior roofing slates and indifferent building stone. Some beds split into large 'planks', which, as a result of the local shortage of timber, were highly valued for bridging, as gateposts and as a means of flooring that required little support. (The last is well illustrated in the early nineteenth-century reflooring of several upper rooms in Castle Rushen.) Such beds were quarried even when, as in the 250ft cliffs of Spanish Head, the extraction of the finished product presented considerable difficulties. Douglas Head and South Barrule are two of the larger and older quarries for other grades. Slate roofing is preserved on the Old Grammar School (St Mary's Chapel) at Castletown.

The red sandstone of the Peel area is the only freestone found in the Island. It was used for many buildings in the town and from an early date, as the tenth-century Round Tower on St Patrick's Isle testifies. Since it was easily shaped it was favoured, particularly in the eighteenth and nineteenth centuries, for details on houses built of other materials—for example, the eaves of several houses on the Parade, Castletown. Creg Malin, at the north side of Peel bay, was the site of the main quarries, and at the end of the nineteenth century production averaged 2,000 tons annually. Unfortunately the sandstone is rather soft and easily eroded by the sea air, so is now of little importance—though it could doubtless be used to colour a 're-constituted' stone.

Granite from the three main exposures—the Dhoon, Granite Mountain (Foxdale) and Oatlands (Santon)—has been utilised in road-building and for paving setts, which still survive in the Windsor Road area of Douglas. Before the growth of competitive milling local granites (glacial erratics might also be used) were fashioned into millstones but in more recent times these have been imported. Chopping troughs for various agricultural uses, such as converting gorse into feed, were also made from local granite. At the present time a large spar deposit, also on Granite Mountain, is being worked; it is a much-used finish for walls and paths.

Carboniferous limestone is found round Castletown and Port St Mary. Among the major buildings in this stone are Castle Rushen, whose earliest surviving parts date from the thirteenth century, and Rushen Abbey. Scarlett quarry provided the stone for the bridges on the southern section of the Isle of Man Railway and for Castletown station. Limestone was also used extensively for harbour works as well as houses but in recent years its chief importance has been as a source of lime (see p 136).

An atypical deposit at Poyllvaish, the so-called black marble, was very popular in the nineteenth century for lintels and steps and for ornamental work such as mantelpieces. The quarry was of sufficient importance to have its own quay, of which traces remain. It is said that the original steps of St Paul's Cathedral in London originated here, but the stone is very soft and they were subsequently replaced. The fine-grained rock can easily be cut into thin slabs and the recently reopened quarry is now supplying ornamental panels for cladding, coffee-table tops, etc, the numerous fossils it contains enhancing its decorative nature. Like most Manx quarries, its products are mainly absorbed by the insular market.

Early History

Little is known about the earliest working of the Manx mines but archaeological evidence from the excavations at Kiondroghad suggests that iron ore was being obtained in the Dark Ages, and remains of what was probably a bowl hearth for smelting or refining iron (apparently dating to the thirteenth or fourteenth centuries) were found at Kirk Braddan. In 1246 King Harald of Mann and the Isles granted the Abbot of Furness and his monks mineral rights, together with 3 acres of land at 'Rakenaldwath' on which to build houses for their men and a storehouse for the ore. Since considerable evidence of lead-smelting and what may well have been a medieval workshop for extracting silver from lead have been found on the Ronaldsway airport site it is likely that the Furness grant related to this area, the ore being obtained from somewhere in Rushen. However, the negative evidence that the Norse rulers, unlike those of Dublin, did not issue their own silver coinage would suggest that silver-lead mining was not well developed.

At the end of the thirteenth century Edward I, now Lord of Mann, granted John Comyns, Earl of Buchan, a licence to dig lead on the Calf of Man to roof eight towers of his castle at Cruggleton in Galloway. Since no evidence of mining exists on the Calf there may have been an obvious exposure which was completely removed. The mineral rights were included when the Lordship was granted to the Stanleys and in 1666, when Charles II renewed the grant after the Restoration, 'the Mynes Royall of Gould and Silver' were added (a mine Royal of silver was one where more than sixty ounces could be extracted from a ton of lead). The mines were worked on a small scale up to the end of the seventeenth century, the Lord's share of all ore raised for 1669 being 32 tons 13cwt. What are likely to be workings of this date may still be seen at Bradda.

At the beginning of the eighteenth century private individuals

were taking leases of the mineral rights. In 1700 the Earl of Derby let
the copper mines to 'Middleton Shaw of Uttoxeter, Co. Stafford,
gentleman' but about three years later the lease was described as
'now broke'. The copper mines were probably at Glen Chass and
other sites in Rushen. From about 1709 to 1713 the Smelt House at
Derbyhaven was dealing with about 30 tons of lead ore a year, on
which the Lord received a duty of three pounds a ton. It is likely
that Bradda Head was still being prospected as the report to the
Mine Adventurers in 1740 indicates that although there was 'great
triall made in sinking shafts all over the hill', it was so long since the
mines had worked that it was impossible to find out what had
happened underground.

It was apparently very difficult to find skilled miners and there
was little in the way of mechanical assistance for removing water.
Whoever held the lease, the mine progressed only as long as the
men were willing to bargain for the work at a rate of so much a
fathom. The only structures associated with the mines at this date
seem to have been smithies for making, sharpening and repairing
tools. Imported coal was used for smelting, though there are references in the Derby papers to using peat mixed with coal, as was
done at Lead Hills in Galloway. In fact, peat never seems to have
been used but the references probably explain the introduction of
the right to cut peat in various draft leases in the Atholl papers. In
August 1739, the Duke visited the Isle of Man (for the first time
since he had inherited) and an intinerary of his tour of the mines
survives. In July, ores from two areas of Bradda, Glen Chass and
Ballacorkish were assayed 'by Mr Joseph Hamilton at Vauxhall',
with very unpromising results.

On 22 August 1739, the Duke of Atholl entered into a co-partner-
ship agreement to work the mines with Sir John Askin, who had
mining interests in Galloway. The terms were very generous. For
the first three years the Duke would take his Lord's dish of one-
seventh of the washed and dressed ore but otherwise he and Sir
John were to share the profits and expenses equally. After that the

Page 53   *Ruins of the engine house at Townshend's mine, Cornelly*

Page 54   *Wooden structures on Beckwith's mine washing floors, excavated 1969–70*

Duke was to have three-quarters of the profits from the mines of the Bradda area while Sir John took a similar share from Glen Chass. The Duke was to take only one-eighth of the ore from any new mines. After the nineteen years of the lease or at the death of Sir John, if the Duke wished to reduce the share of the former's heirs to one-third of the mines, all buildings and equipment were to be valued and paid for. As it happened the Duke did not receive any profit or incur much outlay as Sir John died, heavily in debt, in early October of the same year. After seeking legal opinions about the validity of the contract and means of breaking it the Duke started to look for a new lessee.

Before Sir John Askin died a certain amount of work was done, and the account of his agent, Edward Whigham, of the mines then working is of interest. At Glen Chass Jonathan Hay had two shafts and the ore between them was to be dug out at £1 sterling per bing. William Ross had a shaft 7 fathoms deep and a level was to be driven north/south from this for 10 fathoms in each direction, at 10s per fathom and 5s per bing of ore. Traces of these workings may be seen on the coastal cliffs. The Bradda rate was 25s per bing, all equipment being supplied to the men. The ore already raised was to be dressed and a rate of 2s 8d per bing was suggested for this work. The miners with these agreements continued to work for a short time after Sir John's death.

At about this time investigations were made into the additional profit that might be made if the ore was smelted in Man. An itemised but unfortunately undated and unlocalised account gives some idea of costs, prices and losses in refining.

		£	s	d	£	s	d
Ore & Carriage	To 12 Tons of Lead Ore at £8 per ton	96	0	0			
	To carriage of Do. to the workhouse at 10d a ton	6	0	0	102	0	0
Smelting	To 6 Ton of Coals for Smelting Do. Carriage to the Workhouse	3	0	0	4	9	0

D

		£	s	d	£	s	d
	To Smelting the ore	1	4	0			
	To Wear &c of Tools		5				
	Tons Cwt						
Refining	To Refining 8 8 of Lead produced from the Ore	2	2	0	5	3	0
	To a Ton of Coals for Do	2	0	0			
	To Tests for Do	1	1	0			
Incid^t Charges	To Incidental charges				1	1	0
	Weekly expenses				£112	12	0
	Profits				16	19	0
					£129	11	0

	Tons		
Lead Ore to be Smelted	12		
Waste by smelting (at 6 . . . per ton)	3	12	
Lead to be refined	8	8	
Waste by Refining & Reducing at 1½ per ton	12	½	11
Remains Lead to be sold at £12 per ton	715	¼	17

	£	s	d
By sale of 126 Silver (being 15oz per Ton) at 5s 9d per oz	36	4	6
715.¼.17 Lead (after refined & reduced) at £12 per ton	93	6	6
	£129	11	0

The profits would be enhanced by the difference in duty payable on unrefined and refined lead and the quantities paying duty. Since coal paid only 1s duty when imported to Man it was cheaper to take the coal to the ore than the ore to the English refineries. This account presumably is somewhat idealised, as the last assay report on the Manx ores suggested a yield of only 5oz of silver per ton.

The Company of Mine Adventurers of England became interested in leasing the Manx mines about 1740. The Atholl papers contain documents of this period giving much information about the extent of early eighteenth-century workings and mining costs. It appears that the Duke of Atholl was prepared to offer the Mine Adventurers 'All those Mines & Veins Rakes Pipes and Flatts and other Beds of

Lead Ore Copper Ore and all other Mines Minerals or Metals already opened and discovered and which shall or may be found opened or Discovered in or under all or any of the Grounds & Lands within the sd. Isle of Mann . . .' They were to have complete freedom to 'Work Sink Make Shafts Soughes and Levels and use all other Ways and Means' to find new mines. In return the Duke was to receive a quarter of the clear profits if these were less than £1,500 in a year or one-third if they were higher. These were held to be very generous terms, because 'In England and Wales Adventurers wile nowhere be allowed so large a Tract of Land the Proprietors there seldom granting more than a certain small quantity of meres . . .'

The lessees would also be allowed to build houses for their men and 'Binsteads Smiths forges and storehouses and also Hovels or Buildings for the Dressing Bucking and Cleansing of the sd. ores'. They could obtain the raw materials for building (clay for bricks, and limestone, which they could burn to make lime for mortar) free from the Lord's wastes and commons or from private land for payment fixed by arbitration. Similarly they could cut peat for fuel on the Lord's land and divert water for any mining or smelting purpose. This was not entirely altruistic on the Lord's part, as all the buildings and mining equipment were to remain or become his property on the expiration of the lease and he retained powers to have the quality of the workmanship inspected.

On 17 December 1740, James Grime and James Simpson reported to the Mine Adventurers on their investigation into the Manx mines. After an extremely unpleasant journey they had reached the Isle of Man and done as much as they could to determine what prospects the mines offered. They observed that work had more or less ceased on the death of Sir John Askin and that the local miners lacked skill and experience. The existing smelt house was most inefficient, since 'there never has any water come to the Mill for Smelting nor washing, but their method is this they hired men to blow the Bellows at so much a day'. In any case this building was now owned by someone else so a new smelt would have to be built. As regards the cost of supplies,

> Iron and Steel is bought in Ireland. Viz Iron at sixteen shillings per Hundredweight and Steel thirty shillings per Hundred. Gunpowder about seven pounds ten shillings per Hundred Smith's work generally six shillings English money which is seven Shillings Manx. Coals sixteen or seventeen shillings per Tun generally shipt from either Whitehaven or Workington. Ropes is mostly brought hither from Ireland—

Workmen would be paid 1s a day, or up to 9s a week, but the last lessee had usually allowed the men to bargain for the work at so much a fathom and he took all the ore raised. A mine carpenter received the same rate of pay and would make all the wooden items required (corves, shovels, pick handles, etc). The recently worked mines were Glen Chass, Bradda Head and Green Chambers, Balla-corkish, Foxdale (which they thought the most promising), Glen Maye, near the new church (Patrick), and Glen Auldyn. At Foxdale one ton of ore was reputed to yield 60oz of silver and £8 a ton had been offered for the Glen Chass ore.

On 16 May 1741, the Duke signed an order allowing James Harris to start working the mines for the Adventurers but the final agreement seems never to have been reached and the search for a tenant restarted. A Mr O'Connor offered the Duke an eighth part of all ore raised or a duty of 8s; but in April 1745 Gabriel Griffith of Workington was granted a lease of the mines with the reservation that if the yield of silver went above 60oz a ton he would surrender the ore and merely be paid for its raising. Griffith contrived to work for a time but with so little result that his lease was finally taken over by his creditors, which inevitably led to legal wrangles. By 1791 the rights were back in the Duke's hands and were again let. This struggle to find a tenant who could work the mines satisfactorily continued into the opening years of the nineteenth century and one result was the granting of mining setts rather than the rights to the whole Island as had been offered earlier. The later history will be described under the mines concerned.

Great Laxey

The Laxey wheel, the *Lady Isabella*, is perhaps one of the best known and almost certainly the most photographed example of industrial archaeology in the British Isles (p 18). What is less appreciated is the part it played in the mining complex surrounding it. It is not known when mining operations started at Laxey but the earliest accounts place the date about 1781; for the next forty years there was intermittent work with little result. In 1822 the lease was taken up by Thos Satterthwaite, General Stapleton and others under the name of the Lonan Mining Association. Over the years a number of changes occurred in the partnership; there was also one serious accident, in 1836, when the river broke into the workings and drowned five men. The Laxey Mining Company was formed in 1848 and ran the mines until 1854, when it was reformed into the Great Laxey Mining Company. The last became a limited company in 1862 and, in turn, changed its name in 1903 to Great Laxey Limited.

The formation of the Laxey Mining Company began a period of expansion and success which was to reach its peak in 1874 and did not seriously falter until about 1890. In 1854–5 this mine was producing more zinc blende than the combined output of all the other mines in the British Isles, though in lead it was surpassed by Foxdale. World War I brought the men into contact with militant trade unionists from other areas and in 1919 a strike closed the mines and the old company never reopened. In 1922 a firm of grocers with other interests, Williamson's of Laxey, took over the lease and ran the mines until 1929. They also spent a £4,000 government (Tynwald) grant on exploration in the Grawe area, south of the original workings. The spoil heaps, 'deads', in the valley were removed as hard core, mainly for airport building during World War II, and although an investigation has been made into the possible reserve of metal in the mine it is extremely unlikely that it will ever work again.

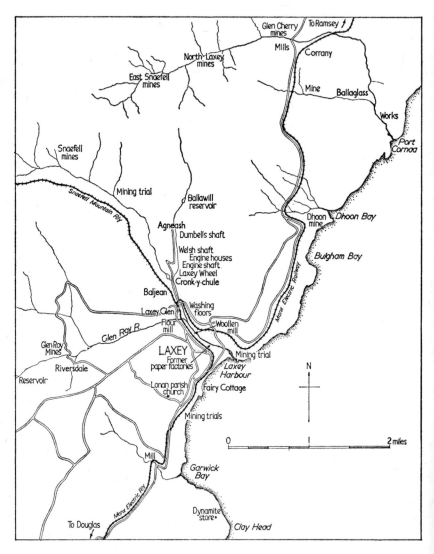

The Laxey area

The Laxey mines produced zinc, argentiferous lead and a certain amount of copper. The mine was worked from a series of shafts connected by an adit along the line of the strike, which ran almost due north/south. The shafts are situated along the line of the Agneash valley and are described here in order from the mouth of the adit. The Corner shaft was sunk in 1862 to open up the southern (copper) ore bodies but by 1887 all machinery was removed and it had become a ladder-way only down to the 30 fathom level, where it was boarded off. A machine house for this shaft, with hauling gear operated by a turbine which used the water from the tailrace of the *Lady Isabella*, stood at the rear of Cronk y Chule farm and a stone-lined tunnel took the winding cables to the shaft.

The Engine shaft housed the pumps driven by the *Lady Isabella* and was also used for hauling, power being supplied from either the Machine house or the Engine house further up the valley. Its maximum depth was 247 fathoms. The Welsh shaft (before 1870 always spelt Welch) was also used for hauling and used the same power sources. At one time a rod linkage at the 200 fathom level took power from the pump rods in the Engine shaft to operate pumps in the lower levels of this shaft, but this practice was superseded by the installation of the Dipper, a large (90gal) bucket with a flap valve in the bottom. It replaced the *kibble* (bucket used for hauling) at nights and weekends and raised the water so that it ran out along the 235 fathom level to the Engine shaft. The maximum depth of the Welsh shaft was 295 fathoms; near its head is the concrete platform on which stood three double-fired steam pumps, which were brought in to clear the mine after it flooded in 1901. The flood was caused when a water-filled 'slide' was struck in the 225 fathom level some 850 fathoms north of Dumbell's shaft. (A slide is an east–west transverse dislocation of the lode and the main concentration of such faults was south of the Corner shaft.) The water reached the 110 fathom level and it was in the checking of the timbers following the successful reduction of the water level that another tragedy occurred, four men being drowned.

Dumbell's shaft was begun about 1860 and was ultimately the deepest, at 302 fathoms. It was driven almost vertically (as opposed to the 10–15 degree 'lie' on the other shafts, which followed the ore body) and cross-cuts were made to the ore. Dumbell's was also used for hauling, and housed compressed air lines and a telephone, for communication between the machine house and the striking boards, which did not operate for very long. Originally power for hauling here came from a waterwheel on the hillside opposite Agneash but this was replaced by a turbine, possibly that removed from Cronk e Chule. Finally, a new winding house was built lower down the slope. The new winding gear was very powerful and could haul faster than it could lower—the kibble was said to go down the shaft on a slack rope. In 1893 a small pump was installed at the 278 fathom level to raise water from the shaft bottom to its own level.

.The Agneash shaft was little used and reached a maximum depth of 59½ fathoms, using a waterwheel for power. The North shaft is only vaguely recorded and reached a depth of only 200ft from the surface (all other shafts are measured from the adit level) and had one prospect, which acted as a drain into Ballawill farmyard. The shaft was filled in 1919.

Mining methods, the 'Lady Isabella' and the 'Man Engine'. The shafts were laddered to the bottom and had levels taken off at approximately 10 fathom intervals. All the levels had a timber sole (floor) and while some ran on the rock others were supported on timbers set in hitches in the rock face. Originally the ladders had to be used throughout the mine, and the men spent nearly as long getting to and fro as they did in working, but in 1881 the Man Engine was installed in the Welsh shaft. This was a hydraulic piston operating under some 250ft head of water, which lifted the man rods on a 12ft stroke. The men, stepping between the platforms on the man rod and fixed platforms in the shaft, could travel up and down with comparative ease and considerably faster than by using the ladders. The man rod is thought to extend to the 200 fathom level

Man Engine, Laxey.

The Man engine

but in its later period of use was only working between the 30 and
110 fathom levels. The rod ran on rollers fastened to the lying face
of the shaft wall. The platforms attached to it were some 20in
square with a metal handgrip at face height above each. There was
a 2ft square shuttle in the fixed platforms, with a bell-shaped hopper
below, so that those coming up came safely through the hole. The
Man Engine was not in use after 1919 but is still in position and
substantially intact.

Unlike many of the other levels the adit ran on the solid throughout
its length, being cut into the bed rock on the east side of the lode. It
started from the Mines Yard and is now marked only by a sizeable
spring draining out of the mine. It rose steadily along its length of
almost 1½ miles, connecting up with each of the shafts in turn.
For almost half its length—as far as Dumbell's shaft—it carried a
steam railway that ran on across the Mines Yard, under the Ramsey–
Douglas road, to the head of the washing floors. The railway was
of 19in gauge and had two locomotives built by Steven Owen of
Poole in the 1870s. These engines, which were greatly modified
during their working life by the mines workshops, were known
affectionately as the *Ant* and the *Bee*; they were 4ft 9in high to the
chimney tops, 8ft 7in long and 3ft wide over the front beam. They
burned steam coal and emitted a vast amount of greasy smoke.
Normally they pulled six to eight wagons, each about 6ft long with
a tapered body of sheet iron and having a hatch at one end, handles
at the other. The ore was tipped out, between the lines, by raising
the end of the truck. The crew consisted of a driver and a boy who
rode the last wagon, undid the hatches and helped to tip the wagons
by lying across the hatch end. Regrettably the engines were sold
for scrap in 1935 but photographs survive.

Between the Engine shaft and the adit mouth the adit was also the
main drainage channel, carrying all the water raised by the *Lady
Isabella*'s pumps; in some places it was channelled to one side but
elsewhere the *Ant* and the *Bee* had a bow wave. Originally the adit
was known as the Horse level, the horses which preceded the

engines having been stabled in a building near the changing room, but later it was always known as the Engine level. The changing house stood on the river bank and was heated by a steam boiler, which also served to dry the men's working clothes. Its ruins, together with the walled-up mouth of the Cross-cut adit, are opposite Mines House. The Cross-cut adit was cut in 1868 between the changing house and the Corner shaft and was a footway only, being the main way in and out of the mine for the men.

The mine was drained by the pumps in the Engine shaft, a series of seven raising the water from tank to tank up the shaft to the adit level. The power for the pumps came from the pump rod on its down stroke, the *Lady Isabella* supplying the power to raise the rod again. The *Lady Isabella* was started on Wednesday, 27 September 1854, by Lady Isabella Hope, wife of Governor Hope, at a ceremony attended by all the local dignitaries (see p 18). It was designed by a Manxman, Robert Casement, though an expert on beam engines called Bowden (his ancestors spelt it Bawden) spent a year in Man advising on it. It is a pitch back-shot wheel, with the water coming from a cistern on the hillside through a 2ft diameter iron pipe, up through the stone-built tower, and out along the timber platform. A by-pass trough made it possible to stop the wheel by diverting the water. A guide published in 1870 gives the following information:

Diameter of wheel	72ft 6in
Breadth of wheel	6ft
Length of shaft	17ft
Diameter of shaft	21ft
Weight of shaft	10 tons
Length of crank	5ft
Length of stroke	10ft
Stroke of beam at pump	8ft
Revolutions—2 per minute can be increased to 4½ per minute	
Estimated horsepower	200

It would appear that the wheel normally ran at 2½rpm.

Many places lay claim to having made the wheel but the metal parts seem to have been manufactured at the following works:

Axle—Mersey Iron Works
Hub—G. Forester & Co, Vauxhall Foundry, Liverpool
Rim—Gellings Foundry, Douglas

Local tradition asserts that the axle was brought into Laxey by boat, dropped over the side at high tide, roped at low tide and hauled on to the beach and up the glen by a team of miners. This would seem likely, for when the Snaefell mines were reboilered at the turn of the century, the boilers were floated into Laxey harbour behind the boat and hauled right up the valley by several teams of horses.

The power was transferred from the wheel through a rod made up of eighteen oak beams plated together and running on rollers; the latter were pairs of wheels not unlike a miniature railway bogie and ran on metal rails set on top of the arched stone viaduct. An inverted T-shaped rocker changed the horizontal movement of the viaduct rod to the vertical movement of the pump rods, which is probably the part of the work Bowden advised on. This rocker is still visible at the head of the Engine shaft. When the wheel was built in 1854, and the pump rods were installed, the mine was 200 fathoms deep. In 1868 the rods had to be replaced with new and stronger rods in order to carry the mine below 220 fathoms. A few years later the intermediate strapping band was added to strengthen the spokes of the wheel. Since the wheel was purchased by the insular government in 1965 the Wheel Management Committee have carried out an extensive programme of repair and renewal; it now looks as it did in its heyday and is once again able to turn. In carrying out the repairs many of the materials and some of the construction have had to be altered but the new work has been 'faked' to look like the original. Considerable work has been done on the watercourses so future visitors will be able to see 'the largest waterwheel in Europe' in working order.

The ore was raised in kibbles, which were large metal-banded wooden buckets about 2ft in diameter and 4ft high. These were hauled up the shaft in a timber duct 'four boards wide and two boards deep' as far as the adit level, where the man on the striking boards pulled them in and tipped the ore into the trucks of the railway. A steam-powered beam engine, installed in 1846 by James Malcolm, operated the winding gear on the Welsh and Engine shafts until it was replaced by the turbine in the lower Engine house in 1862. The beam engine was not, however, removed but remained to provide a useful standby for the turbine in time of drought. The drive from the turbine had one cog-wheel with timber teeth so that should the turbine jam while under full load the easily replaced timber teeth would strip, thus avoiding damage to the rest of the equipment. Signalling from the striking boards was by means of a bell rope or, in the case of Dumbell's shaft after the telephone failed, by 'ringing' on the compressed air pipes with a hammer. A mouse-shaped marker running along the winding room wall gave an indication of where the kibble was in the shaft at any given time but to give accurate control a rawhide thong was spliced through the winding rope when any level was being worked for the first time.

The Carpenters' shop, and the Blacksmiths' shop with its six hearths, were situated in the Mines Yard, together with the Mines Office and House. The original Mines Captain's House is now the Station Hotel, having been largely demolished when the Manx Electric Railway was constructed in 1895. The Powder Houses were also on the Mines Yard, but the Dynamite store was well away from them in a tunnel at the bottom of Cronk e Chule, across the river. On the opposite side of the Ramsey–Douglas road were the Washing Floors with their jaw-crushers, jiggers and buddles (p 18). From here a 3ft gauge horse-drawn tramway carried the concentrates down the Glen Road to the harbour, where they were stored in a walled compound until shipped away (smelting was never carried out except for assay purposes). The company at one time owned its own boats but after the wreck of the ss *Reliance* in 1887, relied mainly on charters.

Two other uses of water power in connection with the mines are worth mentioning—its operation of Switchback and the Haaman. The Switchback, or Browside tramway, was an incline railway built in 1890—and removed before 1914—which took visitors to the wheel; a water tank on one coach was filled until it overcame the weight of the other, thus hauling it to the top of the incline. The Haaman (apparently named after Haaman in the book of Esther, who hanged himself on a high gallows after failing in his plotting against the Jews—or was it merely a Hayman lift?) worked on the same principle but in a vertical tower; it carried trucks of waste for tipping to the top of the spoil heaps, and like the rest of the washing-floor machinery it was sold for scrap.

The Foxdale Mines

The name Foxdale mines is of recent origin. Although popularly thought of as being the area south-east of the Higher Foxdale valley it covers, in fact, five separate mines—Upper Old Foxdale, Lower Old Foxdale, Old Flappy, Maghie's (4, 5, 6 and 7 on the map) and the Louisa (8). The last was also known as Johnson's, Faragher's or Hodgson's mine. Also to be associated with this group are the Far Gin and New Foxdale mines (9 and 10, later combined and called East, or Central, Foxdale) at the Eary; Jones's (11, later Townshend's) at Cornelly; Ballerghy (12, or Clucas's mine or Bell's Hole) on the right bank of the stream lower down the main Foxdale valley, and the Glen Rushen group of Beckwith's, Cross's and Dixon's mines (1, 2 and 3). In addition to these twelve main mines there were a host of trials made by the Isle of Man Mining Co to test the veins running through the area, some of which were later developed but without great commercial success. The company was formed in 1828 by a group of Liverpool, Chester and Flintshire businessmen and was based on Chester, and throughout its history it retained strong connections with that town. It was the first modern mining company to operate on the Island and was responsible for the development of all the Manx mines except for those of Lonan and Maughold. Its operations continued until 1911 but from 1846 the lease was confined to a large area in Foxdale.

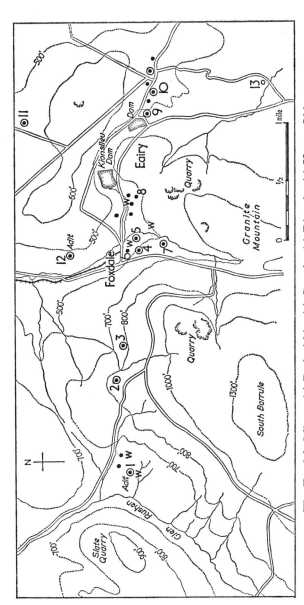

The Foxdale Mines: (1) Beckwith's; (2) Cross's; (3) Dixon's; (4) Upper Old Foxdale; (5) Lower Old Foxdale; (6) Old Flappy; (7) Maghie's; (8) Louisa; (9) Far Gin; (10) New Foxdale (9) and (10) later combined as East, or Central, Foxdale); (11) Jones's (later Townshend's); (12) Ballergy (or Clucas's, Faragher's or Bell's Hole); (13) Ballanicholas trial; (W) known waterwheel site

Trials made westward from Foxdale included a series on Dalby Mountain—developed as the Mount Dalby mine—and on the west coast between Fleshwick Bay and Glen Maye. The most southerly was the Stack trial, but no remains of buildings are visible from the sea. A pocket of antimony was discovered and worked out in the Niarbyl area; the workings, visible as a 'cave' on the shore were unprofitably reopened in the 1880s as the Glen Rushen and Niarbyl mine. The most northerly trials were at Glen Maye, where eighteenth-century trials were extended and again abandoned. The later history of this area is described in the Gazetteer, p 202. To the east of the Foxdale valley there were trials at the Garth and Ellerslie—marked by a chimney SC 328780. These were abandoned by the company but also reopened, as the New Foxdale (also, Mona, Great East Foxdale, Bishop's Barony or Darragh) mine of the 1880s. There was also a trial at Ballanicholas (13) which was never reopened; its site, just upstream of Campbell's bridge, is marked by spoil heaps and much zinc ore.

Upper and Lower Old Foxdale. These mines developed on four main lodes, the most important being the Foxdale Lode running east–west. A companion east–west lode crosses the main lode near the Old Engine shaft and a cross-vein runs north–south (from Old Flappy north, cutting the Foxdale lode near Bawden's shaft). Faragher's vein runs north from Faragher's mine. As indicated previously there had been spasmodic trials in Foxdale at an early date. In 1740 Michael Connor noted five pits, running east to west from the river, the deepest being 17 fathoms and the shallowest 7 fathoms; these were sited on the back of the main Foxdale lode. When the Isle of Man Mining Co took over in 1828 the deepest shaft had reached 40 fathoms and a shaft at Lower Foxdale had reached 13 fathoms.

The three main engine shafts were constructed by this company, and the Old Flappy, Upper Old Foxdale and Faragher's mines were joined and operated as one. Lower Old Foxdale was closed in 1829.

Page 71 *Bradda mines: (left) the engine house; (right) wooden laddering underground*

Page 72　(above) *Netmaking machines at a Peel factory. An example is preserved at the Nautical Museum, Castletown;* (below) *Clinch's Lake Brewery, Douglas in 1969*

The first period of expansion between 1828 and 1835 saw the opening of the Old Engine shaft and exploratory levels driven towards both Old Flappy and Faragher's mines. The mine was closed as exhausted above 45 fathoms and barren below that level in 1835 but was reopened in 1849 on the advice of Captains Bryant and Rowe. A new shaft, Beckwith's, was sunk at the Old Flappy mine and its levels eventually joined those of the Old Engine shaft. The westerly shaft, originally called Sebastapol to commemorate the victory but later known as Bawden's after a prominent local mining family of Cornish origin, was opened in 1855. This, in turn, was connected by levels to the Old Engine shaft, at 155 fathoms. Pott's shaft linked Faragher's mine to Old Foxdale in 1893. When the metal market collapsed in 1902 the shafts had reached depths of 290 fathoms (Bawden's), 170 fathoms (Old Engine) and 320 fathoms (Beckwith's). The engine house complex of Bawden's shaft just east of the Castletown road is well preserved. The brickworks, where the Douglas road crosses the stream, has destroyed the watercourse of the many wheels but the cut-down engine house of Beckwith's shaft survives. Most of the downstream deads and structures have been cleared but up to 1971 the retaining walls flanking the road still stood. Presumably these also supported a bridge for the track along which the tipping trucks ran but documentary evidence for its existence is lacking. The railway built a spur-line to carry the mineral traffic. Although the line has long been closed and most of the Foxdale end has been obliterated in a recent campaign to remove the deads, the station still survives, somewhat precariously, as an office.

Far Gin or New Foxdale—later Central Foxdale. In the early 1820s Michael Knott, one of the most important early exploiters of the Manx mines, discovered lead-bearing veins in an area just over a mile south-east of Old Foxdale. He worked here continuously and successfully until 1828, when the Isle of Man Mining Co took over. He had named his mine Far Gin, after the method used to raise the ore, and by 1827 there were seven shafts—Far Gin (South Vein), Far

E

Gin (North Vein), New String, Corner, Engine, Centre and Crellin's New—and the mine was more usually called New Foxdale. The company dispensed with some shafts: the Centre became the New Engine, presumably with a steam engine; a new shaft was dug on the Far Gin South vein; and development continued at Crellin's New shaft. Work continued until about 1835, when the Engine had reached just under 60 fathoms and the Far Gin about 12 fathoms. Trials were then made on the vein to the east, with work eastwards from the Engine shaft mainly at the 20 and 30 fathom levels, and these continued for not more than a year. Trials made in 1845–6 again tempted the company to reopen the mine for a short period in the 1850s. It would appear that the lease was sold about 1860 but the mine worked for only another three years. The lease was taken up again in 1871, when the mine was named the Central Foxdale and the shafts were renamed Elizabeth, Amy and Taylor's. Work continued until 1883, when the mine was taken over by the Central Foxdale Lead Mining Co. The shafts reached their final depths of 145, 40 and 74 fathoms, respectively, some years later.

Output and Silver Content of Lead Ore from Central Foxdale Mine

Year	Lead (tons)	Silver (oz)	Year	Lead (tons)	Silver (oz)
1872	50	819	1881	400	5,362
1873	135	2,200	1882	450	10,440
1874	58	968	1883	530	15,900
1875	20	280	1884	330	9,839
1876	70	591	1885	325	6,447
1877	198	1,184	1886	319	10,149
1878	360	6,074	1887	418	11,625
1879	360	4,337	1888	250	6,953
1880	250	5,032	1889	92	2,559

The profitability of the mine depended not only on the sheer quantity of ore raised but also on the silver content. As the table indicates this was a variable though high factor.

Old Flappy Mine. The most recent of the three early mines in the Foxdale area, this mine worked on the Old Flappy Vein, a cross vein of the Old Foxdale Lode; it is sited to the south of the Upper Old Foxdale Mine. Old Flappy opened before 1740 and then had only one shaft to Old Foxdale's five. Before Michael Knott took over the lease to mine throughout the Island in 1823, the mine was normally held jointly with Old Foxdale and worked spasmodically at the same periods. Knott reopened it but after some years appears to have closed it in favour of New Foxdale and it was not until the Isle of Man Mining Company took over the lease in 1828 that it was commercially exploited.

The shaft and day level were reopened in August 1828, together with the old workings. By 1829 a small wheel had been acquired from Lower Old Foxdale and the Engine shaft sunk 3 fathoms deeper. Operations ceased again in 1830 but restarted in 1833. Between 1830 and 1838 the mine was deepened and levels were driven towards both Old Foxdale and Maghie's, though there were not actually connections at this stage. The mine remained closed from about 1838 until Captains Rowe and Bryant, in their report to the company, suggested the opening of a new shaft and a link with Old Foxdale. Between 1849 and 1852 this new shaft, Beckwith's, was sunk and the mines joined; and so, from then on, Old Flappy was worked as part of Old Foxdale. The surface remains are insignificant.

Maghie's Mine. The vein on which Maghie's Mine was opened is a cross vein of the main Foxdale Lode discovered in the stream bed. A trial shaft started in July 1834 was intended to reach 15 fathoms, a depth at which a fair assessment of the vein could be made. By early 1835 it had reached 10 fathoms and levels were struck north-west and south-east, a substantial rib of fine lead ore being discovered in the former. During October of that year, with the shaft still under 12 fathoms deep, water became troublesome, perhaps aggravated by heavy rain. The closeness of the Old Flappy Mine provided an inexpensive solution and a line of rods was laid from the Old Foxdale wheel and connected to a series of pumps set down the Old Flappy shaft, from which one of the southern levels would be driven towards Maghie's. Although these drainage works were completed, water was again troublesome in 1837 and a wheel was moved to the mine from New Foxdale. In this year the Engine shaft was at 27 fathoms, with levels east and west at 20 fathoms. Operations continued until mid-1845, when a new waterwheel had to be erected to enable the mine to be driven to greater depths, and not until three years later did underground work restart. Maghie's then worked continuously until 1880, when, with the shaft at 124 fathoms, it was abandoned.

Its well-preserved stone wheelcase, about 9m by 16m, still stands just upstream from Beckwith's engine house. The wheel apparently pumped across the stream but the precise location of Maghie's shaft is uncertain. There is a typical stone mines company bridge across the stream near the wheelcase, and the intact powder house, almost the only one still roofed, lies still further upstream, close to the traces of a granite trial.

Jones's Mine—later Townshend's—at Cornelly. This mine, opened in 1837, was worked exclusively by the Isle of Man Mining Co until it was abandoned in September 1886. There were two main periods of activity: the first, when it was known as Jones's Mine, between 1837 and 1849, and the second after 1878. During the initial period the major works below ground were carried out: three shafts were dropped on the back of the lode, which runs approximately east–west. Because of the steepness of this lode the distance between the shafts is not great—about 92 fathoms. The furthest east, the Mountain shaft, was begun in 1837 but work stopped at 7 fathoms, because of the very watery ground; by 1840 a small pumping/crushing beam engine was installed and sinking recommenced. Extremely hard rock and excessive water again forced the company to reconsider the problem of sinking this shaft, so it decided to install a larger engine and to alter its crushing methods. In 1841 an order was placed with James Sims of Redruth for a 50in/90in combined cylinder engine, modelled on one then in use at Carn Brae Mine, Cornwall. In the meantime the crushing-rollers were replaced by a bank of stamps.

In early 1843, with the engine installed, sinking had started on a new shaft, about 80 fathoms west of the Mountain shaft, which was to be inclined on the course of the lode and to act as the engine shaft. In 1846, with the Engine shaft at about 60 fathoms, it was felt prudent to sink a new engine shaft about 12 fathoms to the west in order to give better access to the lode at greater depths. When the mine closed in 1849, this New Engine shaft had a deep level at 95 fathoms, with a sump slightly below, and connected at the 80 fathom level to the Old Engine shaft. Considerable quantities of lead ore had been raised in this period and the mine was a profitable enterprise. But, because of its barrenness below 80 fathoms it was abandoned in 1850 and the machinery moved to the Old Flappy Mine.

A series of trials was carried out in the area around 1866–8 in an attempt to trace the lode on the surface but apparently nothing of significance was discovered and work ceased. In the hope that, as at Old Foxdale, more ore might be met with at a greater depth the mine was reopened in 1878. The whole surface area was remodelled— plans for this are preserved in the Manx Museum—so that the surviving buildings do not tally with those shown on the 25in map. Those extant include the New Engine shaft's engine house and at- tached boiler house (with the beds of two boilers), and chimney; the Old Engine house (p 53) and its boiler house; the office; chang- ing room block and smithy; the Powder house (well to the west of the Old Engine shaft); a small circular buddle; an oddly designed, rectangular, diagonally divided slime pit; and the large rectangular reservoir that provided water for this hilltop site. Work below ground started in 1879 but the company's hopes were not realised; and althou3h a great deal of ore was raised—mainly from the old 20, 40, 50, 65, 80 and 95 fathom levels—it proved uneconomic, and the new low levels—110, 125 and 140 fathoms—produced little. By 1886, with the deep level in the New Engine shaft at 140 fathoms, the mine was finally abandoned. It is, perhaps, significant that very little ore can be found in its spoil heaps.

Faragher's, Johnson's, Hodgson's or the Louisa Mine. In October 1830 a vein of ore was discovered between Old and New Foxdale Mines and named Faragher's Vein. The mine was opened in late 1831 with a whimsey shaft and day level and an east–west level at 10 fathoms. Even at this slight depth there were pointers to the future potential of this mine: at 10 fathoms a run of solid ore had been discovered, 13 fathoms long and varying in width from 6–72in. Very serious flooding was occurring, however, by mid-1832 with the shaft at only 16 fathoms; so a wheel was sited to the north, below the washing floors, and the sinking of an engine shaft on the Middle Vein begun. In the following year a pumping engine was bought from the Carregboeth Mine in Wales and placed on Kelly's shaft (the old whim shaft), while a ventilation shaft, Harrison's, was opened to the south-east. By 1835 the new engine shaft was at 30 fathoms but watery soft rock hampered progress, doubt was expressed on bearing much deeper and finally the mine closed.

Captains Rowe and Bryant in their 1845 report to the company suggested that the mine be reopened despite the fact that the 30 fathom level was unproductive since they considered the high profitability of the upper levels indicated that more ore could be found at a deeper level. They felt that an increase in depth of 10–20 fathoms would be worthwhile. Work restarted in 1849, under the new name of Hodgson's Mine, the Engine shaft becoming the Louisa at the same time. During the 1850s a new eastern shaft, to be known as Pott's, was sunk; it had reached 67 fathoms in 1866 when work was put in hand to convert it for use as the main engine shaft, operations on the 82 fathom deep Louisa ceasing. In the next thirty years Pott's was deepened to 200 fathoms and was joined to the Old Foxdale Mine at the 127 fathom level. The mine was worked with Old Foxdale and Old Flappy until they petered out in the early years of the twentieth century. Some traces of the buddles, wheelcases, etc, of the Louisa mine may be found just south of the intact Kion-slieu dam, which provided water. Pott's shaft may also be found on top of the large spoil heap parallel to the Douglas–Foxdale road.

Ballerghy or Clucas's Mine—later Bell's Hole. This mine was the furthest downstream of the group in the main Foxdale valley. Work started in 1835 but had to stop early in the following year, with the shaft at 7 fathoms while a wheel from Faragher's Mine was moved to a site across the valley. By July 1836, the wheelpit had been completed and the wheel and lades positioned. A depth of 16 fathoms was reached in 1837 and ore had been discovered at the 7 fathom level in an adit to the west. Work ceased on the 10 fathom level in November 1837, the shaft having reached 38 fathoms, with further levels at 20 and 30 fathoms. Apparently the mine was abandoned about 1839 and the wheel was moved, again, to Beckwith's.

Mining restarted in the 1890s under the name of the Bell's Hole Mine, on a pessimistic annual lease, and soon ceased. The Bell's Hole Mining Co made several trials in the area of the old workings during World War I with no apparent success, the lease being surrendered in 1921. A last attempt to find profitable ore was made in 1924, when the Foxbell Mining Co Ltd spent nearly £6,000 in sinking two new shafts, only to be forced to cut their losses and close down completely in 1926. Remains at the site include a circular concrete buddle and some machinery mountings. The adit entrance is near the small sewage works on the right bank of the stream, SC 279781.

Beckwith's Mine. In 1831 the Isle of Man Mining Co started operations in Glen Rushen by sinking a shaft on the Beckwith Lode, after which both this shaft and the mine were named. An adit driven from a ravine to the west of the shaft was expected to strike it at 18 fathoms. Water was a problem, flooding into the workings from the south, and a pendulum pump was installed early in 1832. By 1836 the company's agent had completed the initial work: the adit and shaft had been joined and a further adit from Shimmin's Vein (also discovered in 1832) had been linked to the infant mine. In driving the adit there had been large discoveries of ore, 650 tons of lead having been raised and reserves of well over 1,000 tons remaining. It was decided, however, that the next stage would be to sink Beckwith's (or the Engine shaft) below adit level. A small steam engine was moved from the Far Gin shaft at New Foxdale to cope with the water. It was not housed and had hardly been installed when more water problems hit the mine: the summer was unusually dry, so the supply of water for washing dried up, while the small pumping engine failed to cope with the water flooding into the workings below ground.

William Jones, the company's managing director and inspecting engineer, decided to cure both problems by diverting the stream running below the mine. Leading it through the floors would provide ample water for washing, condensing and powering a pressure engine—thus releasing the small engine for winding and crushing. At the same time a new engine was ordered from Coalbrookdale, since the shaft was to be further deepened, and by May 1837 it was installed and working; the pumping machinery was coupled on one side and the crushing mill on the other. The Engine shaft was now 7 fathoms below the day level or about 22 from the surface and it was planned to send out new levels at 10 fathoms (ie 25 below the surface). The shaft was at 33 fathoms by November; at 25 fathoms the eastern level was being cross-cut into the vein and the western extended to between 12 and 15 fathoms. During this year a sump, or winze, was also sunk between the day and 25 fathom levels. In November it was decided to sink the shaft below 35 fathoms and then drive levels at this depth.

In February 1838, it had been felt that the present engine would be able to serve this shaft for another 10 or 20 fathoms but by August it was clear that the pumps could barely keep the mine dry, though the shaft was only just below 35 fathoms. William Jones felt that no greater depths could be reached with just the engine, which was also still powering both the crushing and winding machinery; so he ordered the large waterwheel from Old Foxdale to be dismantled and resited in the valley below Beckwith's shaft, thus freeing the engine for its other work. The 25 fathom level had been timbered between February and August and the new low levels had reached 7 fathoms eastward and 10 fathoms westward. Progress was now such that by October 1839 the shaft was at 48 fathoms.

The lack of water on the surface and surplus below ground still caused bother. Beckwith's wheel had been reset and balanced but it only just kept the water under control. By February 1840, the bottom of the shaft was just under 50 fathoms and new east–west levels at this depth had reached about 8 fathoms in each direction. In the following month the lowest easterly level was being driven in a vein 7 feet wide and work was also continuing at 25 fathoms (westerly) and 35 fathoms. A very dry season forced the work of deepening the shaft to cease, as this operation required more water than was available. During the following year the directors opened negotiations with James Sims of Redruth to supply a 50in cylinder pumping-engine but apparently it was never supplied.

The year 1842 proved to be disastrous for the mine. In February, drivings were taking place in the 50 fathom west level and also at 65 fathoms, while the shaft was at 75 fathoms sinking to 80. A further crushing mill was ordered from Belfast in May, a 20in engine being moved from Cross's Mine to power it; both were working by August, giving the mine two crushing mills—which alone argues a profitable site. A 12hp disc engine was bought in this period for winding. Plans were also made for improved water use on the surface. Two new watercourses were to be added, one from the North Gill and the other from the area of Dixon's Mine, while it was intended to move a wheel from Johnson's Mine, Foxdale, to pump the Beckwith's wheel's tailwater up for re-use. However, these plans were made too late and by August the mine had been badly flooded up to the 30 fathom level. Jones still maintained that it would be more economic to improve the water supply than to install another steam engine, since the necessity to import coal made their running very expensive in Man. By November he was forced to reconsider, as it proved that the flooding had caused very extensive damage. Levels had fallen into one another and there were bad roof-falls. A 50in cylinder engine had, therefore, to be bought from Gwernymyndd Mine near Mold, ostensibly for use when it was too dry to use the wheel.

In March of the following year it was decided that the shaft should be sunk to 80 fathoms, when cross-cuts would be made; and by April drivings had been started in the lowest level at 65 fathoms. By July the new engine was installed, being used while the wheel was overhauled, and there were drivings in the 20 fathom (east and west), 35 fathom (east) and 50 fathom levels. Sumps were being sunk in the sole of both the east and west 50 fathom levels and in the following year, in order to test the vein further, this process was repeated at 80 fathoms on both sides of the engine shaft. In May 1844, the company's miners had traced the run of the vein westward and found it appeared in the cliffs near Dalby Point. In November of the same year the sinking of the shaft to 95 fathoms was still in progress and a cross-cut had been made to the north, in the 80 fathom east level, to link with a sump sunk from the 65 fathom east level.

The work of sinking the Engine shaft to 95 fathoms was still in progress in February 1845, as well as driving on the 80 fathom level. On the washing floors a Doon wheel and stamps were erected. Rowe and Bryant also reported on this mine in 1845, stating that a day-level had been brought up from the valley, to the west, to meet the Engine shaft at 23 fathoms; it extended parallel to the vein for 100 fathoms and had three cross-cuts in barren ground and one in ore—the last 30 fathoms to the east of the shaft and running 27 fathoms east. The Engine shaft had been sunk under the adit with levels at 10 fathoms (driven 45 fathoms west and 10 fathoms east), 20 fathoms (54 west, 28 east), 35 fathoms (51 west, 28 east), 50 fathoms (50 west, 45 east), and 60 fathoms (46 west, 45 east). The shaft reached 80 fathoms, where a cross-cut had been made, and the winzes, or sumps, were sunk below the 65 fathom level. A level had also been driven in the North Gill (north of Beckwith's) for 300 fathoms on the course of the vein.

From the observations of Rowe and Bryant it appeared that the vein was dipping 18in south in every 72in of its height. They recommended the sinking of a new engine shaft further south to 150 fathoms and that a day-level should be driven east towards Cross's Mine. In the following year R. S. Bryant reported further on the mine. The Engine shaft was still struggling towards a depth of 95 fathoms but the 80 fathom levels had reached 8 fathoms east and 12 fathoms west. In the 65 fathom level east several fathoms had been driven eastwards on the South (Beckwith's) Vein and a cross-cut north had hit the North (or North Gill) Vein. In the 35 fathom level a further 17 fathoms had been driven east on the South Vein and a cross-cut was only 5 fathoms from the North Vein. It was intended to continue the last on the vein and to deepen the first adit shaft west of the Engine shaft.

In 1849 a trial shaft was being cut on the North Gill Lode (Edmund's shaft) and it was intended to erect a wheel at the bottom of the gill. Taylor reported that Beckwith's shaft had finally reached 95 fathoms and it was felt that the wheel was now inadequate. A new shaft was being sunk to the east and work on remodelling the washing floors was carried out. After this date information is sparse concerning the operation of individual mines, but it is known that in 1867 a drainage level (or sough) had been driven east and it would also unwater Cross's at 70 fathoms and enable the two mines to be worked as one.

Between 1849 and 1879 the mine was drastically deepened in response to the general feeling that in Manx mines the ore improved with depth. A company assay book, which starts in 1857, shows a regular cargo from this group from November of that year until February 1863, after which entries are scarce, the last being August 1870. Nine years later the company ceased operating this mine and sold the area of the sett for £5,000. In 1911 it was estimated that a total of 41,539 tons of ore had been raised between 1831 and 1862, worth, at that time, £535,913. When it closed, the main shaft was at 185 fathoms and a new day-level had been driven in at 35 fathoms.

The older levels (50, 65, 80 and 95 fathoms) had given a vein 10–15ft wide, yielding 15 tons of lead per fathom. Of the newer levels, 110 and 125 fathoms proved barren, as William Jones had stated, but at 137, 152, 167 and 182 fathoms the vein appeared again, in places 20ft wide and producing 30 tons per fathom. There were various attempts to reopen mines in this area, one man going so far as to buy equipment from Great Laxey when it closed; he intended to use one of the air shafts as a new engine shaft but his funds ran out before he had done more than erect two sections of iron chimney. Much of the underground fittings seem to have survived but although some levels are still above water attempts to descend have been foiled by the mass of impacted ladderings and dumped rubbish in the main shafts.

Cross's Mine. The early success at Beckwith's Mine led the company to reopen the Cronk Vane site in the hope of finding an extension of Beckwith's Vein. After an initial survey, work began in 1832 on a shaft to the west of the original working. Two years later, when this shaft (the Engine shaft) was about 10 fathoms, the company negotiated the purchase of a small steam engine from Cornwall at a cost of £450. This, with a 16in cylinder, was to be fitted with a crushing mill on one side and a pumping-crank on the other. The latter was a precaution, as the works were still dry, but the management had had experience with striking watery pockets at greater depths at the Beckwith's shaft and were not going to be caught again with inadequate pumps.

By 1835 the shaft had reached 17 fathoms and it was expected that it would be another 8 fathoms deeper before the engine, which had arrived, was in working order. But water was still no problem and winding was carried out by a gin. A depth of 30 fathoms had been reached by February of the following year but there had been trouble with the couplings between the engine and the crushing mill, and replacements had to be obtained from Chester. A level was started in November 1836 and driven east at 30 fathoms from the shaft; six months later a lower level, at 40 fathoms, was begun. North–south 30 fathom levels were also started and the east level was linked to the old workings higher up. Trouble still dogged the Cornish engine and its boiler had to be supplemented by one from Bradda while a replacement was ordered from Messrs W. Scott of Flint.

Drivings in the east and west 40 fathom levels were continuing in November 1837 without any appreciable deepening of the shaft. The eastern level reached 15 fathoms from the shaft and a cross-cut was made to test the vein. William Jones, after inspection, decided to start sinking the shaft another 10 fathoms; he also arranged on his return to England for W. Charles Morgan 'of the Bog' to visit Man and carry out various engineering repairs and, particularly, to service the Cross's Mine engine.

February 1838 saw more changes at the mine. Arrangements were being made to replace the Cornish engine (for pumping and crushing) with a larger engine from Faragher's Mine, Foxdale. The former would then replace the horse gin, which was unsatisfactory at the present depths, for winding and some crushing. Plans were also made to run pump-rods from the new engine to Dixon's mine; by August, Richard Powning, the company's engineer, had completed the work and the engine was functioning well. Just over a year later drivings were being made from the Engine shaft at 50 fathoms.

On his visit in February 1840, William Jones recommended a replacement engine to take over the work of the Cornish engine and an order was at once placed with the Rhydymyn Foundry. By March, while work continued east and west at 50 fathoms, a rise was being put up in the 50 fathom north level to meet a sump sunk from the 40 fathom level. The Engine shaft was being deepened by a further 15 fathoms. Above ground the foundations for the new engine were being laid and by April the existing horse-whim had been supplemented by another from Ballacorkish Mine, Rushen, since two shafts were now working. It was then hoped that the Rhydymyn foundry engine would be shipped, aboard the *Elk*, within the week.

During 1842 the East shaft reached 65 fathoms and driving continued east, towards Dixon's at 50 fathoms; at the same time a short level was driven west at 65 fathoms, with a sump in its sole. William Jones suspended operations in 1843, ordering the removal of the pumps and timbering from the shafts. Trial trenches were dug to the east and south, and a level started to the east, without success. In the 1845 report Rowe and Bryant reported that the mine was unwatered by a 30in pumping engine. The existing Engine shaft was at 65 fathoms; a level at this depth extended for 50 fathoms, with sumps at depths of 9, 6 and 3 fathoms. An adit from the valley to the east ran for 70 fathoms in barren rock. Rowe and Bryant suggested that a new shaft be sunk to the south but the mine appears not to have reopened until 1866, when it was worked with Beckwith's and deepened to 80 fathoms. The rights were sold in 1881 for £7,000, which argues more promise than the mine's past performance would suggest.

Dixon's Mine. The earliest reference to work in this area is in William Jones's report for 1835, where he records the discovery of Dixon's Vein. In the following year the shaft reached 7 fathoms but water was a problem and work was suspended, it was thought for about twelve months, until a level could be cut to meet the shaft. By May 1837 this had been done, at 20 fathoms, and levels were being driven both east and west at 7 and 17 fathoms from the surface. Since all mining was above the drainage level no machinery was required; the water drained naturally and waste and ore were removed by railroad.

Operations were suspended by 1842 and trials were being cut on the surface, to the east of the mine, to trace the vein. The 1845 report suggested that a level, some 20 fathoms long already, be driven west from Old Foxdale, it being estimated that it would intersect Dixon's at 60ft. In his 1849 report Taylor suggested a new shaft to the south and a waterwheel for pumping but nothing seems to have been done until 1866, when the engine and pitwork were repaired and the shaft was drained and divided. It was estimated in 1837 that the cost of sinking the engine shaft 32 fathoms would be £2,300. In fact by 1868, when operations were again suspended, the shaft had reached 47 fathoms, with levels at 17, 32 and 47 fathoms. A further shaft 280yd to the east (the East shaft) had reached 17 fathoms, with a level at this depth. Nothing came of the plan to link the workings with those in the Foxdale valley and this mine now has the least impressive surface remains of its group.

Surface Remains in Glen Rushen. Most of the shafts of the Glen Rushen mines are on the east bank of the stream, though a spoil heap on the west probably indicates the position of West Beckwith's mine, SC 247777. Of the main group Beckwith's, SC 252779, has the most substantial remains. These include a fine engine house, a crushing plant with attached wheelcase, office and (nearest the Glen Maye road) the mine captain's house. The extensive washing floors are being excavated (1969–70) by the Manx Mines Research Group and buddles, ducts and the water supply for the small wheel that powered some of the washing-floor plant are being exposed (p 54). Half-way down the little glen below Beckwith's are two further wheelcases; the better preserved has a handsome arched entrance to the tunnel up which the pump-rods ran to the main shaft. A sough connects to the same complex from the next side valley seaward. Unfortunately, little trace survives of the extensive network of leads for the water-wheels. The shaft in the still cultivated fields of Ballacottier farm was known as Edmund's and was that selected in an attempt to reopen the mines about 1920. The other mines, moving from west to east, are Cross Vein, SC 262780, with a tall engine house on its Engine shaft and the earlier Whim shaft to the east; and Dixon's, SC 265780, again with the Engine shaft to the west and an East shaft—both with quite substantial masonry remains.

The Mines Labour Force

Fortunately the deficiencies in the mines records are to some extent supplied by the census returns for 1851, 1861 and 1871, which are available locally. Of course they seldom show which mine a man was employed in but the total figures for the main mining parishes are of considerable interest. The enumerators followed their instructions carefully and distinguished, for example, between miners, mine labourers and ore washers. Since strictly a 'miner' was the leader of a gang their numbers are clearly inflated and, since many men travelled considerable distances, the figures given here are not complete—though they are a fair guide to the composition of the labour force at a time when the mines were thriving.

The Mines Labour Force as recorded in the 1851 Census

PATRICK (mainly Foxdale mines)

Lead Mines Agent	William Bawden	*Book-keeper*	John Cowin
Engineers	William Cain Nicholas Woodcock Robert Bridson	*Joiners*	William Kelly Thomas Clucas
		Joiner at *Foxdale Mines*	William Kelly
Engine Worker	Thomas Johnson		
Enginemen	William Bridson Edmund Corteen John Cain	*Miners 87 Mine Labourers 37*[1] *Apprentice Lead Miner* 1 *Learning to be a Lead Miner* 1	
Master of Lead *Ore Washers*	John Johnson	*Lead Ore Washers 19*—of whom 8 have widowed mothers and 3 are Agricultural Labourer's sons.	

OF TOTAL LABOUR FORCE: A. *Sons of farmers*, 5; *Agricultural Labourers*, 5; *Craftsmen*, 3.

B. *Born in England*, 14; *Ireland*, 2; *Scotland*, 2.

C. *Miners, and also farmers of 30 acres*, 1; *20 acres*, 2; *10 acres*, 1; *9 acres*, 1; *8 acres*, 1.

D. *Households with two servants*, 1; *one servant*, 2; *one farm servant*, 1; *one house and one farm servant*, 1.

E. *Lodgers, with miners*, 2; *non-miners*, 2.

[1] Including a woman 64 years of age.

Page 89 (above) *Hill's Royal Hotel, Douglas, c 1850. Note the paddle steamers, the light on the 'Old Red Pier' and the coach office;* (below) *the Royal Hotel area in 1970. Note the bus station and air terminal—above the cargo boat, the iron swing-bridge of 1894, the fluted roof of the new sea terminal at the end of the Victoria pier*

LONAN (mainly Laxey mines)

Manager &			
Proprietor	Richard Rowe	*Mine Agent*	Frank Rowe
Lead & Copper Mines			
Mining Engineer	Robert Casement	*Engineer*	Edward Bawden
Hostler for Laxey		*Lead*	
Mines	William Dickenson	*Wagoner*	John Harrison
Attending machine at		*Machine*	
Lead Mines	James Lawton	*Labourer at*	
		the mines	John Cowin

Miners 136   *Mine Labourers* 61   *Dressers* 2

Master of the Lead		*Lead Ore Washers* 39—of whom
Ore Washers	John Kinley	6 have widowed mothers and 1 is a woman.

OF TOTAL LABOUR FORCE: A. *Sons of farmers,* 5; *Agricultural Labourers,* 5; *Craftsmen,* 14.

B. *Born in England,* 27; *Ireland,* 4.

C. It is known that some of the Laxey miners also had a little land but some of these may have lived in adjoining parishes further from the mines since no acreages are given in this section of the Census.

D. *Households with three servants,* 1; *one house servant,* 1; *one house and one farm servant,* 1.

E. *Lodgers with miners,* 5; *non-miners,* 3.

Most of the 'miners' were between thirty and forty-five, though a few continued to work into their fifties. The very few exceptions in their teens are almost all miners' sons. Otherwise the under-twenties appear as labourers, since, as elsewhere, the payment of the team depended on results and only the strong could keep pace. It is noteworthy that the ore washers belonged to the poorer section of the community and included a number of young boys, who, being fatherless, were working when their more fortunate contemporaries were still at school. In contrast to the tendency towards late marriage often seen in crofting communities, the majority of the miners were married. In Patrick a number of the miners also owned farms, which was apparently usual and may to some extent explain the almost total absence of women among the mineworkers. A few households include servants but some of these may, in fact, be poor relations taken into a slightly more prosperous household, as was the local custom.

F

As is shown by their recorded places of birth, as well as their peculiarly Manx surnames, most of the men were local. The exceptions included a number of Cornish families, notably the Bawdens (ancestors of one of the authors), Groses (Rushen, 1861, Mathew Grose, Lead and Copper Mine Agent, born in Cornwall), Kittos (Rushen, 1861, William Kitto, Mines Agent, also Cornish-born) and Rowes (Lonan, 1851, Richard Rowe, Manager and Proprietor, Lead and Copper Mines, born St Agnes, Cornwall); the last named continued to supply managerial staff for the Manx mines. It is said that both German and Derbyshire miners came to Man but they do not appear at this date, though the Laxey Senogles were of continental origin. There were other Cornishmen, such as Thomas Trewetham and Thomas Penpacton from St Ives. It is noteworthy that although only the country of birth was asked for the Cornishmen were usually more specific. The families mentioned are well known in mining history and the Bawdens are probably typical of those who left the peninsula. (See *Industrial Archaeology of the Tamar Valley* for other Bawdens.)

Edward Bawden (born in Marazion) and his brother Joseph sailed for the Isle of Man when they were both in their twenties; they were shipwrecked on Lundy Island on their first attempt but finally reached Man about 1830. At first Edward was only 'a working miner' but in 1846 he applied for a trial, under inspection, as underground manager of the Isle of Man Mining Co at Foxdale. In May of that year he was appointed at a salary of £170 a year, plus a free house, as manager of the works. Initially this post carried with it certain perquisites but two years later the company curbed these and he was paid a total of £18 6s 8d a month, with a horse and gig to carry him about his work, still with a rent-free house. In 1853 he received a purse of 100 guineas from the Directors 'in acknowledgement of his skill and ability, in bringing the mine to its then prosperous condition, after 23 years of uninterrupted faithful service'. He was a supporter of the temperance movement and an arbitrator in local disputes. 'On one occasion indeed he saved the agent of the Woods and Forests from being seriously maltreated by the incensed miners' in a dispute over the enclosure of common land. He was on the building committee of the Foxdale church and also on the school committee. (The school was largely paid for by the mines company who also paid the teacher's salary of £100 a year.) When Captain Bawden retired in 1865, 'the men presented him with a solid silver service, as a token of their appreciation of his qualities as a master, and as a man'.

His brother Joseph also worked for the mining company. Captain Edward Bawden had married Louisa Ann Walker in 1832. Of his sons, John followed him as manager, Thomas (the youngest) was company secretary, and Edward was under-manager. Since an English-born John Bawden is listed in the 1851 Census as a visitor to Foxdale it would appear that other members of the family had followed Edward and Joseph to Man; but the failing fortunes of the Manx mines affected even the more skilled men and Edward Albert, son of Edward junior, was forced to emigrate to South Africa, and the family's connection with mining in the Isle of Man ceased.

Working Methods and Conditions with particular reference to Laxey

Originally all work in Manx mines was done by hand but by the time Feltham described the methods in his book, *A tour through the Isle of Man*, in 1797, blasting was normal:

> ... A miner sat down here and in about an hour pierced a hole, with great exertion, 16 inches deep. This was partially filled with gunpowder, and forcibly rammed down with proper wadding, to which a communication was made by a long pointed iron, into which was introduced a straw-reed full of prime; the end of the reed had a little brown paper greased and pointed; and with this, lighted like a candel, we retired, when the noise and echo of the explosion was tremendous. On returning we found very large pieces torn by the powder.

By 1900 a compressor house had been built and some compressed-air drills were in use, particularly round Dumbell's shaft, but one miner of this period was still able to describe the working methods of the rest of the mine as follows:

Holes were drilled with jumpers (long cold chisels) driven with a 14lb hammer. About 5 or 6 holes would be drilled, each to a depth of 3′ 6″–4′. The holes would be rodded out and $3\frac{1}{2}$ or 4 sticks of dynamite dropped in— each one being well rodded down. A detonator and length of fuse would be pressed into the top of another $\frac{1}{2}$ stick of dynamite and clayed around, and this put in on top. In a dry area the hole would be filled with dust and in a wet area with water.

The top of the fuse would be split and a chip of dynamite inserted. When all the holes had been charged a slow match was used to light the fuses.

When the air cleared and we returned the ore was broken up by pick and shovelled into wooden barrows to be wheeled away.

The men paid for their own dynamite, powder, fuses, candles and the sharpening of their tools. They worked in a 'pitch' of four men, one of whom was the Bargain man for the pitch, who agreed the rate per fathom with the Captain. On his ability to predict the difficulties of working depended the wages of his pitch. Lighting was by means of multi-wick tallow candles stuck in a ball of clay. This was either held in the hand or stuck to the miner's headgear, which customarily consisted of a felt hat stiffened with clay, under which the men wore cotton caps to protect the hair from dirt and absorb sweat. Several such hats and under-caps survive and one is shown in the Manx Museum. Candles were carried with their wicks tied together and looped over a hook on the breast of the man's overalls. Electric light, allegedly installed in the late 1870s, was used briefly round the man rods but seems to have had little more success than the telephone system.

Perhaps the most dangerous job was that of the 'timber men', who looked after all the timbering, linings and platforms, and repaired them as necessary. During their inspections they carried a ball of clay to smear across cracks to see if they were widening and a pocketful of pebbles which they threw ahead of them as they went, knowing from the sound whether the timber was safe to walk on. It is said that Clay Head, to the south of Laxey, got its name from a small seam of clay which proved very useful to the miners.

Records of the progress of the work were kept, surveying being carried out with a 5in compass fitted with a sighting rail. Plotting was carried out without apparent regard for adjustments of magnetic variation, which was revealed when Jespersen, while writing his book on the *Lady Isabella*, attempted to correlate the surviving plans with the surface remains. He subsequently redrew the plans, allowing for variation. Regrettably most of the companies' records have been lost. (The Laxey mine is now flooded up to adit level and although Jespersen has worked out a scheme for using modern pumps to drain the mine it is unlikely that this would be allowed even if funds were forthcoming. Moreover, the amount of impacted timber and rubbish is such that it is desirable to allow it some time longer to decay before an entry is attempted.)

Conditions in the Laxey mine were generally safe but wet. In the 1870s the company provided free medical attention for its employees and, through the Mines Club, which stopped 1s a week from their pay, operated a sickness benefit scheme. Anyone injured underground was brought up in the 'dead box'—a large coffin-like wooden box with a hinged lid, a cut-out panel opposite the head of the occupant, a seat and leather restraining strap. The dead box was attached to the hauling ropes in place of the kibble and hauled up the shaft while men walked the ladders beside it. Older and seriously disabled men were normally found surface work and a few pensions were paid.

Housing

As has been indicated it was not unusual to combine ownership of a croft with work in the mines. It is apparent from the census returns that about a quarter of the men employed in Manx mines were not born in the Island. Presumably it was to accommodate these that the mine companies erected housing, notably at Foxdale and Laxey. At the latter the terrace above the bridge, on the right bank, often called 'Ham and Egg Row' because of a former preponderance of eating places, was named, after one of the directors, Dumbell's Terrace.

Many of the crofts on marginal land at the head of the valleys were once the homes of miners and were abandoned when the mines closed; there were a few houses even at such remote sites as Glen Roy and Snaefell.

Mine captains had more impressive dwellings. Although reduced in size the Station Hotel, Laxey, shows how handsome a house was thought appropriate. Brookfield at Foxdale, built and owned by the Bawdens, is noteworthy for the quality of its interior woodwork. Only the shapely gable is preserved at Beckwith's mine, Glen Rushen, but the plan (pp 97–8) suggests what was likely at a rather less important mine—Townshend's mine at Cornelly, c 1880. Although extended, the house is still substantially as designed; it is built of carefully dressed and coursed local stone with brick surrounds to the windows. It is perhaps worth pointing out that an indoor lavatory was provided upstairs, though it is not clear how water was originally lifted to supply this or the boiler and sink in the scullery; the house stands very high so some form of pump was presumably necessary. The largest ground-floor room, 12ft by 16ft, was intended as a boardroom for the directors.

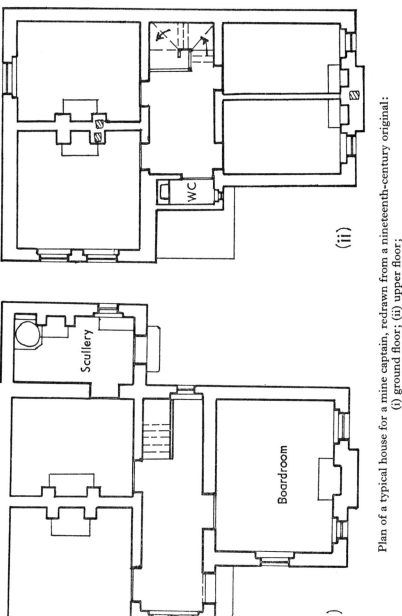

Plan of a typical house for a mine captain, redrawn from a nineteenth-century original: (i) ground floor; (ii) upper floor;

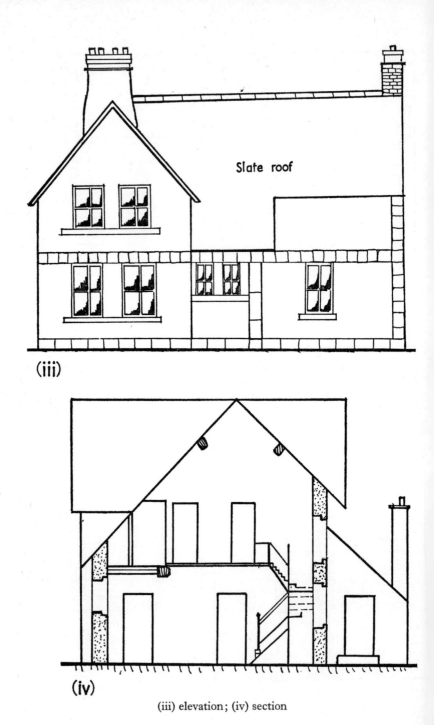

Slate roof

(iii)

(iv)

(iii) elevation; (iv) section

CHAPTER FIVE

The Tourist Industry

A VERY high proportion of the industrial monuments of the Isle of Man owe their existence to the tourist industry. Without the need to disembark, house, entertain and transport its visitors the Island would probably have remained as 'undeveloped', and doubtless would have become as depopulated, as the Scottish isles. Manx tourism was a product of nineteenth-century improvements in transport coupled with the establishment of the custom, particularly in the northern textile industry, by which whole towns took their annual holidays in a 'Wakes Week'. The Isle of Man seems to have become a popular resort fairly early: it has been stated that even in the 1830s some 25,000 people visited the Island annually, which compares favourably with the numbers at the then fashionable resort of Brighton and greatly outweighs Blackpool's mere 1,000. In its early days as a resort Douglas had visitors throughout the year, as sea bathing, for which it was highly commended, was held to be beneficial even in winter. These hardy visitors also botanised, studied the marine biology, walked and investigated the antiquities of the countryside. Like the poet Wordsworth and his sister Dorothy, they were undaunted by the miseries of the sea-crossing, which might take a full day even in summer.

Sea transport soon improved, however. Within seven years of the launching of the first British-built steamship (Henry Bell's *Comet* in 1813), the steamer *Robert Bruce* was calling regularly at Douglas en route from Greenock to Liverpool. At this time intending passengers were rowed out to the boat at Liverpool and, if the tide was low, might have to scramble into a rowing boat again in order to land at Douglas—hence the Royal Hotel's assurance, '. . . a safe boat belonging to the establishment and manned by regular Harbour Pilots lands passengers upon the Pier, free of charge . . . .'

The Isle of Man Steam Packet Co Ltd, so named in 1832, was founded in 1830. The paddle steamer *Mona's Isle* (I), its first vessel— built by John Wood of Glasgow with engines by Robert Napier—was advertised as carrying thirty-two passengers and took 8hr for the crossing to Liverpool. After this there were always Manx-owned boats offering a regular service which became ever swifter until in 1882 the *Mona's Isle* (III), another paddler, reduced the journey to 3hr 35min.

The population of Douglas rose as the number of visitors increased: there were about 6,000 inhabitants in 1820 and 12,500 in 1861. The Princes Landing Stage at Liverpool was built in 1857, by which time the city had been linked by rail to the industrial Midlands and North; but at the Douglas end the Victoria Pier was not completed until 1873. Once there was regular, fast, comfortable travel the numbers of visitors swelled; in the first year for which official statistics were kept there were 183,000. The special cheap fares of the Steam Packet's Jubilee Season brought these up to 348,000, with a slight decline when the fares returned to normal. The Island entered the conference trade early, when delegates from all parts of the United Kingdom assembled in Ramsey to form the first Grand General Union of Operators and Spinners in 1829.

From 1895 there was again an increase, the number of visitors reaching the record of 634,000 between May and September 1913. World War I, however, struck a blow at the Manx tourist trade from which it never recovered. Even during the post-1945 boom in holiday traffic, when the results of legislation regarding statutory paid holidays were finally apparent elsewhere, the Island could only attract a maximum of 624,747 people. Since then there has been a decline to about 400,000 and the population of Douglas has settled at about 20,000. But the building of some new attractions, such as the swimming-pools at Peel and Ramsey and the holiday centre complex at Derby Castle; and the provision of twin car ferries, the *Manx Maid*

(1962) and the *Ben my Chree* (1966), each of which can transport eighty cars on her main deck, may reverse this trend.

ACCOMMODATION

When the tourist trade started there was something of a shortage of accommodation, since the closely interrelated insular community had found little need to buy hospitality. At first existing buildings were adapted. Some sixty lodging houses found it worthwhile to advertise in the guidebooks of the 1830s. Castle Mona (built in 1804 by John, 4th Duke of Atholl and Governor-in-Chief of the Isle of Man) opened as a hotel in 1832 and 'Buck' Whaley's handsome eighteenth-century house, Fort Anne, suffered a similar fate in 1846; both are still operating. In 1840 the Castle Mona recommended the sea bathing and offered board and lodging at 2 guineas a week (servants £1 5s) with a reduction of one-half between 15 October and 15 April. By 1852 the number of advertised lodging houses had risen to eighty and the usual charge was a guinea a week or 7–10s a day, according to the position of the room—for a sea view already meant a higher charge. A day excursion to Ramsey (16½ miles) cost 5s return and to Peel or Castletown (about 10 miles) cost 2s.

The next two decades saw a major building boom. The *Manx Sun* recorded that in 1870 there were 1,500 lodging houses in Douglas alone. (The cheapest of these had to be controlled by Act of Tynwald in 1865 as they were beginning to be a health hazard.) The handsome crescent of the Loch Promenade at Douglas (see plate, p 107) was built between 1876 and 1878 on land reclaimed from the sea along the original sea front of Sand (later Strand) Street; £25,000 of the £30,000 cost of the work was recovered by the sale of the building plots, on which were erected houses of a more or less uniform design, though varying in size and detail. The Villiers Hotel, then the largest in the Island, opened, though unfinished, in 1877–8 with

200 bedrooms and 20 sitting rooms; and by 1889 it was advertising 300 rooms. At a time when an average London hotel charged 5s 6d for bed and breakfast it was charging 2s 6d to 3s 6d for bed and attendance, 2s for breakfast and 3s for dinner. There was little rise in prices for some considerable time. The Mount Murray Hotel, a pleasant mansion with a 'wild garden' and a small lake (now to be replaced by a motel), offered a week at £2 9s od in 1886. Three years later the Villiers charged £3 3s od, which would still pay for a week's board in Port Erin in the 1929–30 season.

At the end of the century lunch was served from 1–3pm and a 'table d'hôte' dinner at 6.30 or 7pm. A considerable number of servants looked after the visitors: in the 1871 census (out of season) the long-established Royal Hotel had a hotel keeper and assistant, a female housekeeper, two barmaids, a cook, a waitress, three house-maids and three kitchenmaids. The slowly rising costs of the servants' wages probably helped to force on the hotels a price increase of about 3s a day each decade. Boarding houses, being largely family-run, held their charges more nearly constant. In 1900 an average charge was 8s 6d a day and in 1936, with 'electric light throughout', it had become 10s 6d, during which time the hotel prices had crept up from 9s to about 17s 6d. Since 1945 prices have spiralled and, despite the absence of Selective Employment Tax, the daily rate is now about £1.25. Even the modest charges of the nineteenth century were too much for some and Cunningham's Young Men's Holiday Camp was founded to meet their needs in 1887; this camp has a good claim to have been the initiator of the great holiday-camp boom, as the canvas tents were soon supplemented by weatherproof chalets.

Douglas was not the only Manx resort where there was building to cater for the rising tide of holidaymakers but its position as the main landing place for visitors assured its pre-eminence. The Mooragh Promenade, Ramsey, was started about 1888 but never completed. Castletown, Port Erin and Port St Mary all have some fairly large hotels dating from about 1900, though the first, like Peel, is not yet a major tourist centre. Many country houses like Ballacooil, Ballacallin House and Ballachrink near Glen Maye were rebuilt or extended to accommodate visitors between 1900 and 1910. There has been little subsequent building and the tendency now is to convert older premises into self-catering accommodation, though the handsome new casino hotel is a welcome indication of future trends.

The Fittings of a Typical Boarding House about 1900

Lighting: Gas: halls, landings, kitchens and sculleries usually flat-flame, rigid fittings. Dining, sitting and other main public rooms usually chandeliers supplemented with wall brackets. It is likely that the Loch Promenade development had gas-lighting from the time of its building.

Water: Service to kitchens with large earthenware sinks. Each landing would have a cold tap and lead-lined sink for filling ewers, usually hidden in a doored cupboard which might be recessed in the wall. Hot water would be heated in the kitchen and carried to guests in cans.

Sanitation: Normally not more than two indoor toilets, with round earthenware bowls in box fittings. There would be a staff toilet in the yard or under the front steps.

Cooking: On open coal-burning ranges with heavy iron kettles and pans; the ranges, like the gas and plumbing fittings, would often be locally made by firms such as Gellings Foundry.

Heating: A coal fire in almost every room, with a charge of about 1s a week for those in bedrooms.

Laundry: Small establishments would have similar equipment to an ordinary household, with one or two coppers. Large hotels, like Milne's Waverley, Queen's Promenade, Douglas, would have a specially built laundry and the necessary staff.

The plans of the Belvedere Hotel, Loch Promenade, Douglas (shown here), were copied from the originals prepared when the hotel was built. The layout is fairly typical of the medium-sized establishments on the Loch Promenade, in contrast to the 200 room Villiers, and is almost exactly double the size of single-fronted boarding houses in the same development. It was planned as a temperance hotel. It is difficult to believe that it could be run by fewer than six (manager, cook, scullery maid, two housemaids and 'boots') but there appear to be insufficient bedrooms unless the attic was also used. Laundry maids may well have come in as required.

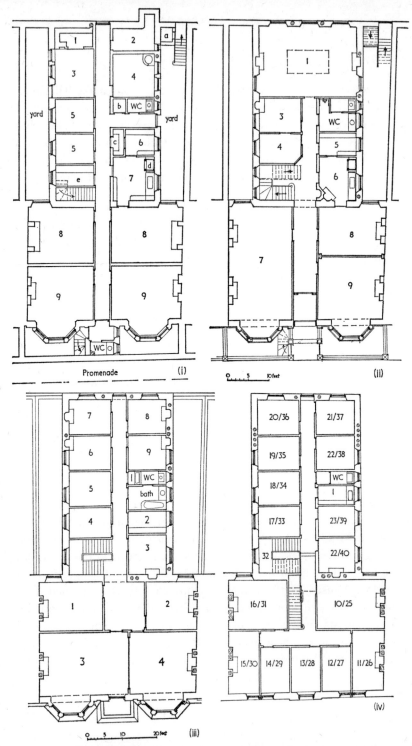

The Belvedere Hotel: for plate captions see page 105

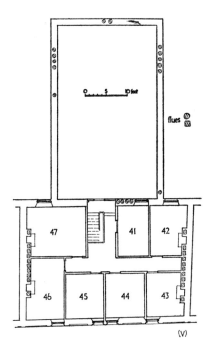

(V)

The Belvedere Hotel

(i) Basement: (1) drying closet of laundry; (2) coal store; (3) laundry; (4) wash-house; (5) servants' bedrooms; (6) pantry; (7) scullery; (8) kitchens; (9) stock rooms: (a) ash pit, (b) wand (ie broom) store, (c) store, (d) food-lift, (e) boots room under stairs

(ii) Ground floor: (1) billiard room; (3) private sitting room; (4) office; (5) pantry; (6) still-room with food-lift from basement; (7) dining room; (8) coffee room, can be divided into two

(iii) First floor; (iv) second and third floors; (v) attic

The small numbers are the original room numbers. Room 32 is situated over the stairs on the third floor as there is no attic at the rear.

(1) housemaids' closets on first, second and third floors; (2) linen closet on first floor; (3) drawing room, and (4) sitting room, both with glass-panelled doors

The public rooms included a large billiard room, sitting room and drawing room. The coffee room could be divided to give an additional sitting room which, like that behind the office, could be rented by a party. Presumably the manager or proprietor would use the private sitting room when it was not let. The most noteworthy feature of the fittings is the existence of a bath. There is no indication of how water was heated for this but gas may have been used or cans brought from the cooker in the basement. Like the other Loch Promenade hotels the Belvedere has been extensively modernised but, as the illustration shows (p 108), its façade has been changed very little apart from the doorway.

The Douglas boarding houses kept pace with changing circumstances as may be seen from the sketch plans (pp 109 and 110), which were compiled from information collected during the preliminary industrial archaeology survey. It is hoped ultimately to obtain more detailed and accurate data as part of a fuller study of the holiday trade.

Plan (i) shows the basement. The first alteration was the provision of a kitchen annexe, which resulted in one staff bedroom having no outside ventilation. The food lift was also resited. In 1969 the whole of the cooking and serving of food was replanned so as to be on one level and to take advantage of modern equipment. The modernised kitchen and still-room have wipe-clean surfaces, neon lighting, and easily cleaned non-slip floors. The walls, which are also washable, have a special finish that kills pests such as cockroaches, which tend to appear where there are bulk foodstuffs. Public-health inspection is strict and regulations are enforced—note the separate basin for washing hands at the end of the main sink unit.

Plan (ii) shows the ground floor. The initial alterations provided an annexe as the smokeroom and the original smokeroom became a lounge. For a short time this had a bar, which was later removed. (The number of licences for the sale of drinks to residents only has tended to increase.) While food was still hauled up to the first-floor dining room on the lift a pantry was necessary, but when the dining

Page 107   The Loch Promenade, Douglas in 1968. Notice the tracks for the horse trams

Page 108   *The Belvedere Hotel, Loch Promenade, Douglas in 1968*

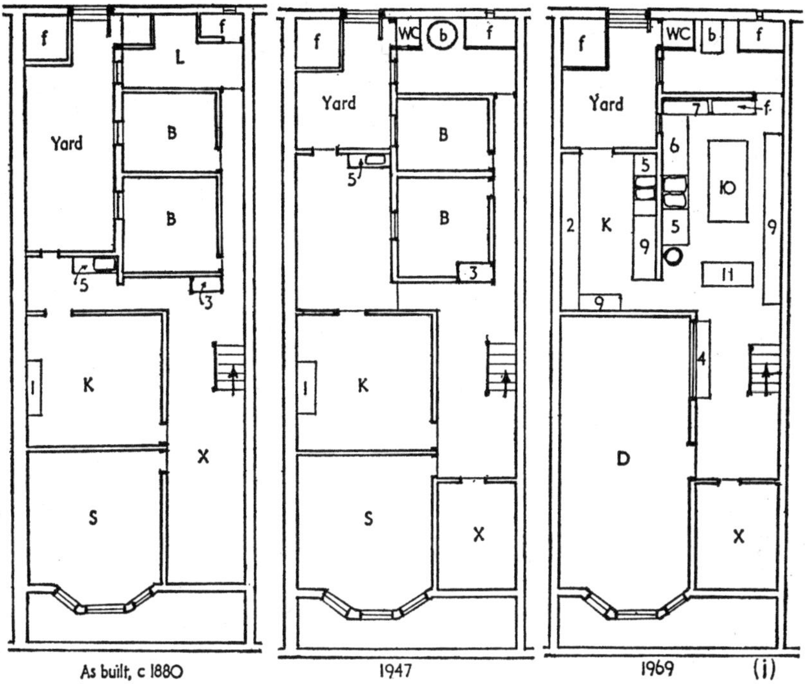
f
f
L
Yard
B
B
5
3
1
K
X
S
f
WC
b
f
Yard
B
5
B
3
1
K
S
X
f
WC
b
f
Yard
7
f
6
5
10
2
K
5
9
9
9
11
9
4
D
X
As built, c 1880
1947
1969
(i)

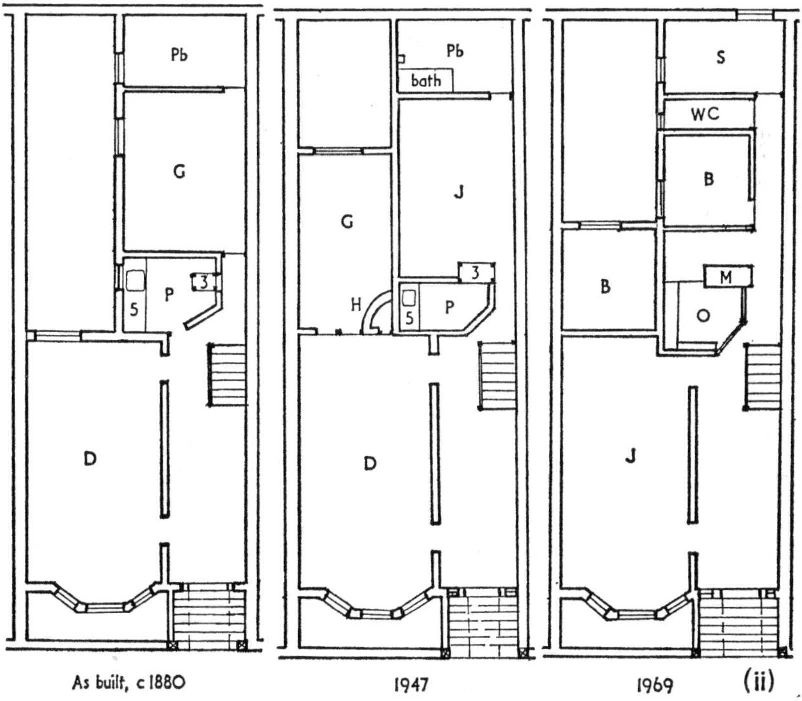
Pb
G
3
5
P
D
Pb
bath
J
G
3
H
5
P
D
S
WC
B
B
M
O
J
As built, c 1880
1947
1969
(ii)

G The development of a boarding house: for captions see page 110

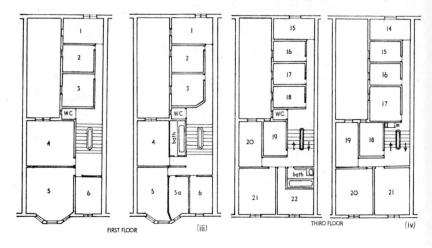

FIRST FLOOR   (iii)   THIRD FLOOR   (iv)

The development of a small boarding house in Douglas

(i) Basement; (ii) Ground floor
(B) staff bedroom; (b) boiler; (D) dining room; (f) fuel stores; (G) smoke room; (H) bar (1947 only); (J) lounge; (K) kitchen; (L) laundry (as built); (M) broom cupboard; (O) office (1969); (P) pantry; (pb) proprietor's room; (S) staff sitting room; (X) store
(1) coal-fired range; (2) modern cookers; (3) food-lift; (4) heated cupboard and serving-hatch; (5) sinks, earthenware as built; 1969 stainless steel units; other modern equipment mainly in reorganised still-room; (7) deep freeze cabinet for long-term storage; (8) large refrigerator for short-term storage; (9) cupboard units; (10) working table; (11) clothes cupboard
(iii) First floor; (iv) Third floor (*left*) as built; (*right*) in 1969

room was moved downstairs this area became the office. The bath shown in the proprietor's room (which was also fitted with a hand-basin) in 1947 was then the only one on the premises and was apparently not available to guests. In the most recent replanning the front room became the guests' lounge and the staff were provided with adequately ventilated bedrooms. Like those of the guests these were equipped with handbasins having hot and cold water. The public rooms on this floor were probably the first part of the hotel to be lit by electricity. As late as 1936 some smaller establishments still supplied their guests with a 'candle to light them to bed', though 'electric light throughout' was a proud boast on the Loch Promenade in the 1920s. One unusual feature of Douglas sea-front boarding houses, which mainly lack gardens, is the provision of seats up the front steps on which guests sun themselves or chat in the evenings. To some extent this communal seating may reflect the tendency for whole towns to holiday together, guests knowing fellow guests and those in adjoining establishments. Whatever the origin of this custom it started fairly early, as comic postcards show.

Plan (iii) shows the first floor. The second floor is essentially similar but the room over 4 is divided in two, as on the third floor (see Plan (iv)). These plans show the heroic measures necessary to insert even a minimum number of bathrooms and lavatories without sacrificing too many rooms. Even in 1969 there was no bathroom on the second floor, though the maid's cupboard, on the plan, has been replaced by a lavatory on the upper floors—to supplement the original fitting, now modernised, on the first. All rooms now have running hot and cold water, electric lights and either gas or electric (or, less commonly, central) heating. Electric heating may be only through a coin meter—a survival of the 'shilling for fires'. Decorations and furnishing are usually in a pleasant modern style.

PLACES OF ENTERTAINMENT

By the end of the eighteenth century the Island attracted sufficient wealthy people to support assembly rooms in which subscription balls and other entertainments could be held. Two are known to have existed in Douglas about 1780, one in Fort Street the other on the North Quay close to the Parade. About 1810 Banks Dancing Room and Playhouse (sometimes called Downward's Long Room, it being 50ft long and 40ft wide, or Downward's Assembly Room) stood at the opposite end of the North Quay near Clinch's Lake Brewery (see map, p 150). Other assembly rooms, sometimes also used as theatres, stood on the sites now occupied by St George's Chambers, Atholl Street and the old British Hotel in the Market Place. The sole survivor used for something like its original purpose is the Assembly Rooms, Wellington Hall (now the Golden Goose Club) in Strand Street. St James's Hall, Atholl Street, which also housed a library, is now an auction rooms. Outside Douglas, assembly rooms were combined with hotels: the Albion Hotel, Ramsey —now the Ascog Hall—and the George Inn, Castletown, are perhaps the more notable examples.

As the popular nature of the holidays offered in the Isle of Man became more apparent, monster ballrooms, initially as an adjunct to 'pleasure grounds' (with mazes, streams, wild gardens, bicycle riding, wine, cake and fresh strawberries), were erected. Derby Castle, once the residence of the Pollock family, was the first of these new attractions; it was opened in 1877 by A. N. Laughton, a Douglas advocate, and largely rebuilt and extended in 1884. Its ballroom could hold 5,000 dancers, but in time its extensive gardens were cut into by roads and the original structures were recently swept away to make room for a much needed indoor swimming-pool and elaborate modern amenities. However, the renamed operating company continues to control a sizeable share of Manx attractions including a majority of the cinemas. Falcon Cliff, once elegantly known as 'Cremorne', was opened in 1882 with similar facilities to Derby Castle; its enormous dancing pavilion has long disappeared but the hotel, with its picturesque tower, is still a prominent landmark. Traces of its upper turnstiles and the lift, operating only in summer, still survive.

The Palace, SC 383762, the youngest of the old triumvirate of giants (1889), is the sole survivor. The ballroom was destroyed by fire in 1920 and rebuilt in 1921; it has 16,000sq ft of parquet floor, sitting room for 5,000, dancing space for 6,000, and was claimed to be the largest ballroom in Europe and the finest in the world.

Olympia, with its pony-trotting track, has given way to a housing estate, though steps, etc, belonging to it still survive. Belle Vue, whose attractions included a bear pit and a full-size replica of Nelson's *Victory*, was largely built for the Manx International Exhibition of 1899, but has now been transformed into the sports fields of King George V Park. Both Belle Vue and Falcon Cliff featured circuses at one time or another, but no trace of them survives, nor of Harmston's Grand Continental Cirque, which stood on the corner of Hill Street and Church Street where the Atholl Garage now is. The Hippodrome Circus of Varieties, which stood on the Douglas Eiffel Tower and Suspension Bridge site, has been replaced by the Isle of Man Steam Packet Co's warehouses. Outside Douglas, Ramsey also had its Palace, which eventually became a cinema.

About the turn of the century and later, there was a return to the building of ballrooms like the short-lived Marina on the site of the Gaiety Theatre and the Pool Ballroom, Ramsey. The Palais de Danse, Strand Street, is now a supermarket, most traces of its interior fittings, apart from a few mouldings and stained-glass door panels on the upper floor, having been obliterated after a fire in 1967. Many small dance-halls have shared a similar fate, including that on the first floor of Burtons, Victoria Street, SC 381755, a typical provision by this firm in a seaside resort, as may be seen at Weston-super-Mare; it retains its floor but is now the Rural Library.

Other resorts sprang up in quite surprising places. In the days when the chief means of transport for visitors was a horse-drawn vehicle, it was necessary to provide good facilities for spending a day while the horses rested for the return trip. The railway encouraged these resorts and many have survived the internal combustion engine. They usually provided pleasant walks, a dance-hall, restaurants and bars, and a variety of entertainments, as the following contemporary advertisements indicate:

Now Open FORT ISLAND Hotel and Pleasure Resort, 30 acres of grounds surrounded by the sea and the Castletown Golf Links (*Manx Sun*, 3 July 1893).

Visited in Thousands Daily 'Riviera of Manxland!' GLEN HELEN Pleasure Grounds and Rhenass Waterfall. Largest and most charming resort. First Class String Band. Dancing on the Lawn. Bowls, Swings, Trout Fishing etc. Excellent fully licensed hotel. Special Tram and Car Services (*Mona's Herald*, 20 June 1900).

Beauty Spot of Mona. LAXEY GLEN GARDENS. By Electric Tram or Horse Car to the Gates. Dinner, Luncheons, Teas, Cake and Wine, Cycling, Boating, Shooting, Bowling, Billiards, Tennis, Croquet, Strawberries and Cream, Music and Dancing. Beauty Spot of Man, Laxey Glen Gardens (*Mona's Herald*, 27 June 1900).

At Injebreck, SC 358849, only quartz-bedecked fountains and shrubbery survive of the well-displayed gardens; but at Laxey, SC 430844, Glen Maye, SC 235795, Glen Wyllin, SC 316901 and Glen Helen there are more substantial traces. Groudle Glen had sealions, whose pool remains, SC 420785, as its chief attraction; while at Port Soderick, SC 348727, there was a raised walk over the oyster beds and a 'Smuggler's Cave'. The most recent is the Douglas Corporation's Villa Marina, SC 384763, originally the Kursaal, dating from 1913 and improved in the 1930s, whose Royal Hall holds 2,000 people.

Cinemas and Theatres

The earliest dramatic performance in the Isle of Man of which we have any record took place at Castle Rushen in 1603, when Lord Vaux's Players, one of the lesser Men's Companies presented a play. Douglas had a theatre in the mid-eighteenth century about which nothing is known, but in 1788 a theatre was built in Douglas by Captain William Barton Tenison, a member of a well-known Irish family who had settled in the Isle of Man. According to the actor S. W. Ryley, 'it was a pretty little place, built for private amusement'; and the Duke of Rutland states that it was 'formed from an assembly room'. Until quite recently the building still stood in Fort Street; the site is now occupied by Osborne's store. About 1800 many buildings and large rooms were occasionally adapted for the performance of plays and concerts, but all have long disappeared. Edmund Kean and Mrs Siddons are known to have appeared here, the former at the Theatre Royal, British Hotel, and the latter at the New Theatre, Atholl Street. Eliza Craven Green, the authoress of *Ellan Vannin*, also appeared at the New Theatre.

About 1820 buildings were erected by a number of gentlemen between Strand Street and Wellington Street. The lower floor, now largely occupied by T. H. Cowin Ltd, appears to have been intended as a public market, while the upper floor, now the Cabin Ballroom or Golden Goose Club, was to be used for assemblies. It was soon, however, made to serve as a theatre, for a time being known as the Waterloo Theatre and later as the Theatre Royal and the Prince of Wales Theatre. Towards the end of the century it was called the Wellington Hall, which name can still be made out above its old entrance in Wellington Street. Among those who appeared here were the 'Female American Serenaders', who gloried under the names of Mesdames Cora, Jumba, Woski, Miami, Yarico, Womba and Rosa; and Mr (later Sir) Henry Russell, the composer. About 1875 the hall was 'converted into a skating rink, frequented by the "elite of the town" '.

The Oddfellows Hall in Atholl Street was built in 1847 to a design by Henry Robinson of Douglas, the foundation stone being laid by Sir William Hillary. The building was called the Prince of Wales Theatre from 1849 to 1853, and is now the Douglas Court House. In 1858 John Mosley built the Theatre Royal, Wellington Street, on the site of the sailcloth factory of William Fine Moore. According to the *Manx Sun:*

The entrances to the boxes, pit and gallery are separate and distinct; they are situated in 'Wellington Street', nearly opposite the Wellington Hall entrance . . . The house will contain an audience of 1,000 persons of whom 200 will be seated in the boxes. The boxes on the grand tier are open more than two-thirds round the circle, and laid out with very commodious benches, covered with handsome scarlet cloth . . . ; the private boxes are at the other extremity. The pit is large, the benches backed and of convenient form . . . The gallery, with its double wings, will accommodate nearly as large a number as the pit. The proscenium is lofty, and is handsomely decorated . . .

Soon after 1880 the theatre closed its doors for the last time, becoming first a store and then the citadel of the Salvation Army, who vacated it in 1933, at which time the gallery, etc, was torn out. The building which once echoed to the voice of Sir Henry Irving now houses a waxworks exhibition.

Irving also appeared at the Victoria Hall, which was opened by a Mr Everard in 1862 and is now occupied by the South Douglas Old Friends Association. In its time it played many parts, but it was more often a theatre than anything else; in that capacity it was variously known as the Prince of Wales Theatre, the United Services Theatre, and the Gaiety Theatre—which name it took on 4 July 1881. At this time the building was entirely remodelled and decorated in the Pompeian style: flanking the stage, with its splendid new proscenium arch, were handsome and capacious private boxes; a new dress circle and orchestra stalls were put in; the stage was raised; the pit lowered; the floors were sloped and the orchestra sunk, so that an uninterrupted view could be obtained from any part of the theatre; whilst ugly wooden supports to the galleries were replaced by slim but strong iron columns. The building's entrance was in Prospect Hill through what is now a photographer's shop. The date 1881 on the façade relates to this reconstruction. Happily, the old building has not been entirely forsaken by the drama, for in recent years a Little Theatre has been constructed within it, though this is not now continuously used and the whole area is being 'redeveloped'.

The opening of Victoria Street brought strong competition to the Theatre Royal and the Gaiety Theatre in the form of the Grand Theatre, which, standing at the entrance to the new thoroughfare, was opened in 1882 by Thomas Lightfoot. It gradually eclipsed both the older houses and eventually became the Grand Cinema. Finally it was extensively rebuilt by the Palace and Derby Castle Co and opened in June 1935 as an up-to-date cinema called the Regal,

SC 381756; it still has films throughout the summer but no longer has its Compton Unit Organ, with the first Mellotone attachment to be fitted in the British Isles. Having been built as an integral part of the Grand Building, the façade, seen by itself, is undistinguished, but it fits in well with its companions. There have been moves to refurnish the building as a theatre.

The Masonic Hall, Loch Promenade, was used by concert parties towards the close of the nineteenth century. Spence Lees opened his 550 seat Bijou Theatre, Regent Street, on 19 May 1893; its name was changed eventually to the Mona Theatre and then the Empire Theatre. Finally, early in the present century, it became a cinema, the Empire Electric Theatre, and so remained until it closed in 1929. It is now a betting shop. The Marina ballroom had a short unhappy life, which was not prolonged by the change of its name to the Pavilion, but about 1900 a metamorphosis into the Gaiety Theatre, Harris Promenade, brought a change of fortune. The Gaiety is now by far the longest surviving theatre on the Island, still staging summer shows and amateur productions.

Two theatres have stood on the Palace site: the 'Opera House', which was built in 1892, held 1,000 people but was gutted by fire in 1920 and now houses a bingo hall, while the Coliseum, which was built to replace it, was demolished to make room for the Casino. There was also an Opera House at Derby Castle.

Mention has been made of the Empire and Regal Cinemas. Other cinemas in Douglas, moving from south to north, include the Royalty, SC 384753, in Walpole Avenue, built in 1927 on the site of the Pier Pavilion, a wooden erection opened about 1905. It has a fine façade, in moulded white ceramic with swags, enlivened with stained glass; and has recently been used as a live theatre and for model car racing as well as films. The Picture House, Strand Street, extended in 1933, is one of the few Manx examples of applied pseudo half-timbering. Its near neighbour, the Strand, now an amusement arcade and automatic cinema, was built about 1913 and reopened after interior reconstruction in April 1930; it has an interesting vertically elongated façade, with twin towers, carried out in white brick. The Crescent Cinema, opened 9 June 1930, SC 385764, stands isolated on the promenade without its intended twin theatre. It is unusual in having preserved its splendid 'romantic' interior décor of painted tapestries, flambeaux and portcullis after the installation of a wide screen; it has dressing rooms and stage fittings, and has occasionally been used as a theatre.

Outside Douglas there are several examples of 'small-town functional' in cinema architecture, including the Pavilion, Peel, the Strand, Port Erin, and the Avenue (or Continental), Onchan, now a builder's store, all dating from about 1936. The Plaza, Ramsey, formerly the Ramsey Palace Ballroom, is more pretentious, but the town's second cinema, the Cinema House, is now a garage. To complete the tally, the Cosy, Castletown, SC 265675, has been reconverted into a factory. Mention should also be made of the Crescent Pavilion, which stood next to the Crescent Cinema on the site of Buxton's Pierrot Village; the Onchan Head Pavilion, destroyed by fire in recent years; and the Open Air Theatre, Douglas Head. Finally, buildings outside Douglas known to have been used for performances at one time or another include Old Cross Hall, Ramsey; Castletown Town Hall; Victoria Hall, Laxey; and the George Hotel, Castletown.

Two further 'places of entertainment' are worthy of mention: the Iron Pier and the Douglas Head Camera Obscura. The former was 1,000ft long and 17ft wide and cost £6,500; it was opened on 19 August 1869 but dismantled and sold to a Welsh resort before the end of the century. A few rusting iron stumps mark its site. The Camera Obscura is, however, still working, one of the few such relics to survive in the British Isles. Otherwise the once-elaborate artificial amusements of Douglas Head—'mutoscopes, electrical machines, and other appliances *ad nauseam*'—are much reduced in number, which would doubtless please the author of the earlier Ward Lock guides.

Music Halls

Music halls operating in Douglas in the 1890s and the early 1900s included the Star Music Hall, Prospect Hill; John Woodruff's Music Hall, Strand Street ('which is visited by thousands of Yorkshire and Lancashire people every year'); the Grand Music Hall, Victoria Street ('adjoining the [Grand] Theatre . . . will seat 1,000 visitors; underneath is a large room 72 ft. by 48 ft., occupied in the season as a bazaar'), absorbed into the Grand Hotel about 1902; and the Douglas Head Hotel Music Hall and Dancing Pavilion.

Swimming-pools

For an island with many excellent safe beaches, the Isle of Man has had a remarkable number of artificial bathing places. The oldest which survives in use is at Traie Menagh in Port Erin; 50yd by 32yd, it was built by High Bailiff Laughton about 1890. Nobles Baths, at the bottom of Victoria Street in Douglas, were adapted from Lightfoot's Baths between 1906 and 1908. Accommodation consisted of twenty-four slipper baths, Russian bath, gentlemen's bath (75ft by 30ft), refreshment buffet, laundry, ladies' bath, cistern room, boilerhouse, and engine house. The architect was Frank Cottle, the Borough surveyor. The baths have recently been replaced by a new nationalsize pool at Derby Castle. Other modern pools are at Ramsey (a 25m pool designed by A. J. Davidson and opened 27 June 1968), Peel (opened in 1959) and at several hotels. There are derelict pools at Peel and Ramsey. The latter had an area of 12,400sq ft at low tide and 13,600sq ft at high tide; four retaining walls at graded levels surrounded it, the outer one 14ft thick and the others 6ft thick. On the outer wall was a valve with a 12in pipe running 150ft out to sea to discharge water. The pool was 10ft deep at its seaward end. The architect was J. T. Boyde, FIAS.

Towards the turn of the century there was a private bathing

establishment, Waddington's Hydropathic Baths, in Castle Street, Douglas, behind the Masonic Hall, where there is now an aquarium. Mention should also be made of Port Skillion, a creek fitted up as a gentlemen's bathing place by R. Archer of Douglas in 1874. The creek was carefully divided up by concrete walls into enclosures of different depths, from shallow pools to others deep enough to allow safe diving, and dressing rooms were provided.

International Exhibition

One major event of the nineteenth century that may appropriately be mentioned as a visitor attraction was the Isle of Man International Exhibition of 1889. This was held '. . . To bring before the public in a popular manner Manufactures and Inventions of all descriptions of this and other Countries, to foster Home Industries, *to encourage the attendance of Visitors to the Island*, and to promote Industry, Sciences Art & Education generally'. Its general manager was Henry W. Pearson, subsequently Superintendent of the British Exhibits at the Chicago World Fair of 1893. Large buildings to house the exhibits were erected on the site of the Belle Vue pleasure grounds and exhibitors ranged from the predictable giant producers of chocolate and beef extract to retailers of souvenirs. A great many of these souvenirs survive including printed handkerchiefs, engraved glasses (names added under the purchaser's eye), japanned tea caddies and various publications. A great attraction was a full-scale replica of Nelson's *Victory* as she was after Trafalgar, a sure way to Manx hearts, since a local naval hero, Captain Quilliam, served on her at the time of the battle. If an interesting oil painting showing the exhibition is to be believed the events arranged for the year included balloon ascents, which certainly were listed among nineteenth-century entertainments in Man, as advertisements show. It is perhaps ironical that this exhibition seems to have marked the beginning of a decline in Manx industry, particularly the mines.

Visitors have always wanted souvenirs of the places they visit and the Isle of Man has always provided these. Most of them were, and are, of the type manufactured elsewhere and localised only by a crest or 'A present from . . .', but one or two were unique to the Island. At the end of the nineteenth century Broughton's of Douglas sold pottery teapots, probably made in Staffordshire but possibly Scottish, in the form of a three-legged man. In the commoner type he is a sailor seated on a coil of rope. Another version has him in a frock coat, with the three-legs ornament, astride a tree. Curiously enough this figure is known in both a standard Staffordshire colouring and in a more refined imitation-porcelain style of painting. Although many examples have been traced no real information about their origin has been obtained. Much of the souvenir china was of continental origin and, as with the glass paperweights with glued-on printed scenes, a particular picture might survive in use longer than the scene it depicted. One unusual china souvenir is the cup with a translucent view in the base, in the manner of a lithophane; this seems to be of an early twentieth-century date.

So-called Laxey silver cutlery, in reality plate, was apparently intended to trap the souvenir hunter, though it also enjoyed a good local sale. It is nearly always in the fiddle pattern and the usual marks are *Laxey Silver* between two three-legs emblems, *D & A* and various marks relating to the type and quality of the plate. The initials have been identified as those of Daniel & Arter of the Globe Nevada Works, Birmingham. The firm changed its name several times, explaining other initials, but, although it survives as a producer of motor-cycle parts, all records of the date of manufacture (probably c 1890–1905) of the cutlery and retailers have been lost. The implication behind the name *Laxey Silver* was apparently that the silver used in plating came from the Laxey ores, but cutlery with the identical maker's mark and of the same pattern is also known to have been marked Russian, Nevada and Portuguese silver, so it is debatable how much of the silver used in the Laxey-marked pieces was really of Manx origin. Pieces marked *Manx Silver* are also known but, despite local belief to the contrary, no piece of hallmarked silver known to be made from Manx ores has yet been found.

At the close of the nineteenth century Cottier & Cubbon, a Douglas drapers, sold attractive handkerchiefs (or 'head squares') printed in, apparently, printer's ink with Manx scenes. Some of these, like the one produced for the Steam Packet's jubilee, are representational; others, like the 'Manx Cat Puzzle' and the 'Complete Manx Tourist' (three-legged, leading a Manx cat and a Manx hen and carrying a box of kippers) are more closely related to contemporary children's book illustrations. One example, 'King Orry on his Tynwald Mount', may be a political satire on the then members of the House of Keys. Examples showing non-Manx political figures also exist. It is likely that these handkerchiefs were locally produced, possibly by Brown's, the Douglas printers of newspapers, guidebooks and almanacs. A painting of the King Orry design preserved in the Manx Museum lends weight to this suggestion. Indeed it is possible that some of the equipment of the Port e Chee cotton factory was finally used for this purpose; certainly handkerchiefs were one of its chief exports.

Isle of Man Rock

One of the most popular souvenirs is seaside rock. There is some dispute as to where and when it was first made but several firms were operating in the Isle of Man at an early date. Thomas Cubbon's of Rushen Abbey exhibited at the Isle of Man International Exhibition of 1889, though their main products were preserved fruit and jam, which are still made there. Gore's, in whose shop it is still possible to watch the rock being made, was established in 1893. So great is the present demand that some is imported from Blackpool and there seems little likelihood that the production of this unsophisticated sweet will decline in the near future. In addition to the familiar pink sticks with a red three-legs kicking all the way through, other colours are made, as well as novelties. Proof that these novelties are not so new was forthcoming when a local foundry closed, for among the old patterns salvaged was one for making a toffee kipper.

MINERAL-WATER MANUFACTURERS

Most of the mineral-water manufacturers on the Island depend for their sales on the holidaymakers, so it is not inappropriate to deal with this industry here rather than among the more traditional manufacturing trades. The brewing of ginger beer started early, followed by soda water. As the plant required was not very elaborate, firms came and went rather rapidly and their existence is often indicated only by surviving bottles (see Appendix Six). By the end of the nineteenth century there were at least fourteen firms in existence, of which four still survive—Downward's, Irving's of Peel, Kelly's, and Qualtrough's.

Qualtrough's is the longest established, as its advertisement in *Mercantile Manxland* (1900) insists:

Qualtrough & Co.
The big, ever-growing demand for pure and refreshing aerated drinks is capitally met in the Isle of Man. The works are equipped with a thoroughly up-to-date plant and every precaution being taken against possible metallic contamination, the absolute purity and reliability of all Qualtrough's products have naturally secured for them a wide and ever increasing popularity:—their old-fashioned stone ginger beer is a positive luxury.
Qualtrough & Co. who are really the oldest firm of makers in the island having been established for nearly half a century.

A court case between a mineral-water manufacturer, his creditors and a firm from which he had obtained equipment gives a very good idea of what machinery was used in the nineteenth century.

Summary Court, Douglas   Jany 20. [18]96

There is a concrete floor . . . bolts are placed in the concrete floor & there are holes in the machinery corresponding to these bolts—The machine is then dropped on the bolts & secured with nuts & washers screwed on to the bolts. The washers are of iron. . . . all the other parts of the plant lead up to that.

Behind the machine, between it & the wall, there is a water regulator . . . that is fixed to timber which is let into the wall.

The next piece of machinery is the Gas Holder . . . connected with pipes. It contains the gas which is used to impregnate the water. This is connected with a third machine called the Gas Generator . . . [which] is connected with an acid tank.

. . . Then there is the little wonder filling machine which stands near the pump. This is connected by pipes both with the filling machine & the soda water machine.

The next machine is called a 2 doz: bottle rinser. We only supplied the rinser and not the trough.

We supplied also one slate tank . . . it supplies the soda water machine by a pipe. Upstairs it is connected with a filter. . . . inside an enamelled iron tank. . . .

The next machine is a 30 gallon sugar boiler . . . [an] enamelled iron cooking pot. . . . There are 4 other mixing tanks . . . connected with the filling machine by black tin pipes. There is also a syrup junction. . . . The various articles are used for distinct purposes & can be purchased separately & put with other systems of machines. . . . For instance [the main machine] not only supplies [the little wonder bottle filler] but supplies also 4 other fillers made by other makers. . . .

There are two floors the ground floor extending the whole length of the building and the other at ⅓ of the ground floor. The 2nd floor is called the syrup room and the four syrup tanks . . . are connected with the other machinery by pipes which come down to the syrup junctions. . . . All the water used passes through the filter . . . connected by a pipe with a slate cistern below by means of couplings *all the manufacturing parts of the machine are connected with this slate tank.*

The firm concerned was one of the larger ones in Douglas and it gives some indication of the size of the trade at this time that it had four complete runs of machinery.

Page 125   (above) *The waterwheel at Ballacorris tuck mill, Santon, c 1951;* (below) *a town mill: the twin waterwheels at Pulrose near Douglas, c 1921*

Page 126   *Cronkbourne village:* (above) *the front terrace, c 1860;* (below) *the rear terrace in 1968*

CHAPTER SIX

Traditional Manufacturing Industries

UTILISING INORGANIC MATERIALS

Metalworking

ARCHAEOLOGICAL evidence of dark-age metalworking has been
found, notably at Braddan, Kiondroghad and Ronaldsway. During
the early period of working in the southern mines (see p 51), an
attempt was made to smelt the ore in Man, which, at the time,
should have been cheaper than sending it away (see p 55), but the
work does not seem to have been done very efficiently. In 1668 a
lease had been granted of all Manx mines together with permission
to erect a smelter. This may have been John Murrey's smelt house
at Derbyhaven, since the Mine Adventurers' inspectors reported
'there never has any water come to the Mill for Smelting or washing,
but their method is this they hired men to blow the Bellows at so
much a day'. Tradition also records that smelting took place on Port
Erin shore.

Accounts survive for the building of a new, apparently water-
powered, smelter in 1793 (see Appendix Two); this probably stood
on the left bank of the stream at Rhenwyllin, since in the 1795 Deed
of Sale Rhenwyllin mill is said to stand on ground near the 'Old
Smelting House'. The smoke from the smelting caused considerable
annoyance, as recorded in the Atholl Papers, 137, 10:

Ballahurry
    June 12th 1794
Charles Small Esq.
    This week I have been under the necessity of taking one of the peoples
Cowes that lives near the Mill she being a little Sick with the Smoak &
was oblig^d to pay more than the value of the cow; I would recommend to

you to get a settlement with Mr Gawne respecting the place as these people will never be satisfied, my opinion is that if you could rent the Land at a fair price that there would be very little loss as the Smelters would pay the rent and take the loss upon themselves. I see clearly that we will get but little smelted till the corn is got off the ground: The vessel that went with the Black Jack is come to the Island again.

I should have waited upon you myself with these but for the plague I have with the smelters, they now expect a Guinea per Week whether they work or not & ever since they came to the Island; I promised them that the time they were in erecting their Hearth but no more, nor after a tryal do I think one of them is even fit for a smelter we have many upon the place better than him I have set him to the Mines & if he will not take his chance as another Miner I will have nothing more to do with him.

> I am Sir your most Obed. & most hbl.
> Servant
> *John Summers*

and 137, 11:

Charles Summers Esq.
> Smelting Mill 13th May 1795

This morning Mrs Gawn by order of Mr Gawn her son discharged us from Smelting any more let the wind blow from where it will till he have a settlement with you respecting the same.

I met with Mr Gawn yesterday who told me he intended it should be settled; that he did not mind how it was settled if it was but done, he was plagued with the Tenants but I know very well that he is plagued with the people in his own house & specially the Brewer his Brother. I am also fully persuaded he expected to have some appointment from his Grace and that if his Grace would have thought it fit to give him a promise of the comptrollership at Castletown when vacant the terms would have been left to yourselves: he is also much unhinged that his Grace took no notice of him now when His Grace was at Castletown, therefore he is determined to have an immediate settlement that there may be a right understanding in the future. I know very well he does not wish to go to law but that he is persuaded he ought to receive some mark of distinction for giving his Grace the above accommodation.

I have laid the whole of the Business before you I hope you will take such steps as we may get forward: as the Mill being stoped when we are refining will be a very great loss and nearly the same in the Slag Hearth. I owe Mr Gawn my rent which is £45 which was due this week & desire you to let me have some cash that I may be able to pay him.

> I am Sir Yours
> *John Summers*

The Duke of Atholl purchased Rhenwyllin mill and a parcel of land on which to build a further smelting house in 1795 and came to an agreement that between 12 April and 1 August (sss October 1795–57) each year no smelting would take place if the wind was inshore, that is blowing from the mill towards the surrounding houses.

It was not only the neighbours who were affected as in 1796 the Duke was petitioned as follows (Ms 669A, p 262):

> The humble Address and Appreciation of
>   Robt. Foster   Smelter—
> Humbly Sheweth
>   That your Petitioner has been employed in the Smelting Business up-wards of two years in the Parish of Rushen which he cheerfully undergoes whilst it pleases the Almighty to grant him his Health—but it so happened sometime past that your Petitioner was afflicted with such excruciating Pains both in Bowels & Bones for a quarter of a year following owing to the pernicious smoake of the smelt Mill as rendered him incapable of pursuing his work being confined to his Bed & room the most part of the time.
>   That upon the re-establishment of your Petitioners Health he renewed his work as formerly but was again attacked with the same Disorder so violently that his Life was several times dispaired of & was prevented from Smelting for ten Weeks by which Losses of Time your Petitioner has suffered so very considerably in his circumstances besides the Expenses he has been at paying Doctors Bills amounting to five Guineas & upwards as may be made to appear, that he is reduced toward & Poverty Your Petitioner begs leave further to Observe that in Smelting places in other Countries the Smiths in the Case of Sickness have the Doctors Bills generally paid for them by the Gentleman concerned in the Mines . . .

Despite these hazards the smelt seems to have worked for a little longer since John Feltham records in *A Tour through the Isle of Man in 1797–8*: 'the lead-mines at Brada—ore is brought to PORT-IRON river (in boats), where there is a conveniency for cleansing it, it is then conveyed by land to the smelting house, near PORT LE MARY at BUN ROOR'. The smelt seems to have drawn its water from the same dam as Rhenwyllin corn mill since there are no accounts for a new dam head. However, the troubles over the leases were such that the mines virtually ceased operation and the smelt fell into disuse, leaving only its name to the area. The Castle Rushen papers,

'Receipts and Disbursements', contain a good deal of as yet un-published information on the early working of the mines and it is likely that a careful study will bring to light further information about the smelt houses.

The Smelthouse, Derbyhaven, SC 285673, probably dates from 1711. Its owner, John Murrey, made the first known Manx coins, which subsequently were made legal tender by Act of Tynwald. Despite its name the Smelthouse seems to have been mainly a metal-working shop. A metal foundry on a similar scale to John Murrey's was set up temporarily in Castle Rushen to produce part of the 1733 coin issue. It is possible that these coins were made in Man because considerable scrap metal in the form of guns was available. The accounts for the minting in the Castle Rushen papers, 'Receipts and Disbursements', were transcribed in the nineteenth century. All the equipment and two skilled coiners, Amos Topping and Samuel Dyall, had to be imported at considerable expense. Three furnaces were erected together with a press and some equipment to make blanks, the furnaces being fired with a mixture of peat and coal. The evidence for this mint is both archaeological and documentary; its site seems to have been against the outer wall but that has not been adequately explored. The most entertaining section of the accounts records: 'for Rum for cleaning the Dyes and Screws duering the whole time of the Coyning' 14s Manx and 'for other liquor given the Coyners on Extraordinary occasions' a mere 12s. One wonders how much of the rum was really used to clean the dies. The two skilled workmen were, incidentally, not employees of the Royal Mint, though in 1708 Isaac Newton, the then Master, while refusing to make coins for the Lord of Mann, had given permission for Mint craftsmen to make designs for Manx coins.

About 1760 one John Stole (Stowell), 'Iron smith of Ballasalley', erected 'a Tilting Mill or Plating Forge' on a rivulet, presumably at Ballasalla. (This use of the term 'Tilting mill' is thirteen years earlier than the first cited in the *Oxford English Dictionary*.) It is probable that this mill was on a tributary of the Silverburn which enters just upstream of the Abbey mill; there are still appropriately sited stone buildings but no real trace of machinery. The mill presumably made spades and similar implements and does not seem to have lasted long. There was a second short-lived spade mill at Kewaigue near Douglas, long since destroyed, and a newspaper advertisement indicates that there was a third at Ballig in Braddan or Ballahig in Patrick.

In the nineteenth century there were several foundries in Douglas, and at least one of these, Gelling's of the South Quay, made quite sizeable items including mill parts, heavy mining machinery and a very wide range of street furniture. Domestic equipment such as kitchen ranges, grates and hinges were also produced locally. But it is clear that more rural households continued to depend on the blacksmith rather than the foundry to supply their needs in traditional forms. It is perhaps worth noting that among the fourteen nailers that were found in a cursory study only one, the Parade Iron Foundry, appears likely to have been a factory rather than a home industry.

Gearing Patterns from a Manx foundry. The wooden patterns shown on p 90 were salvaged from a Manx foundry and are probably typical of the larger work done at the end of the nineteenth century. All the parts were thought to be from corn mills when collected but J. Kenneth Major is of the opinion that some belonged, in fact, to mining machinery. His description is as follows:

> *Great spur wheel* from a corn mill. Designed originally to be used with an iron upright shaft but subsequently re-fashioned with a print (means of making a hole) for an octagonal wooden upright shaft.
> *Great spur wheel* from a corn mill. Designed to be used with an iron upright shaft.
> *Bevel gear* as used in a dressing machine or to give power from a lay shaft in a corn mill. *Spur gear*, a heavy iron construction probably from a mine machine such as a crusher.
> *Spur gear* with six spokes, light-weight construction, possibly from a lay shaft drive for corn milling machinery. *Upper spur gear*—a stone nut from a corn mill. *Lower spur gear*—from a piece of heavy, probably mining, machinery.

Other patterns from this foundry included many railings, balusters and similar decorative items, fire grates, stoves and ovens, ventilation grilles, boat fittings, agricultural machinery parts, lettered stamps and brands, and items from amusement arcades such as the balls for pintables, the ducks for the shooting-gallery, and the mould for toffee kippers.

Brickworks

Although there are abundant deposits of glacial clay, the shortage of local fuel for firing and an excess of lime, which caused very high kiln losses, restricted their use. Galena-glazed tiles from the site of Rushen Abbey, a Cistercian house at Ballasalla, are the earliest extant examples likely to have been locally made and must date from well before the dissolution of the monasteries in 1540. Elizabeth Eames has suggested that another type of tile used in northern Cistercian houses was made by itinerant craftsmen and this may explain why there is no continuing tradition in Man. The first recorded brickworks was built at Castletown in 1692 at the instigation of the Earl of Derby, but its precise location is uncertain. From its position in the Castle Rushen Inventory of c 1694 it was thought that the kiln was somewhere near Bagnio House, but in James Webster's *Valuation of the Isle of Man*, dated 1826, one of the fields of Red Gap Farm, about ½ mile to the south-west, is called 'the Brickfield', a name it still retains. It was arable in 1826 so, although excavations at Bagnio House yielded many waste bricks used as paving, it is likely that this field was the site of the 1692 clay pits rather than a later works. Since it is marked with the Lord of Mann's 'I.D.' cipher[1] (also on his standard and the coinage), a single brick preserved in Castle Rushen almost certainly dates from this attempt to establish the industry. It is unlikely that the Castletown kilns had a long life, though crude handmade and presumably local bricks were utilised in repairs to a number of old buildings in the area. The following extract

[1] I = *Ioannes* or *Jacobus*; D = *Dux* or *Derby*.

from the Derby Papers explains the difficulties which were encountered:

> My Lord there are now a hundred thousand of Brick burnt in the ovens.[1] The workmen say they are as good as those made at Knowsley but the great rate of coal here makes them dear vizt. at 15s per thousand in coal & workmanship, besides casting up the clay & other charges which if not done by your Lordship's tenants for boon service would make the bricks dearer but the other way of burning in clamps, if your Lordship think fit, would save £5 in every 40 thousand. I would not alter the first method without Your Lordship's particular order.

Neither documentary nor archaeological evidence of eighteenth-century brickworks has yet come to light but by 1802 'Bricks made at Finche's Brick Field, adjoining Douglas' were offered in the *Manks Advertiser*. In the *Manx Sun*, 10 July 1832, 'Bricks from the Kiln in the field above Mona Terrace, Finche's Road' were advertised at '£2 British per thousand', an indication of the value of the Earl's boon service! No surface trace remains, for the House of Industry was erected on the site, but it is reasonable to suppose that bricks from this source were used in the extensive early nineteenth-century development of this area of Douglas. With the growth of the town the brickmakers moved further out. Ballanard was perhaps the most important, supplying building materials for a good part of the later nineteenth-century expansion (eg, the backs of the houses in Hyldesley Road, Douglas). It ceased work in the early years of the present century but in 1900 its products still included:

> Bricks of a fine warm colour . . . Vases, window-boxes, rustic garden chairs and tables, brackets, finials, key-blocks, lettered and figured panels etc. though domestic requirements are not overlooked as witnessed by the useful bread-pan, the pig-trough, the manger etc. A novelty lately introduced in this department is in the form of a butter-cooler, of highly improved type, although simple in design. The 'Ballanard' butter-cooler, being made extremely porous, and therefore more perfect in action, must undoubtedly become a most valuable adjunct to the pantry whether in mansion or cot . . . the body of the Ballanard terra-cotta is extremely durable and the general colour a delicate and *even* red . . .

[1] In 1694 there were still 'At ye Brick Kiln Bricks computed to ninety thousand'.

The Andreas brickworks also played an important part in supplying the needs of the nineteenth-century builders. In the 1851 census Thomas Casement of Ballacoarey describes himself as 'Brick and Tile Maker' and Thwaite's 1863 *Isle of Man Guide* similarly lists William Christian at the same address. Alfred Christian had succeeded the latter when *Brown's Directory* was published in 1894. The kiln marked near the main road on the 25in OS map probably belonged to the earliest period. Work ceased as a result of World War I but in 1925 an attempt was made to restart on a scale that would yield 8,000 bricks a day.

Jones & Sons of Buckley contracted to erect a fourteen-chamber Hoffman continuous kiln from which waste heat was led to a 100ft chimney, and both still stand. Despite improvements to the firing, much still depended on hand labour and, if the contemporary account in the Manx press is accurate, the clay was not adequately weathered. It was dug with pick and spade, flung into trucks and hauled by means of a rope railway to the upper floor of the main building; there it was ground in a wet grinding pan installed by Buchanans of Bootle. The paste then passed through multiple grids to the rolling and pug mill below, when additional water might be added at this stage. A spiral worm forced the prepared clay from the pug mill into a mould, usually twelve bricks in length, and the bricks were cut with wires. The green bricks were barrowed to the drying sheds, which utilised the waste heat from the boiler that powered the grinding machinery and from the kiln. The firing temperature was 1,000°C, at which heat Manx clays colour to a pleasing red. Production continued for only one full year, though some time passed before all the bricks and portable plant were sold.

There were also brickworks at Regaby Beg (*Brown's Directory*, 1889, 'Quayle, John, brickmaker and owner'), St Jude's and West Craig. In 1900 the last was stated to be able to produce 5 million bricks a year, 'common pressed or facing bricks, or other patterns to order, besides a large proportion of drain-pipes, roofing, ridge and floor tiles etc'. Nevertheless, it only employed some fourteen men.

The clay pit was about 20ft deep and the clay was hauled out in trucks by a steam engine on the edge. The preparation of the clay was powered but the bricks were hand-moulded and moved in barrows. After firing they were taken in 'stiff-carts' to Sulby Bridge railway station for transportation to Douglas. The kiln has been destroyed but one of the sheds survives, and it is said that the machinery was exported to New Zealand. The bricks had a poor reputation locally because of the friability resulting from the presence of pockets of lime. When Lamplugh made his geological survey about 1900 he recorded traces of other clay pits and it is likely that bricks for a single building were fairly frequently fired where they were to be used, though there is no proof that this was the practice before 1800.

There were a number of attempts to exploit the glacial deposits in the St John's area although most of these were short-lived. The Abbey (or Ballawyllin) brickworks was of particular interest as its pug mill was apparently powered by a waterwheel, for a wheel from this site was subsequently sold to a woollen mill. It has been suggested that this works closed in consequence of some disturbance, possibly to its water supply, caused by the building of the railway. A brick, stamped BALLAWYLLIN/ST JOHNS (No 5426) is preserved in the Manx Museum.

The only firm still making traditional bricks in the Isle of Man is the Glenfaba Brick Company (1927) Limited of Peel. Despite vicissitudes such as 'the extraordinary expense of removing the overburden at the quarry' at the foot of the inland slope of Peel Hill, which caused a price rise in 1926, the firm continued production of burnt shale bricks from 1866. Bricks are made from crushed shale obtained now from a new quarry, on the same strata, opened in 1946. The plant consists of four grinding mills, and the same number of brick presses, with two twenty-chamber Hoffman kilns for burning. The 1968 output was 120,000 to 150,000 per week, all the bricks being used on the Island. Since 1965 concrete bricks—using cement and aggregates from the Poortown (granite), and Billown and Turkeyland (limestone), quarries—have been made, the 1968 output being 100,000 per week. Again the product is used locally. In fact much of Manx building now depends on this firm, bricks being imported rarely and reluctantly.

Lime Burning

The burning of lime for sale was one of the manorial rights of the Lord of Mann, though tenants claimed to be entitled to use the limestone on the land they held for the improvement of their own or their neighbours' property. While the Lord had a direct interest in the lead mines the right to burn lime for use in mine buildings was included in the leases. By the beginning of the nineteenth century the agricultural use of lime was increasing in the Island and profit could be made from its sale. In consequence, at least one kiln proprietor, Jefferson of Ballahot, was presented for offering lime as merchandise without permission; but despite injunctions he was not put out of business and in 1823 he was offering lime at 2s British a barrel—the standard rate at this time—or, delivered in lots of 20–30 tons, at 20s a ton in Ramsey and 21s at Dogmills. In 1810 he was using kilns at Derbyhaven but later he seems to have worked nearer his Ballasalla property, presumably at the oldest quarries on the site now more usually called Billown; this site is marked as Ballahot quarries on the 1861 map prepared for the Disafforesting Commission.

J. Proctor opened a kiln at Scarlett in 1808 and those at Port St Mary were working at least as early as 1822. In 1829 A. Bridson erected a rival kiln to Jefferson's, also at Ballasalla. Five years later 'the New Lime kilns on the South Stockfield (the property of Thos Moore)' commenced burning and by the time of the 1851 census this 'Farmer of 300 acres & Limeburner' employed '40 labourers and 6 boys'. His quarries and kilns carried on a thriving business, and surviving structures include a tall, stone-built engine house. The use of burnt lime declined rapidly in the twentieth century and the Billown kilns alone are still working. A new quarry was recently opened at Chapel Hill, Balladoole to provide a fresh supply of raw material for the future.

Both lime and limestone (which was less unpleasant to handle) were normally moved about the Isle of Man by sea and the Manx newspapers are full of references to cargoes of lime which might, on occasion, go for export. The shortage of fuel was one reason why lime kilns were built away from the limestone areas. The growing town of Douglas had its kilns, shown as two isolated circular structures on the South Quay, just west of Gellings's Mona Foundry, on John Wood's 1833 plan. In 1809 the *Manks Advertiser* records:

> A Lime Kiln on a plan altogether new, has lately been erected at Kk. Michael, by *Mr William Ray*, by which there is an actual saving of at least one third of fuel. It is contracted at the top upon which a moveable cast metal head is placed. By the proper adjustment of this the draught is increased or diminished; and the heat reflected—it is well worth the attention of Lime-burners, in this country; and reflects much credit on the assiduity and spirit of the proprietor.

Despite the saving of expensive imported coal the new type does not seem to have caught on and all the known Manx kilns are extremely simple stone-built structures, their only refinement being the way in which the slope of the ground is used to facilitate top-loading. The two earliest are probably one of which the only traces are lumps of vitrified stone on the shore near the site of Ronaldsway farm, Derbyhaven, and a better-preserved example just above the Monk's Bridge at Ballasalla.

Ballasalla Ochre and Umber Works

John Grellier, the editor of the *Manx Sun*, leased the Ballasalla Flax Mill (SC 248708 GBM 24/071, built by John Quayle c 1767) about 1833 and converted it into a colour works. Grellier seems to have worked the mill for a short time but the Crown Agent was unable to persuade him to pay the dues on his raw materials. The following letter comes from the Crown Receiver's Letter Book in the Manx Museum:

13th June 1836

Dear Sir,

I request you will get your friend, if he can spare as much time, from raking up the ashes of the dead and defaming the living, to make out, and send me a statement, of his sales of ochre in order to ascertain the Lordship due to the Crown—I write to *YOU*, because I understand you undertook some time ago, to have this done.

The Lords of the Treasury have acceded to the Coal and Freestone Lease which is in preparation, and you will please to communicate this to your partners.

James McCrone

Edward Forbes, Esq
Banker

The source of the ochre, if such it was, is unknown. Although the mill was henceforth known as 'the Ochre and Umber Works', no indication that it really processed the former survives. The 1837 Directory still gives Jas Grellier & Co as an 'umber & ochre manufacturer', with Thos Pearson as agent in Ballasalla.

Grellier was succeeded by the long-established Douglas firm of Gavin Torrance. Joseph Torrance was the Ballasalla agent in 1843 and Thomas Muncaster (presumably one of the well known watch-making family) in 1852. By 1846 the manufacture of Roman cement had been added to the company's activities—it also owned ships, including the *William* built in Prince Edward Island in 1860, and traded regularly with Glasgow. At the end of the century it was also producing polishing powders but demand for what were apparently inferior local products declined and the works closed about 1898. In 1900 it was bought and converted into a private house.

During this conversion a circular area paved with about twelve wedge-shaped limestone blocks and some 8ft in diameter was found in the basement. This was probably the colour-grinding floor, though it may have also been the base of the original scutch mill. The colour was ground in water and then run into rectangular settling tanks, and when it had dried it was dug out with spades. Some of the dry powder was exported, hence the name 'Umber Warehouse' for the firm's building on the north quay at Castletown.

This building, the miller's house at Ballasalla and all the mill fittings have been destroyed, but the cut-limestone dam survives, together with the mill dam and part of the watercourses.

'Umber' was obtained from several sources. Between 1887 and 1893 an olivine-diorite dyke, stained because it intersects the Drynane haematite vein on Maughold Head, SC 497914, was mined but this product may have been exported untreated. The original source of the substance processed at Ballasalla seems to have been a pit near the Billown quarry, SC 268702, but by 1848 the main supply was obtained from an outcrop of decomposed, black, flaggy limestone about a mile distant, SC 277712. According to Lamplugh the rotten stone was a 'fine argillaceous silt, which has accumulated, apparently by rain-wash, in a boggy depression on the moorland between South Barrule and Cronk Fedjag' (approximately SC 245750, now planted over). Examples of this material were also found in the excavation of South Barrule hillfort. No real traces of any of these quarries survive. The origin of the ingredients for the 'Roman cement' is unknown, though a water tank lined with it was uncovered in Atholl Street in 1955.

The Ramsey Salt Works

The Manx Salt & Alkali Co started operations about 1901; its works, with chimney and evaporating pans, was in the old shipyard at Ramsey, which has again reverted to its original use. Salt was discovered in the Triassic marls of the northern plain in the course of unsuccessful boring for coal; it was tapped and pumped into a reservoir from which it was carried by gravitation in an iron pipe along the shore to Ramsey. It is alleged that the disturbance caused by laying this pipe, which may still be seen, caused an increase in coast erosion. The salt was both used locally, mainly in fish-processing, and exported, but production proved uneconomic in the face of modern mechanised plants elsewhere.

Chemical Works

The local directories and the large scale OS maps indicate the existence of a number of chemical works in Man. These processed imported raw materials and were mainly short-lived. Among premises so used were a mill in Glen Auldyn, SC 432931 GBM 24/091, and a number in the Douglas area. The existence of automated factories elsewhere has ensured that such 'do-it-yourself' operations no longer exist, and also explains the absence of paint and colour works until 1970.

INDUSTRIES UTILISING ORGANIC MATERIALS

Fish Preserving

As witness the Deemster's oath (p 20), the herring fishery was the most important to the Isle of Man from an early date. There is definite evidence for its existence in the thirteenth century, every tenant of a quarterland farm being required to provide himself with fishing nets. The church and the Lord of the Isle both claimed a share of the catch, much of which was preserved for winter use. By 1610 a Water Bailiff was appointed to oversee the herring fishery, which started in early July off Peel, moved south to its peak in August south-west of the Calf and ended in September–October off Douglas. An export trade in the preserved fish probably started as early as the sixteenth century, but it was not until the markets of the New World developed that this became important. In 1760 nine Manx merchants petitioned the Duke of Atholl to get them leave to export to the North American colonies, which an old British law prohibited; but he was not wholly successful, since in 1788 a cargo sent to St Christopher in the West Indies was seized and sold, together with the vessel carrying it, because it was not from Great Britain. Nevertheless, in 1824 the local Press was commending South America as a market and until the abolition of slavery in 1833 vast quantities of herring went to feed the plantation slaves.

These fish were preserved by salting, or salting and smoking, the latter producing 'red herring'. The first smoke house for red herring was erected by 1769 and in 1771 Mr Woodhouse of Liverpool introduced 'the Yarmouth method of curing'. Other herring houses were erected at Port St Mary by 1770 and at Derbyhaven in 1771, and by 1798 there were fourteen in the Island. Normally there were at least four working in Douglas (at the seaward end of the North Quay, several on the South Quay and more dotted about the older part of the town), four at the head of Peel harbour and more in the town, and at least one at Derbyhaven. By the beginning of the nineteenth century the annual production was about 150,000 barrels a year and as many as eight vessels loaded with salt might be sailing for the Island at one time, though they were delayed in Liverpool by an embargo in 1803. In 1826 there were 250 fishing boats crewed by 2,500 men. There was a temporary decline following the abolition of slavery (200 boats in 1835) but in 1837 Holme's works in Peel reopened and by 1864 there were 300 boats employing 2,800 men, the annual product being worth £70,000.

It is not known when the kipper, a split smoked fish, replaced the red herring, which was smoked whole, but literary evidence points to about the middle of the nineteenth century. In 1883 it was estimated that about a quarter of the Island's population depended for a living on the fisheries and their ancillary trades. A new curing station opened at Port St Mary in 1909 but by 1914 the number of Manx fishing boats had declined to 57—35 nickies and 22 smaller nobbies. Between 1925 and 1939 67 per cent of the herring catch went to pickle-curers and 30 per cent to kipperers. Between 1951 and 1966 more fish were kippered than pickled but recently continental pickle-curers have been purchasing Manx-landed fish. In 1939 there were only nine Manx boats against 163 non-Manx and in 1947 there were ten. Since then there has been a revival of interest in fishing and though only six Manx boats were licensed for the 1968 herring season a total of eighty vessels actually landed catches in Man. There has been a marked improvement in the efficiency of the fleet in the number of man-hours fished for a given return and by comparison the very large fleet of the 1860s was uneconomic.

A herring for kippering is split and placed in brine for about half to three-quarters of an hour, according to its size and the time of the season, which affects oiliness. It is then placed on frames of tenter-hooks and put into the kiln to be smoked. There are now only six or seven firms working, ranging from J. Rice of Peel, the last one-man business, to Moore's, whose kilns hold 30,000 pairs and whose machines can split 21,000 fish an hour; the hand rate is 2,000 fish per person per day. In the 1930s dredging for scallops (*Pecten maximus*) for sale in shell at Billingsgate market, London, started in earnest, though a scallop dredge had been exhibited in the 1883 International Fisheries Exhibition. After 1947 there was a steady improvement in the dredging gear and by 1968 thirty boats were engaged in this very profitable fishery. In the last few years attention has turned to dredging 'queenies' (*Chlamys opercularis*), mainly for the American and continental markets. There has been a com-plementary development of freezers and packers and several old dock-side premises have been converted, including a National Coal Board yard in Douglas where remains of the original 1771 Red Herring houses can still be traced. Herring houses can still be seen also at Derbyhaven; and the 1909 Port St Mary buildings are fairly well preserved.

Brewing

An old Manx proverb that spoke of a person 'going about like a brewing pan' originated with an old custom by which one kettle for brewing, often the property of the parish, served a whole neighbour-hood, passing from one household to the next as often as a fresh supply of 'home-brewed' was required. For the liberty to brew

Page 143   *The Great Snaefel Mine:* (above) *c 1895;* (below) *the waterwheel*

Page 144 (above) typical farm mill, Port e Chee near Douglas; (below) t Rhennie Laxey (Dhoon) wheelcase 1970

the Lord of the Isle was paid a charge, collected together with the Lord's Rent, called a *bras rent*—from *brasseur*, a brewer. The Manorial Roll of 1511–15 shows that no less than 193 individuals were paying this rent, many of them millers, since they had excellent facilities for malting. The mills, because of the considerable space available, thus became popular meeting places.

Alehouses, each of which brewed its own beer, came to be strictly controlled. By a law of 1576, re-enacted in 1637, no person was allowed to retail any wine, beer or ale unless considered fit 'by the Lord and in his absence by the captain or his deputy, and by the comptroller and the water bailiff or by some three of them, whereof the captain or his deputy to be always one'. In addition such a person was required to obtain a licence from the Governor, or his deputy, and to enter into a recognisance in the sum of £3 (about three month's wages for a labourer) to keep good order in his house and observe the assizes respecting the price of corn. The duty of granting licences was eventually deputed to the coroners, who empanelled juries each year to go through their sheadings fining offenders and reporting on suitable people. It was anciently provided also that if any alehouse keeper sold liquor in a can or measure which had not been tried and sealed by the Comptroller, the Great Enquest or any other authorised person, the guests had the liberty to drink as much as they pleased of the liquor so retailed and pay the house nothing for it.

Good as an alehouse's product might be, nineteenth-century developments brought about its end. The growth of a more sophisticated society, which started with the influx of half-pay officers and insolvent debtors and continued with the rise of the tourist trade, meant a demand for larger quantities of beer of a consistent quality and a greater variety of liquors. In consequence there was a trend towards large commercial breweries which might even import their ingredients (brewing malt could not be imported until after 1747), and middlemen selling imported beers.

By 1793 there were no fewer than eighteen breweries, of which

I

nine were in Douglas. A very extensive brewery was being built near the small north-western village of Ballaugh; it was operated for some time by the partnership of Quayle, Taubman & Moore, who issued 'card money', a local attempt to overcome the shortage of coin, from this address, though the firm is better known as bankers operating from Bridge House, Castletown. There were twenty-two breweries by 1810 and twenty-three in 1837: nine in Douglas, two each at Laxey, Peel, Ramsey and Ballaugh, four in Castletown and one apiece in Michael and Rushen (Mount Gawne). Although the total numbers at any one time did not increase much there were about eighteen premises in Douglas which were once used as breweries. These included the Nunnery; the Howe, which imported Scottish barley in 1793, then progressed to selling Barclay's London Stout and in 1846 suffered the indignity of becoming the preserved potato works; the Union, which specialised in October ale; James Robinson's in Hanover Street, which was 'capable of brewing twenty-five barrels of ale' in 1812; the larger premises in Society Lane where, between 1813 and 1829, 'forty-five barrels were brewed weekly with the aid of two men only'; and one at Kewaigue which was offered for rent at 20 guineas a year in 1824, an indication of the profits to be made even if 'superior ale' retailed at only 'a guinea a barrel'.

The product at this date was not always all that might be desired. A correspondent writing to the *Manks Advertiser* in October 1825 complained:

> I wish there was any mode to compel our Brewers to do justice to the public, in giving good ale for good money; not making a pretence of a low price for serving a bad article. If they cannot brew a *good* beverage, to be retailed at 3d per quart, let them advance their prices at once. Really the stuff now to be got at the public-houses, under the name of Ale, deserves no other name than small beer of a disagreeable flavour—I had been complaining the other day to a friend of this circumstance, who stared at me with astonishment, saying 'did I known no better than to expect good ale this season of the year!' Upon which I confessed my utter ignorance of any cause why it should not be rather better in this season than any other, as 'October store', is a term frequently used in our English writers for good

ale. My friend, however, to my great surprise, undeceived me by the information that a certain sort of ale has been brewed in this Island, called by the natives 'jough flodd',—Anglice, 'drink for the fishermen'!! If the herring catchers are to be put off with such a mixture, still there ought to be provision made for respectable house-keepers in a different way . . .

After the turn of the century there was a decline in the number of breweries but those that remained prospered. Among the more important was that which came to be known as Clinch's Lake Brewery (see plate, p 72), founded modestly enough in 1779 when a little *thie gymble* was built on the North Quay at Douglas, close to the *Lake*—a swampy river-flat where the Railway Station now stands. This brewery changed hands many times: in 1824 it was owned by Robert Cochrane, in 1837 by Robert Curphey & Co, and by 1843 John Hogg had taken over. By 1846 he had taken a partner and traded under the name of Hogg & Co until the premises were taken over by John Williams Clinch in 1868. Under the latter's control very extensive alterations and improvements took place, 'bringing the brewery abreast of the times in all respects, so that a more compact or better equipped little brewery does not exist'. Deep tube-wells were sunk and subsequent advertisements cited the analysis of their 'plenteous supply of pure water'. Brown's *Directory* of 1882 gives a complete description of how the brewery was organised:

This establishment was first opened as a brewery in the year 1779. . . . The present proprietor took the business in the year 1868; and since then the plant and machinery have been entirely remodelled, a new Brewhouse built and an abundant supply of excellent water procured by putting down tube-wells on the premises. . . . The water is forced to a large cistern on top the main building by means of steam pumps which are in duplicate to provide against breakdowns. The premises are all supplied from this cistern, and there is also another large one in which water to supply the malting is stored. The barley is taken in from farmers' carts &c., by an entrance level with the upper floor of the barley granary, in Bigwell-Street, and after passing through the malting process, is stored as malt in granaries, shown in the engraving, facing the quay. Storage for hops is also provided in these lofts. The malt after cleaning and weighing, is placed for the requisite time required by the Manx Act of Tynwald, under which duty is levied, in an 'entered room,' as it is technically called, in the basement of the Brewhouse. It is then lifted to the top of the same building by the steam hoist and crushed in a grist case commanding the mash tun, which is cast iron. After passing through the process of mashing the grains are discharged into carts by the spout shown in the engraving. The boiled worts, after cooling, are first fermented and then cleansed in a very complete apparatus, on a modification of the celebrated Burton system; after which they are racked off into carriage casks and stored until required for consumption in the spacious cellars at the back of the building.

From newspaper accounts it appears that the steam hoist, boiling tanks for brewing and washing casks, etc, were powered from 'a Cornish boiler placed in a separate building and communicating with the (old) brewhouse by a bridge over the private road adjoining. In the Boiler House, coals are also stored being tipped from the carts through a gateway opening on Bank Hill'. The main building still stands (see p 72) and the spout down which the waste was dumped is still visible; the building is largely of local stone with a slate roof and has a corner site. The ground is much higher at the west side and rear and, as indicated above, advantage of this fact was taken in that coal and barley were initially moved only on the level.

Clinch's motto was *Glen as Lajer* (clean and strong) and a device showing three brawny mail-clad arms, each terminating in a clenched fist, was used. When the firm became a company in 1897 this device, with the motto *Troor Duirn* (three fists), was registered as the trademark. Clinch's Brewery Co Ltd was dissolved in 1948 and the buildings are now used as a store by a large UK brewery. Another interesting brewery which flourished in the eighteenth and nineteenth centuries was Mount Gawne, Rushen. The proprietor, like the owners of the Ballaugh brewery, was a banker who issued notes showing his residence and it appears that the same vignette was used on the bottle labels. The house still stands but of the brewery only a few walls, forming part of the Shore Garage, Gansey. Peel quay brewery, now the 'Vikings' long house', was horse-powered.

With growing ease of communication and better transport containers, the preference of holidaymakers for the product of their local breweries could more easily be met. Whatever the cause, by the end of the nineteenth century there were only five breweries left in Man. A plan for a great amalgamation of breweries and hotels (even premises not offering food or accommodation are normally so called in the Island) was initiated about this time, but it was not a success and at the 1902 annual general meeting the shareholders of the Isle of Man Breweries Limited were told that there had been a loss of £3,000 on the year's working. Liquidation followed and eventually, in 1904, the concern was taken over by Boddington's (IOM) Limited. This firm also operated the Castle Rushen, or Castletown, brewery, established just across the river from the castle about 1830 by John Quayle to replace his original premises on the Parade. This brewery, the home of 'Castletown Ale of Man', is still working well and its odd collection of buildings, enlivened by a crenellated arch with a handsome three-legs emblem, always brightly painted, are a familiar landmark to visitors.

The only other surviving brewery still brewing its own beer is Okell's Falcon Brewery, Douglas. Unlike the other breweries its buildings form a group built more or less at the same time, though there have probably been some alterations. The main block, recently repainted in an attractive cream with its many trimmings picked out in light blue, is dated 1857, and was erected by William Okell. With persistence, traces of other Manx breweries can be found—a wall and a chimney at Poyll Dhooie, Ramsey, for example, or the fragments of perforated tiles from a malting floor (probably late seventeenth century) excavated near the Parade, Castletown.

The Sulby Glen Starch Works

This once thriving concern ceased work at the end of the nineteenth century; its building was gutted and the chimney destroyed when it became the Northern Water Board's filter plant in 1935. The mill is on the left bank of the Sulby river, SC 381934 GBM 24/094. Its initial use is uncertain but it was rented by the Southward family

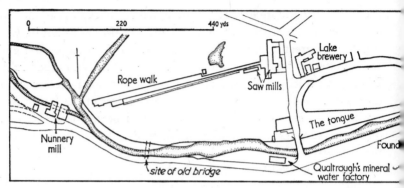

Douglas c

of woollen manufacturers, who installed a new waterwheel, about 1831. They rebuilt another mill to which they moved in 1834. In February 1846 the local Press reported that 'a company from Manchester have erected a commodious building at Sulby for the manufacture of starch'. By the 1851 census an English-born family of starch makers were in occupation: 'Thomas Stott, Starch Manufacturer, employing 18 men, aged 28, with two house servants', and 'Robert Stott, aged 35, Starch Carter', with 'H. Y. Rowe, Starch Maker and Margaret Murphey, Starch Packer' as part of his household. The chief source of starch was potatoes, up to 50 tons a day being processed, while cornflour was also made from maize. The residue of both was sold as pig-food. Examples of its travellers' cards, boxes and posters and other relics of the factory are preserved in the Manx Museum and most of the watercourse can be traced on the ground. George Hall, Starch Manufacturer, Carran mills, Lezayre, is listed in the 1857 *Directory*, so presumably the firm soon changed hands.

The Douglas Patent Preserved Potato Works

At least two firms manufactured a 'patent preserved potato' for use on ships. In October 1846 the Howe brewery, South Quay,

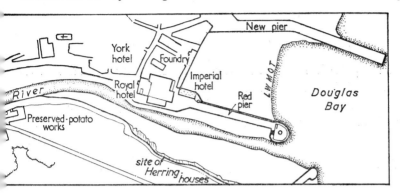

Douglas was converted for manufacturing farina from potatoes; this involved erecting a tall chimney and the plant later included a gaso-meter and large water tanks. At the time of the 1851 census 'Edward Downes, Patentee for preserved potatoes, employing 16 men and 24 women' lived at Falcon Cliff. Up to December 1872 the Douglas Patent Preserved Potato Co retained these works on the South Quay (see plan, above). Local tradition records that many of the girls working for the firm were Irish. Their appearance was greeted with the rhyme:

> They used to call me Saucy Nell
> But now I'm just a spud mill girl.

The potatoes were shredded, dried and sealed in large tins. It is alleged that the Royal Navy was among the purchasers of this early precursor of 'instant potato'. At the time when this firm and the Sulby Starch mill were founded the Isle of Man produced a large surplus of potatoes which had hitherto to be shipped away for sale, but despite the ravages of blight, often mentioned by the local Press, the surplus was apparently sufficient to support several manufac-turers. Little is known about the second potato processing firm except that it was also in Douglas.

Tanneries

During the late eighteenth and early nineteenth centuries news-papers and directories list about twenty tanneries scattered over the Island. Some were short-lived and in the country districts usually small. Tanning might be combined with other trades such as brewing (William Killey, Castle Street, Douglas), the sale of imported leathers and made-up leather goods (the enterprising Ann Kennaugh, Strand Street, Douglas), or boat building and fish curing (John and Caesar Corris of Peel). A verse about them ran:

> John and Caesar, live for ever,
> Best for boats and best for leather.

Hides were imported and exported—there was a fell-monger in Douglas throughout the nineteenth century—and bark, for use in the usual tanning process, was also imported. Two water-powered bark mills have been noted: one in Ballasalla, probably at the Creg or Abbey mills, and the other, which worked up to about 1837, attached to a tanyard in Glen Tramman. Although bark was also used on fishing nets it is likely that the Ballasalla bark mill served the tannery there. The only site with substantial remains is that occupied from at least 1843 by Thomas Cain on Well Road Hill, Douglas; this long-established firm exhibited at the Isle of Man International Exhibition. The shell of the main building, with a tall brick-capped stone chimney, survives but all trace of tan pits, etc, have been swept away to provide parking space and it is likely that demolition will be completed in the near future.

MILLS

Grain and Feed Mills

Because of the paucity of documents it is difficult to trace the early history of milling in Man. It is clear that the Norse type of mill in which the wheel and the top stones turned in the same plane (the so-called sideshot or horizontal mill) survived until a comparatively late date. Grist, Soaken, Toll and Mulchure were among the manorial rights inherited by the Lords of Mann from the Norse kings, and it is likely that the first mills were originally built and owned by the Lord and leased out. Ultimately, they became fees of inheritance but still subject to a yearly Lord's Rent (see Appendix Four for the earliest complete list). All landholders were bound as tenants to a mill and could be fined for failing to grind there; they were also obliged to keep it in repair—to provide straw for thatch or help to transport new millstones for example—but, as long lists of tenants 'presented' to the court show, these duties were not always performed.

D. H. Jones has begun a study of surviving Manx mills and has already shown that they can conveniently be divided into two groups —the small 'upland' type, which still served the surrounding farms, and the larger 'town' mills, which provided flour for the ever-growing number of townspeople. The typical 'upland' mill (see Grenaby, p 188) was a small stone-built structure (most ultimately had slated roofs) on three floors. Usually there is a drying kiln attached, a feature which goes back at least to the medieval period. The grain was hoisted to the top of the mill, fed from there to the stone floor and thence, as flour, to the ground floor. Normally there were three pairs of stones, though very small private mills such as that on the Calf might have only one, and a pearl barley stone, all powered from a single wheel. The equipment was usually completed with flour sifters and a threshing machine, often housed on the lower floor.

Cornaa Mill. The Cornaa (or Ballaglass) mill is fairly typical of the upland type and is also one of the best documented Manx mills because of the litigation concerning its ownership and tenants. In one of the pleas it is alleged that the mills 'are by undoubted reputation as ancient as the Grinding of Corn in that parish' and were 'Anciently the Lord of the Isle his own Milns . . . for the supply of his Houses & Garrisons'. Cornaa means 'mill river' in Norse, some indication of its real antiquity. In the 1511 Manorial Roll John McCristen (ie Christian) appears as the tenant but he was forced to go to England on business, so, in 1535, *Liber Vast* records that his servant, Lewis David, took over the tenancy. John Christian died in England leaving an only daughter, Joney. She was still a minor when her father died and it was not until 1613 that her son, Deemster Samsbury, succeeded in recovering the family estates.

Jane Samsbury, the Deemster's widow, sold the mill to Deemster Ewan Christian in 1642 and he settled it on his second son, the Manx hero Illiam Dhone, who was executed in 1662. His eldest son, George, persuaded the Prince of Wales to restore the Christian estates but in order to do so had to stay in England, leaving his brother Ewan as his agent in the Isle of Man. In George's absence a plot was hatched to sell the mills' tenants to a newly built mill at Lewaigue, a double impossibility since Ewan did not have power to dispose of his brother's estates and such a sale of tenants was contrary to custom. On his return George took seventy-one actions for damages against the inhabitants of Ramsey—probably the total of his mills' bound tenants there—for grinding at the more convenient Lewaigue mill, but the dispute was not settled for a considerable time.

The mill went out of use in 1951 and is now being converted into a dwelling. The present building is largely of local stone with a roof of imported slate. The corn-drying kiln, on the downstream side of the main building, has bright red handmade bricks in its walls and much iron in its construction—lintels, joists, perforated floor, etc—presumably as a fire precaution. The last-used millstones were all imported: one Welsh pebble, one millstone grit, and one French burr with four iron weight pockets (Patented Mill-wheel balance, Clarke & Dunham, 1859).

For the last 100 years the millers were members of the Gelling family (*Thwaite's Guide and Directory*, 1863, Thomas Gelling; *Brown's Directory*, 1882 and 1894, John J. & Thomas Gelling) and they presumably were responsible for most of the surviving fittings. Like the stones already mentioned these were designed to help the mill compete with the larger town mills. There was a winnowing machine in the basement—with a vent for the chaff in the downstream wall—and a pearl barley stone. The last was used to supply the Knockaloe Internment Camp during World War I when it hardly stopped working. Together with a few documents, some hand tools and most of the fittings from the stone floor, it has now been deposited in the Manx Museum. The following bills give a glimpse of the charges made in the twentieth century.

1938		
4 Bush Oats crushed	1	0
8 „ „ „	2	0
3 „ Barley do		9

14 Nov 1944		
3 Bush Barley Crushed	1	3
„ „ „ Ground	2	0
2½ „ Oats „	1	8
17½ „ „ Crushed	7	3½
	12	2½
14lb Barley Meal	4	0
	8	2½
½ crush oats	10	0
	18	2½

Town Mills. The earliest town mill was probably at Castletown near the site of the present Meadow Mill. Like Cornaa it is well documented because of litigation, and the mills on this site can be traced back at least as early as 1511. Probably the earliest Lord's mill stood here, though there are slight traces of a tide mill in the basement of Castle Rushen—the place usually shown as Bishop Wilson's prison. The owners of the Castletown mills were usually progressive and added other water-powered manufactures to corn milling. These certainly included flax scutching and fulling and are reputed to have included snuff and powder grinding.

Rhenwyllin, for part of its later history, and the Creg and Abbey mills at Ballasalla were other mills in the south of the Island which took up commercial rather than service milling. The main town mills, however, were at Douglas, near the developing centre of population, and Laxey, which had particularly abundant water power. *Mercantile Manxland*, 'reviewed and up-to-date', published in 1900, gives a good idea of the competition between the main firms.

The Nunnery Roller Mills, Douglas

Almost the first objects one notices on leaving Douglas by the Castletown Road are the extensive 'Nunnery Flour Mills' of W. and T. Quine. . . . Many mills have no doubt succeeded the first one, those at present in use dating back to the early years of the present century. Still the silver stream of the 'Dubhglaise' flows on, gently but forcibly revolving the massive water-wheel. . . . In these days of progressive changes, the Nunnery Mills have been changed too. The old water-wheel has been supplemented by a powerful steam engine, and the roller system has been adopted.

T. Corlett The Laxey Glen Roller Mill

To the traveller standing upon the viaduct at Laxey, Corlett's lofty stone-built mill, embowered in verdant foliage, with the dark background of Pen-y-Pot in the distance, forms a striking and prominent feature of the lovely landscape.

The Laxey Glen Corn Mill is, structurally, undoubtedly the finest mill of its class on the island . . . unexcelled by any of the largest mills across the water. . . . The Glen Roy stream is harnessed to a turbine, from which as much as 40-h.p. is derived. This force, however, has long been found in-sufficient to cope with the heavy machinery and a powerful steam-engine by the late noted firm of McAdams, of Belfast, is also put in requisition. This engine, we may remark, was originally intended for pumping water for irrigation purposes on the Nile . . . The capacity of the mill—which has been fitted up by Harrison Carter's of London, with a plant second to none in the kingdom, on their improved roller system—is very large . . .

This mill still stands and still produces flour for the local market, where its price is slightly lower than that of imported products.

Quine & Son, The Silverdale Corn Mill, Castletown

. . . came into the possession, some thirty years ago, of William Quine & Son, by whom it has been fitted with a modern steam plant of effective character.

The new Ballaughton mill also had a progressive owner who was prepared to install a patent mill while most of his fellows were still struggling with the old type of wheel. His testimonial, quoted in

James Whitelaw's *Description of the New Water-Mill*, Paisley, 1843, gives a clear indication of the amount and type of work Manx mills undertook at this date.

Ballaughton Mills, Isle of Man
10th April, 1843

MR JAMES WHITELAW.

DEAR SIR,—Having one of your patent water-mills, and feeling particularly well pleased with its working, I have been testing its power, by drawing a comparison between our mill and Pulrose Mill, situated about 400 yards below us, on the same stream of water. The following results will convince every person who understands the subject, that your patent water-mill will work to very great advantage on a low fall, compared with the common water-wheel, and any person desirous to see both mills at work can satisfy himself at any time by calling on me:—

Our fall of water is 8 feet 6 inches, and the water-mill is 9 feet 6 inches diameter—it has four arms, and works in tail-water. When the 4 arms are open we drive 6 pairs of stones, each 4 feet 6 inches diameter, viz.: 2 pairs grinding wheat, 2 pairs barley, 1 pair making oatmeal and sifting at same time, and 1 pair shelling oats with the scree and fanners. With 3 arms open —2 pairs—1 pair barley, and 1 pair oatmeal, as before. With 2 arms open— 2 pairs wheat, and 1 flour cylinder. With 1 arm open—1 pair wheat, and 1 flour cylinder. Our flour cylinders are 18 inches diameter and 7 feet long. The quantity of wheat we grind per hour on each pair of stones is 6 bushels, and of barley 4 bushels, and oatmeal 10cwt.; on each cylinder 16cwt. of fine flour. It may be as well to observe, that all our barley is kiln-dried before grinding, and is ground into a very fine flour for making bread; consequently it is much harder and takes more power than wheat. The speed of the water-mill, when working as above, is exactly 54 revolutions per minute, our stones 108 revolutions, and our flour cylinders 470 revolutions per minute.

Pulrose Mill has a fall of 7 feet, and is worked by an undershot water-wheel 15 feet diameter and 5 feet wide. It is only 4 years old, and is made on the very best principle, and there is no loss of water between the two mills. When our 4 arms are open, at Pulrose Mill they have more water than they can consume. Our 3 arms give the exact quantity required by them to drive 1 pair of wheat-stones, 4 feet 6 inches diameter, grinding five bushels wheat per hour; and 1 pair barley grinding 3 bushels per hour. When our 2 arms are open they have barely enough water to work 1 pair of wheat-stones, and one flour cylinder (16 inches diameter by 5 feet 10 dressing 8 cwt. fine flour per hour. When 1 of our arms is open, they are scarcely able to grind 3 bushels of wheat per hour, without any other part of the machinery at work. You are at liberty to make what use you think proper of this letter, and to refer any person for further information respecting our mill to, dear sire, yours very respectfully,

ROBT. DONALDSON

A further testimonial in the *Description of the New Water-Mill* relates to a threshing mill, a reminder that in the Isle of Man, with its shortage of fuel, water power was utilised for many farm tasks. At least three windmills used for threshing are also known.

Kirk St Anne, Isle of Man
22nd March, 1843

Mr James Whitelaw.

SIR,—It affords me great pleasure to be able to give the following particulars respecting the patent water-mill made by you, and which was erected by me in this island, on the estate of Ballabrooie, the property of Caesar Bacon, Esq., in the parish of Lezayre.

The mill has two arms or jets, and when they are both open, is calculated to give 9½ horses' power, and is used for the purpose of driving an ordinary machine for thrashing corn.—The two arms I find to be altogether too powerful, consequently I partially closed one, leaving it about one-third part open—this would leave 6⅓ horses' power to work the machinery, which is quite sufficient for my purposes. We were thrashing oats at the time, and the quality not of the best description, the straw being long, and the ear not well filled. In one hour we threshed 88 bushels of oats, Winchester measure. The grain was well cleaned, and free from chaff.

The threshing-mill, feeding-rollers, are 4½ feet diameter, with two shakers and one pair of fanners.

Having had a great deal of experience in setting up thrashing-mills, I can speak with some degree of certainty of the advantages of your patent water-mill in this instance, over ordinary overshot water-wheel; and I believe it to be the first of the kind applied to this purpose, I trust it may meet the notice of all farmers desirous of making the most of the water in thrashing, especially in dry seasons. Having made most of the thrashing-mills with water-wheels on the south part of this island, I can with truth say, I have never been able to get out of a thrashing-machine, worked by an over-shot water-wheel, having the same advantages as to height of fall and quantity of water that your machine has, more than 58 bushels of well-cleaned oats an hour; the balance in favour of your mill is therefore 30 bushels per hour, or, in other words, a saving of one-third of the time ordinarily taken. You are at perfect liberty to refer any person to me for further information on the subject.—I am, Sir, your most obedient servant,

THOMAS BAIRD

Papermaking

Papermaking was introduced into the Isle of Man in the eighteenth century by an Irishman named McDaniel. He was probably a member of the family of Michael McDaniel who started a mill near Tallaght, County Dublin, about 1775. According to a draft memorial to the Lord of Mann among the Bridge House papers in the Manx Museum library, McDaniel had great difficulty in starting work. He was unaware that, since imported paper paid a duty of 3d and 1d, respectively, on a ream of writing or brown paper, he would have to obtain a licence.

> That your mem$^{st.}$ for yrs past has been frequently sollicited by most of ye Merchts and some other considerable persons inhabitants of this Isle to carry on there in the Paper-making Trade.
>
> That your mem$^{st.}$ being induced by such sollicitations and promises of Encouragement and not having been appraised until by yr Hon$^r.$ of any Cause of Interupption brought hither from Ireland (where yr. mem$^{st.}$ was settled in ye sd. Business) both his Family and the proper Utensils for manufacturing paper the Freight & Land Carriage of which Utensils (being very ponderous and unwieldy) came very high which with the support of a numerous Family in a State of Inactivity since last Michaelmas very much hurt yr. mem$^{st.}$ in his circumstances . . .

Whether or not this document was ever presented is unknown but McDaniel—no extant document gives his first name—was finally given permission to start making paper providing that he paid an annual rent at least equal to the previous receipts from the duty, some £13 to £14 a year.

He apparently confined himself to 'the manufacturing of coarse brown papers, fit only for covering of Teas Suggars &c'. According to Governor Wood, who came to Man in 1761, 'he having neither Capital nor Industry failed in about a year', and his mill did not work again. Like many of his contemporaries he evaded his rent, in this case fairly simply since his agreement to pay was only verbal. Although much is recorded about his mill it cannot be precisely located; it certainly stood in, or near, Plot 2864, Malew (see map, p 186), but the course of the river has been considerably altered in the last 150 years and the area disturbed by the building of the railway. After heavy rain, water lies in several depressions, which probably indicate the lines of its watercourses. The name 'Paper Mill Farm' was still used after all the original buildings had been destroyed by the Quayle family's early nineteenth-century agricultural improvements.

According to the Report of the Commissioners of Enquiry, 9,514 reams and 151cwt of bundles of paper were exported from the Isle of Man during 1784–90. This was probably all made by William Powell Buck, 'of or near Cockermouth in the county of Cumberland and Kingdom of Great Britain paper maker but at present in the Town of Douglas in the Isle of Man . . .', as he was described in a deed of sale of the White Lion Inn, Douglas, dated 8 November 1791. Alexander Lewthwaite, another Cumberland man, came to the Island from Egremont in 1789 bringing with him his four younger children. He took a lease of an existing mill and probably took over Buck's business; about 1793 his son-in-law, Patrick (or Peter) Roche Farrill, a refugee from France, joined him. Buck died about this time. From evidence given in a dispute between Tromode and Ballaughton mills in 1854 it is clear that Lewthwaite's mill, usually known as Ballabeg mill because he rented Ballabeg in Braddan parish, was on the site later used for Moore's Sailcloth works (see p 172), which is now occupied by Clucas's laundry.

The Isle of Man Paper Mill Company solicited the custom of local shopkeepers for 'woolen grey, tea-paper, bag cap &c.' in the *Manks Advertiser* of 8 July 1809. The firm continued to work under a variety of names at the Woodside mill, built on the site of a flax mill at Ballaoates, presumably to take advantage of existing water rights. In February 1816 Mark Antony Mills, an Irish solicitor, set up the Phoenix Press in the Parade, Douglas, and came to an agreement with the proprietors of the Woodside mill to supply him with paper, which they did for eighteen months from May 1816 until a dispute arose about the amount Mills owed them. An account prepared for the use of the Chancery Court shows the sizes of the paper produced and the prices:

	£	s	d
1 Rheam fine post		14	0
1 Rheam royal	1	5	0
1 Rheam 3rd foolscap		13	0
1 Rheam News royal	1	11	0
1 Rheam folio post	1	4	0
1 Rheam 2nd foolscap		19	0

The 'News royal' was used for the *Isle of Man Weekly Gazette* and paper watermarked 'B. & Co. 1815', costing 30s a ream, was supplied for the *Ancient Ordinances and Statute Laws of the Isle of Man*. After the dispute this work was completed on paper marked 'W.W. 1821'.

Profits from the mill declined and there were several involved lawsuits over debts. On 15 August 1825 the mill was taken over by the owners of the New Paper Mill, Laxey, whose own premises had been gutted by fire and two years later they renewed the lease for a further twelve years. But by March 1830 they wanted to let 'Woodside Paper and Flax Mill with Immediate Possession given, with the Moulds and Felts . . . from Ten to Twelve Tons of Raw Material may be had at Valuation . . .' (*Manx Sun*, 12 March 1830). The mill did not work successfully again until the 1850s. In *Slater's Directory*, 1853, John Demeza is named as the principal in the mill; it was later taken over by the Carooins family—probably the same Carooins listed in the 1851 census as papermakers in Laxey. They produced wrapping papers until 1885, when the mill was sold to Charles Litt of Douglas. It was subsequently used by Bimson's soap works and Litt's fertiliser factory; the latter firm is still in occupation and in consequence this is the only Manx paper mill at which substantial buildings have survived.

In 1816 John Gelling, one of the partners at the Woodside mill, had sold out to the others. Three years later he built a new paper mill on his own land at Ballamillaghyn which was to be known as the Baldwin Vale Paper Mill. Alexander Lewthwaite left the Woodside mill to manage the new works and the Lewthwaites took over

K

complete control in 1822, though *Liber Assed* shows that the Gellings retained some interest, since they continued to pay a share of the mill rent. One of the firm's frames with the watermark 'A L 1826' is preserved in the Manx Museum.

The abundant water power available in the Laxey valley was used by two paper mills (see map, p 60), the earlier of which was the Laxey Glen Mill. A notice appeared in the *Manks Advertiser* on 2 November 1820 stating that William Walker '. . . has rented the large Spinning Mill, situate on the Laxey River, which he intends speedily to convert into a Paper Mill, and expects to be able to supply the Public with Manks Manufactured Paper, of a good Quality, and on the most moderate terms'. The mill was working by the following July—it supplied the balance of the paper for Mills's *Laws* . . . and a warehouse was opened near the Market Place, Douglas. Thomas Topliss, who had been manager at the Woodside mill, was Walker's agent at the New Paper Mill and seems to have been a partner.

The firm suffered a setback in February 1824, when the mill, '. . . together with the old machinery for spinning linen yarn, and a considerable quantity of paper, rags &c. . . .' caught fire. For-tunately, the Norwich Union Fire Office paid the amount of the insurance 'with the greatest promptitude and alacrity', so the mill was soon repaired and in both the *Manks Advertiser* and the *Manx Sun* for 22 June 1824—

> Walker and Topliss take this opportunity of returning their most grateful thanks to their friends and to the Public, for the encouragement they have received since they commenced the above establishment; and beg leave to acquaint them, that having completed the erection of the mill, upon the most modern and improved Kentish Principle, they feel confident in stating, that they are enabled to manufacture all descriptions of paper in a style much superior to anything ever attempted in the Isle of Man.

The 'Kentish Principle' refers to that county's connection with Henry Fourdrinier, who introduced continuous papermaking to England and thus, together with Bryan Donkin, spread the use of machines in what had previously been an unmechanised industry. It is likely that the new equipment for the mill was an 'ingeniously constructed piece of insular manufacture'.

From the *Manks Advertiser* of 27 June 1837 it appears that Thomas Topliss surrendered control of the Laxey mill to his son William, while remaining at the Woodside mill which they had acquired after the fire. However, the business did not prosper and the *Manx Liberal* had to report on 10 October 1840: 'We regret to record the death of Mr Topliss, paper-maker, Woodside, near the Strang, who was found on Thursday last in his own mill, suspended by the neck and quite dead'. Not surprisingly William soon left the trade but in 1846 Dillon's *Guide* mentions that 'At Laxey an excellent paper mill is in operation under the management of Messrs. Walker and Tilsley. Their paper is exported in large quantities to Liverpool, where it is speedily bought up'. The mill was finally converted into a power station for the Manx Electric railway and only its shell survives.

Before Thomas Topliss left the firm he had bought from James and Ann Quayle, according to a deed dated 13 April 1829,

> . . . lands calld. the Claddagh together with the little Mill and tuck Mill adjoining with seven yards of Crott Norris Brew for the use of a Mill race a part the sd. property on the North side of the river and joining Phill Hoggs rent joining the river on the North from the old dam head down to Laxey Bridge Joining the Bridge on the South East and own garden on the South and Thos. Fargher on the South West and Charles and Philip Skillicorns on the South West and Crott Norris Brew on the South West . . .

This purchase secured water rights which might otherwise have been difficult to obtain in the Laxey valley.

A new mill was apparently soon built, for when Topliss was forced to sell his property included:

> . . . certain Lands and Premises purchased by me from James Quayle and John Moore situate in the said Parish of Lonan with the Mill, Machinery, Improvements, Buildings and Prems. lately erected upon part of the said Lands which deed bear date respectively from sd. James Quayle on the thirteenth Day of April one Thousand eight Hundred and twenty nine and from the sd. John Moore on the thirty first Day of July one Thousand eight Hundred & thirty four.

Walker paid out £1,400 to his former partner's creditors but apparently ceased to work the mill. On 14 March 1846 William Broughton (the new owner and probably the Douglas china dealer) leased it to John and Alexander Lewthwaite & Co; these men were sons of the Alexander Lewthwaite who made paper at Tromode.

In the 1851 census Alexander Lewthwaite appears as 'Paper maker and employer of ten labourers', though only five other people in Lonan parish claimed connection with the trade. Early in August of the same year fire again took its toll of the vulnerable buildings with their piles of rags and this time the insurance cover was only on the stock, with the Caledonian Insurance Co, for £300. Papermaking could not be resumed and in 1852 the brothers were sued for their outstanding rent. At the Deemster's Court they were ordered to put in repair the damhead, millrace, floodgates and fences, a matter of some £10 to £20 judging by contemporary bills, and to pay the costs of the case. No major repairs were done, for in 1862 'the said concern and premises consisting of the lower Laxey Paper Mill (several years ago destroyed by fire)' were sold to James Bridson Milburn, brewer, together with the land for £105. The surviving traces are slight.

It is likely that only the abundant water power and a supply of flax as a raw material made papermaking an economic proposition in the Isle of Man. After 1833 the bounty on the growth of flax was withdrawn and even before this there may have been a shortage of material for making better-quality papers. The following appeal appeared in the *Manks Advertiser* for 11 September 1802:

> The inhabitants of the Isle of Man are most particularly requested not to destroy their Linen and Woolen Rags: as a Continuance of the Importation of these Articles, must be attended with a rise in the Price of Paper. There are persons now employed in Collecting Throughout the Island, Materials for making paper.

The quality of the early Manx paper is good and a considerable amount has survived. Study of the watermarks indicates that there were other short-lived partnerships besides those mentioned but it is clear that this was never a very profitable trade. Despite the ingenuity of local foundries in producing equipment, so small and insecurely based an industry could not compete, even on a craft basis, in the nineteenth century and is most unlikely to be revived, though descendants of some of the craftsmen still live in the Island.

Fulling Mills

Fulling was the first process connected with textile production to utilise the abundant water power. Tuck, or walk, mills are listed in the first complete surviving manorial roll, but the survival of at least one 'waulking' song may indicate that their use did not at once become universal. It has proved almost impossible to locate the early fulling mills but some were apparently attached to the old manorial grain mills and may even have been powered by the same wheels. Their numbers increased steadily and by the end of the nineteenth century the handloom weavers relied on mechanical fulling. Local tradition has a good deal to say about the noise of the fulling stocks, which drove the 'little people' away from the remote glens, and how, in a dry period when the water was low, there would be a long pause between strokes. Unfortunately there is considerable confusion as to which mills were used for fulling. *Tuck* mill is often used to indicate a flax-breaking mill and the Ordnance Survey's abbreviation *T. mill*, may designate a threshing mill. In addition an existing wheel might be used successively for a variety of processes. So only a few of the fulling mills will be mentioned.

In 1643 Thomas Moore, who owned the Castletown mills, was licensed to build a walk mill just upstream, on what had been Abbey lands. This may imply that neither of the monastic mills at Ballasalla had been equipped for this purpose. Moore's mill was converted into a paper mill about 1760 and has now disappeared but there were at least two other fulling mills on the Silverburn. That at Mullin y Carty, SC 272717 GBM 24/074, was built by William Christian, gentleman of Jurby, William Mylechreest and Robert Kewn of Malew in 1739. The rectangular granite building, approximately 23ft by 40ft, was originally thatched like most Manx mills but was re-roofed with imported Welsh slates about 1880. Each of the builders had a 'tucker' and worked the mill for a week, in rotation. By 1794 one John Shimmin had acquired full rights to the mill and his surviving mill accounts (see Appendix Two, p 231) give a good in-dication of the expense of maintaining a waterwheel and dam at this time. John Shimmin seems to have given up about 1814 and the mill was subsequently used, according to the 25in OS map of c 1868, for carding wool. The 1837 *Directory*, however, still lists Robert Mullen, the then occupier, as a cloth-scourer, so perhaps, as at Union Mills and Southwards', Sulby, a variety of processes was carried out. 'Mullen, the weaver', according to oral tradition, was the last occupier. The building is now a roofless shell and virtually all trace of the associated dwelling has gone. The ochre and umber mill already described (p 137) was probably also used for fulling at one period, as well as for flax processing. Those fulling mills which form part of a woollen manufacturing business are dealt with in the section on woollen mills that follows.

Woollen Mills

In the nineteenth century, in addition to the fulling and dyeing mills, there were a number in which every process from scouring and carding the fleece to dyeing and finishing the web was carried out. The history of Southward's Sulby mill is typical. About 1830 the Southwards moved to Sulby, probably from Laxey where Corlett & Southward had a bleaching and carding mill (also described as 'a Tuck mill and Dye House') about 1830–55. At first they leased the building which later became the starch works, SC 381934 GBM 23/094, where they installed a new waterwheel. In 1843 they rebuilt another mill, SC 282928 GBM 24/077, and by the time of the 1851 census Thos E. Southward was employing six men. It is not clear whether these were in addition to his sons Thomas (cloth finisher) and Francis (apprentice wool-carder). Thomas's household also included another apprentice wool-carder, an apprentice handloom weaver and his brother-in-law, a weaver. It is likely that his labour force was completed by one or more of the weavers living in the neighbourhood. It is clear that already all stages of cloth production were being carried out.

The mill flourished through several changes of ownership and was particularly noted for its flannel. At the end of the nineteenth century the dyer, William Fargher, favoured simple reliable shades of blue, brown or black. The dyestuffs used were mainly imported vegetable colours such as indigo and logwood. Machine-knitted stockings were also made on the premises. During World War I only singlet flannel and sock wool were made. Taylor took over the mill in 1925. It was badly affected by floods five years later. Howarth & Penrice were the last firm to run it and though they added tartan travelling rugs, for the souvenir trade, and attractive fashion tweeds to their range, they closed in 1956. The building now houses Manx Construction Ltd.

William Kelly's Union Mills, SC 354778 GBM 24/073, were also on a fairly small scale. In June 1807 he was appealing in the *Manks Advertiser* for twenty experienced woollen weavers and in the following year he announced that as little as 10lb of wool would be accepted for processing. In 1809 he was offering to make blankets, etc, from the customer's own yarn or to produce rolls (for hand spinning) or spun yarn. A cart was sent round the countryside to collect orders, including items for dyeing. Kelly became involved in a lawsuit with the Lord Bishop and the premises were damaged by fire in 1828. They seem to have been rebuilt by James Grellier, the newspaper editor and one-time proprietor of the Ballasalla Ochre and Umber mill. It was then taken over by Dalrymple and continued to work almost until the end of the nineteenth century. In addition to the usual tweeds and flannels, drugget was made. There was also a corn mill powered by the same water supply, hence the 'Union

Mills At the sign of the Flail and Fleece' on the card money issued by the first owner.

Of the surviving mills St George's mill, Laxey, SC 434844 GBM 24/111, is exceptional in that it was founded to give reality to Ruskin and William Morris's notions of an ideal economy. Great stress was laid on craftsmanship and the fact that, as had always been true in Man, anyone could bring wool for processing and receive it back as cloth. The original manager was Egbert Rydings and it has been stated that the building was specifically built, though it is likely that existing water rights were acquired. Most of the wool is now imported and chemical dyes are used. Products include fashion tweeds, various mohair items, travelling rugs, ties, socks and knitting wool, and outlets include at least three retail shops in the Island.

The Tynwald mill, St John's, developed from a number of wool-processing mills in the area. There was a fulling mill near Ballig bridge in 1703 and one with a calendering machine by 1790. Mr Craine built a new fulling mill about 1798, probably SC 285827 GBM 24/076. Ann Killey of Ballakilley also built a fulling mill, SC 279824 GBM 24/079, in 1820. The Crellins of Ballig worked a mill here until 1843, when it was taken over by John Moore, who had married Jane Crellin; he enlarged and extended the weaving and dyeing business and built a three-storey mill and dyeworks in 1846, while Ann Killey's mill was used for carding. His grandson built the present electrically powered mill, SC 283824 GBM 24/078, about 1920. Ann Killey's mill then became a wool store. Products still include flannel, tweeds and travelling rugs, which enjoy a good sale locally and to tourists.

Although the history of the other small woollen mills is less known, they will be listed here rather than only in the gazetteer, in the hope that further information will be forthcoming. Matthew Senior's Ballabrooie bleach mill (so-called 1812), SC 262821 GBM 24/083, had become 'Mrs Stephenson's woollen mill' by 1838 and seems to have been used for this purpose for some time. Also fairly long-lived was Hugh Bell's carding mill near Castleward and there was another in the same parish of Braddan, at Ballawyllin, SC 361747 GBM 24/081, run by Philip Kelly. There were wool-processing mills in Onchan (Bowring mill, SC 396796 GBM 24/075 and Ballacreetch, SC 369792 GBM 24/082) and elsewhere in the Laxey valley apart from St George's mill. George Lawton had a mill in Glen Auldyn, SC 434934 (possibly site GBM 24/045), in 1860. As mentioned previously Mullen carded wool at the Ochre mill and later at Mullin y Carty, Malew. There were also several dye works in the Douglas area, including that, now destroyed, at Kewaigue, SC 361747 GBM 24/080, which may also have served as a spade mill.

As has been indicated the handloom weavers took advantage of the mills' machine-made yarn and mechanised fulling but they did not commonly, as had occurred in Ireland, group themselves into cottage industries. A number of machine-knitting and clothing firms have had small factories in Man from time to time since the old mills closed but such small-scale works are of purely local significance.

Cotton Mills

During the eighteenth century there were several attempts to manufacture cotton goods in the Isle of Man, the earliest being the printing works started at Port e Chee, near Douglas, some time before 1772. This printed material was made by local out-workers from raw Jamaican cotton purchased in England by the factory. A certain amount of flax and linen was also handled, together with imported cloth; the printing was in one, two or three colours from blocks imported from England. There were two or three changes of ownership and the business started and stopped with each. In its last period the main product recorded was handkerchiefs, some of which were exported to Madeira and illegally re-exported to South America. The business foundered about 1780 in a welter of debt and all trace of the factory building has gone. The equipment was sold and it is possible that some of it was purchased by Abraham Delapryme for the factory he was building near Ballasalla, though he used water-powered spinning frames in contrast to the entirely hand-operated machinery used at Port e Chee and by its out-workers.

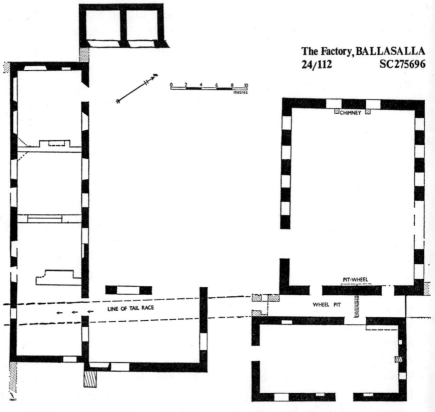

The factory at Ballasalla, erected about 1778 (sketch plan from IA record cards)

On 12 January 1780 Thomas Moore, 'his Majesty's Deemster of the Isle of Man', signed an agreement with Abraham Delapryme and Francis Wheelhouse. Moore was to erect a building (34ft long, 26ft wide and 30ft high) on his own land and he was to find, 'Slates, Mortar and Workmanship, for slating the said-intended Mill; and likewise cause the Walls of the said Mill to be plaistered in a work-manlike manner.' He was also to build a dam and a place for a shuttle, though the other two signatories were to pay for the shuttle itself. (A shuttle here means the control of the water supply.) The annual rent payable to Moore was 12 guineas and Delapryme and his partner were also to pay the annual Lord's Rent fixed by the setting quest:

> We whose Names Ensue Being the Setting Quest of the Abby Lands of the Parish of Malew have appeared on the Premises Within Mentioned in Order to Settle a proportionate Part of the Cheiff Rent on the Same Do Settle thereon the Sum of Sixpence half penny Manks to be Yearly Cheiff Rent of sd. Premises and to be paid by the proprietors Thereof yearly and Every year And this we Give for Our Verdict in the premises this 17th April 1782
>
> $\qquad$ *Signed* Christopher Bridson
> $\qquad\qquad\quad$ John Harwood
> $\qquad\qquad\quad$ Christopher Bridson
> $\qquad\qquad\quad$ Jno. Quayle

Several buildings of local stone survive (see p 170), though it is very difficult to decide precisely which was Moore's original mill and which the house and outbuildings built by Delapryme a few years later. The spinning of cotton probably started about 1782 and continued with moderate success until about 1792, in which year there was an instruction to the Douglas custom to pass, free of duty, cotton goods manufactured by Delapryme (Atholl Papers, 128-, 13). When cotton spinning ceased the mill seems to have been used for a short time for spinning thread for making fishing nets. It is called a flax mill in 1818. Very large timbers in the smallest streamward building suggest the foundations of fulling stocks, which may indicate another subsequent use. The wheel was finally used to power a threshing machine which was unfortunately destroyed by vandals comparatively recently.

Flax-processing and the Linen Trade

Linen was a fairly late arrival in the Manx economy but it would be difficult to overestimate its importance in the eighteenth and nineteenth centuries. The Duke of Atholl, Lord of Mann, and the Manx Society share the credit for fostering the trade. The latter, with the Duke's assistance, distributed seed and gave spinning equipment to the poor; as a result the exports rose from 12,000yd in 1765 to at least 100,000yd in 1767. Before flax can be spun it has to be retted and scutched. Virtually every lowland Manx farm had a 'flax dub', or pool, in which the plants were soaked before the fibres were separated from the waste. At first the latter process, scutching, was done entirely by hand but later simple machinery was introduced and water-powered mills appeared. As has been indicated it is difficult to disentangle references to scutching mills from those relating to fulling works, as both tend to be called 'tuck' mills. As yet, no machinery comparable to that extant in Ireland has been found.

Spinning and weaving were again largely hand processes but a few factories did exist. Moore's (Tromode Works) was the longest-surviving firm and one of the few to introduce a real flavour of industrialisation to the Isle of Man. Its products show an interesting development from a wide diversity of household goods to a specialisation in sailcloth, which was of so high a quality as to warrant an Admiralty contract and to be used on Brunel's *Great Britain*. Many of the workers came from Ireland and were housed in a small 'Industrial Estate', virtually unique in Man. Very strict rules, comparable to those in English textile factories, were enforced. As Strutt told the Factories Inquiry Commission in 1833, 'small fines' were used to maintain discipline. The 'crimes' also show a similarity to those recorded in Strutt's Quarterly Wages Book, 1801–5, though the Manx fines seem to have been lower. The Tromode hands were provided by their employer, with a cricket club for the summer and a reading room, for the winter, so possibly conditions were less harsh than in England. There is certainly no record of the employment of very young children or pauper apprentices.

Since the majority of workers lived in the tied cottages of 'Cronkbourne Village' (see Gazetteer, p 201) the census returns are a good guide to the origins and composition of the mill's labour force. In 1851, of a total of about eighty manual workers, some thirty were Irish, two English and one Scots. From the evidence of the birthplaces of the children, it is clear that some, like one of the master weavers, had been in Man at least sixteen years while others were recent arrivals, showing that the recruiting of skilled workers from the Irish linen trade was more or less continuous. At the time of the same census the inhabitants of the village also included two millwrights (one with his son as apprentice), a mechanic and a boilermaker. Otherwise the trades obviously connected with the mills were as follows:

Hecklers 4 (Boys, 12–14) *Flax-dressers* 6 (2 Boys, 16;
Spinners 17 (6 Girls, 13–15; 2 Men, 26, 50;
    8 „ 16–20; 2 Women, 21, 36)
    Women, 22, 28, 42)
Quillers 2 (Girls, 18, 20) *Spoolers* 2 (Girls, 18, 24)
Reelers of sail-cloth yarn 2 (Girls, 21, 25) *Warpers* 1 (Woman, 40)
WORKERS 5 male (3 Boys, 12; 1 Boy, 14; 1 Man, 29)
    23 female (10 Girls, 12–19; 5 Women, 20–35; 8 Women 40–54)
Weavers 18 male (6 Boys, 16–20; 6 Men under 35; 6 Men, 36–64)
Bleachers 2 Men (65, 66) *Overlooker* Samuel Craig

In 1861 William Moore is recorded as employing 150 men in all. Hand and power-loom weavers are differentiated only in the later census but it is clear from the 'Rules and Regulations' that both were also employed in 1851. Similarly Sack-cloth weavers are enumerated in 1851 only but it is believed that the mills were still producing sacks when they closed. It is perhaps noteworthy that, though a school was provided, far more children are recorded as working than is the case in the mining communities. It seems likely that this reflects to some extent the greater prosperity and independence of the miners rather than the putatively more physically exacting nature of the work.

The *Manx Sun* for 28 September 1850 gives a lengthy account of the factory in its early days.

The motive power is derived from an iron water-wheel . . . 19ft diameter and 9ft wide, the water is applied on the overshot principle. When the supply of water is plentiful the motion is entirely derived therefrom, and even in times of scarcity the water is by a peculiar contrivance, husbanded, as it were, so as to give an adequate supply for a few hours in the morning. . . . When the water fails to communicate the required motion recourse is had to a horizontal steam-engine of 16 inches cylinder and 3ft stroke. . . . The wheel was made by John Rowan and Sons of Belfast. . . . The motion of this wheel . . . is conveyed by internal and external contrivances . . . to the rooms containing the different machines. . . .

We come now to the heckling. This operation is for the purpose of removing the tow or short fibre. . . . A quantity of the flax is arranged in a sort of case, and introduced at one end of the machine. Speedily the first operation is effected—that of getting rid of the coarser matter. In this state, the portion of the flax is passed, by the machine itself . . . into another division, and then to another, in each of which a different degree of fineness is produced, till, at last, every particle of extraneous matter is removed, and the whole of filaments arranged in distinct even and parallel fibres. . . . The heckling machine was manufactured by Samuel Lawson and Sons of Leeds, upon their patented principle . . .

The next process is accomplished by various drawing machines. The drawing is for the purpose of straightening the fibres. The first result of the drawing is what is called the sliver, a beautiful, glossy, ribbon-like arrangement of the fibres. The subsequent drawing is for equalizing this sliver. . . . The product is then ready for roving.

The roving throws the sliver, thus arranged and equalized, into coarse thread, twisting it slightly, which thread is then ready for the spinners. The spinning is conducted in upper rooms, where there are 636 spindles . . . Here the coarse thread, derived from the roving, is spun and is afterwards reeled. The spinning and preparing machines were made by Samuel Lawson & Sons and Peter Fairbairne & Co of Leeds. . . .

The yarn is also bleached on the premises. This department contains a plash-mill, washing reels, wringing hooks, and weft beating machine driven by a water-wheel. After bleaching process is accomplished, the yarn is in summer hung on poles in the neighbouring green to be dried, and in winter, this is effected by means of a stove. During the night time, and in rainy weather, the yarn is carried into a shed 180ft long and hung up there. The drying may now be supposed to be completed.

All is now ready for the weaving. This important part of the process takes place in a separate building . . . it is in reality one room. The roof consists of a number of divisions a peculiarity adopted for the due admission of light. The whole of the Northern aspect of each division is glazed . . . the power looms are by C. Parker of Dundee. . . .

The workrooms were originally gas-lit, the gas consumed being made on the premises. In 1882 electricity was substituted, from a Compton dynamo—voltage 110,200 amps working at 888rpm. The works closed in 1905 and the site is at present occupied by Clucas's laundry.

SECTION TWO

Gazetteer

CONTENTS

THE members of the Field Section of the Isle of Man Natural History & Antiquarian Society have started compiling a card index of all industrial archaeological sites in the Isle of Man. It will be some years before this work is complete and it will require supplementing with considerable research before a complete account can be written. This gazetteer, therefore, is merely a field guide to areas of particular interest, to be used in conjunction with Sheet 87 of the OS 1in Series. As far as possible the international mill survey numbers (beginning GBM 24 or 25) have been given for all sites with waterwheels in the hope that this will promote interest in their recording. It is for this reason also that many entries consist of little more than a grid reference. Offers of help and completed record cards would be welcomed by the Secretary of the Field Section, c/o The Manx Museum, Douglas. The entries here are grouped in sheadings working from south to north.

SHEADING OF RUSHEN

The Calf of Man

This 616 acre island is owned by the English National Trust but administered by the Manx National Trust, an insular government body, primarily as a nature reserve and bird observatory. Until about 1955 it was actively farmed and the self-sufficiency that isolation imposed on the farmers has left many traces. Gravel for road repairs and building, last required for the new lighthouse, 1966–7, was obtained from a small pit in the centre of the islet, SC 161659. A small pool on Caigher, SC 155653, marks the site where turf was cut for fuel. Of the mill only a roofless shell remains, SC 155653, but its dam is well preserved and all the watercourses can easily be traced; one of its single pair of stones is used as a garden table at the Observatory and the other lies broken, downstream of the mill. A small tower silo, with a railing improvised from the supports of a treadle sewing-machine, forms an addition, unusually early in the Isle of Man, to the farm buildings, all of which are of stone quarried on the islet. Its lighthouses and jetties have been described (p 34).

Southern Mines and Quarries

Nothing can be seen even from the sea to indicate the location of the Sloc trial, SC 211734, the most southerly of the Foxdale workings. The great quartz vein visible in both faces of Bradda Head was described by Sir W. W. Smyth as 'the noblest surface exhibition of a mineral vein to be seen in Europe'. At North Bradda, SC 180707, surviving remains include an engine house with chimney, smithy and adit, and shaft entrances on a platform about 20ft above sea level. Exploration underground has been started by the Derbyshire Caving Club and the Manx Mines Research Group, and laddering, supporting timbers, rails and many small metal items have already been photographed or recovered (see p 71). Similarly at South Bradda, SC 186697, the engine house and entrance to the Thirty Fathom Shaft are on a platform about 15ft above high-water mark. It is likely that investigation of some of the workings visible high in the cliff face may reveal traces of the earliest workings. The South Manx Mining Co worked here about 1850–63, producing 178 tons of lead and 146 tons of copper. Between 1866 and 1875 the Bradda Mining Co managed to extract 364 tons of lead and 193 tons of copper. The mine was last worked by the Bradda United Mining Co Ltd, who secured 478 tons of copper in the brief period 1881–3 but nevertheless apparently failed to make a profit.

There were many trials in the southern peninsula but the only

major mine was at Glenchass, SC 200670. Like Bradda this was
worked early, for copper, the original adit starting from the cliff
face at 'Collooway'. Two chimneys of local stone are the main
surface remains, though there is considerable spoil, with virtually
no trace of ore, in their vicinity. Just south of this mine at Spanish
Head, SC 182658, was the slate 'lintel' quarry from which were
extracted the beams used in reflooring some of the rooms at Castle
Rushen, in supporting the floor of the Abbey and Mullin y Quinney
mill kilns, and in many other buildings. There are quarries of various
dates above Glenchass, SC 198673, at Cregneash, SC 190673, and on
the Mull Hill (for spar), SC 192678. This last had a tramway to the
main road running south but was worked only for a short period.
The little powder house above the Marine Biological Station at Port
Erin, SC 188689, also belonged to a quarry in the area.

Two shafts, North and South, are visible at the Ballacorkish,
Rushen or South Foxdale mine, SC 220700. (This should not be
confused with the Glen Rushen mines of the Foxdale group.) Some
structures survive but the source of water for the much denuded
washing floors is doubtful. Dr Garrad believes that the large dams
may have powered the Scholaby farm mill in the valley to the east,
but water pumped from the mine by steam engine may also have
been used and there is also a small silted dam behind the spoil
heaps. Like Bradda the mine was worked early, but profitably, and
again about 1862–94, in which period 3,693 tons of lead, 2,869 tons
of zinc but a mere 138 tons of copper were returned by the Rushen
Mining Co. The Belle Abbey shaft, SC 224706, is on the left bank
of the little stream on which the Scholaby mill stands. There is a
very large area of deads, considering the known size of the mine.
It reached only to 72 fathoms. It appears to have produced little—its
output for 1872–8 was 23 tons of lead, 16 tons of zinc and 59½ tons
of copper—and it is possible that there were more rewarding early
workings in the same area. Local rumour suggests that a sough was
driven into the Ballacorkish mine from the main road near Colby
Level, SC 223697, but documentary evidence supporting this is not

available. As it is also stated that an 'underground passage' reached as far as Kentraugh, too much credence should not perhaps be given to this story. The limestone quarries have already been listed (p 136), the more notable being Ballahot, Billown, Chapel Hill, Poyllvaish, Port St Mary, Scarlett and Turkeyland.

Langness. On the road from Derbyhaven to Langness the first buildings of note are the now disused herring houses (on the seaward side of the road in Derbyhaven village, SC 285675). The steadily diminishing building at the right turn, SC 286673, is John Murrey's Smelt (see p 186). There is also a sizeable nineteenth-century lime-kiln on the shore just opposite the turn. On the upper shore where the road reaches Castletown Bay is a large slab of concrete marking the site of an unsuccessful attempt to find coal by 'a Mr Dickett from Africa'; his pumps failed to cope with the water and his shaft was utilised as a source of freshwater for King William's College.

Just beyond the ruined farmhouse the road rises and a stone-built structure may be seen in the field on the left, marking the engine shaft of Langness copper mine. The concrete slab on the seaward side of the road caps the laddered travelling shaft down which the men climbed to their work. The structures at the top included a smithy and changing rooms, now destroyed. The first ladders, turning about every 10 ft, went to 6 fathoms; the men then walked along a level towards Castletown for about 100ft and then went down to the 20 fathom level. There was also a lower level at 40 fathoms but this was flooded during the last period of working. The mine followed the ore, which might be 'as thick as the body of a horse', and the maximum distance reached from the shaft was about 300 fathoms. This mine worked much later than most. Dynamite used for blasting was stored in the powder house, the double-walled structure on the top of the hill. The ore ran from the conglomerate into the 'black slate', which was very hard to drill. Precautions were minimal: when a shot was fired the men merely retired to a wide spot and stuffed their fingers in their ears, and if they were in the travelling shaft they felt 'as if they would be blown up it'. After the shot was fired the walls 'shone like gold with the peacock ore'. Underground the ore and waste were moved in trucks on metal rails, the trucks having a light on the front. The ore was crushed by machines bedded on stone or concrete blocks that may still be seen. It was hoisted by means of ropes running over a wheel on sheerlegs on the engine house. On the wall was a large indicator showing where the kibbles of ore and buckets of water were in the shaft. Waste was dumped from trucks over the cliff. The crushed ore was exported for smelting, usually to Wales, but fragments may still be picked from the dry stone wall beside the road.

In addition to the two shafts there is a day-level, primarily intended for drainage, running to the shore; this was cut after the shafts had reached this level. Heaps of deads and buildings (further out on the peninsula, SC 282654) mark the site of other trials, and copper has been found outcropping on the shore. It is alleged that considerable amounts of ore remain in the mine but recent expert opinion does not support this suggestion. It seems to have been economic, however, to work this mine with a few men, despite the fact that all winding was done with a coal-fired engine whose fuel had to be carted from Castletown after being imported, and not cheap water power.

Windmills

Windmills were never common in the Isle of Man, perhaps because, as the repeated accidents in the nineteenth century to Castletown mill would seem to indicate, the winds might rise swiftly to gale force and damage the sails. The earliest yet discovered, but not located on the ground, is one for which Philip Moore was paying mill rent in the 1780s (*Liber Assed*). This was apparently at Ballakermeen, Onchan, Sheading of Middle. Castletown mill was built in 1828 (see p 186) and there was another large commercial mill in Ramsey, SC 445952, Sheading of Ayre.

Several farms in other sheadings had small mills to work barn machinery, usually thrashing machines. Traces of towers of local stone survive near Ballacorage in the Curraghs, SC 348956; Baldromma—or Windmill—farm, Maughold, SC 490913; and at Ballawhane, NX 398012. At least two quarries seem to have had wind-powered machinery. The row of cottages now converted into garages at Billown were at one time known as Windmill cottages, apparently because there was one on the hill behind where an engine house was later erected. There was also an early twentieth-century attempt at harnessing wind power for quarry uses at Billown. At South Barrule slate quarries, SC 270768, the tower is still intact and sections of the iron rim on which the cap turned may be found at the base. In looking for further quarry mills it is as well to remember that at least one Manx limekiln was similarly provided with a cogged iron rim on which a wind-scoop turned to provide an induced draft. It is probable that further windmills may come to light but they played only a marginal part in milling in Man.

Watermills

The Mills of the Silverburn. The Silverburn rises on the slopes of South Barrule and reaches the sea at Castletown. It is one of the most important and probably the first used sources of water power in Man. The earliest documentary source, the manorial roll of c 1511, lists Grenaby and the Castletown mills and thirty years later a post-dissolution document mentions the monastic mills at Ballasalla. The main period of mill building in the area was the eighteenth century, though the handsome weirs of dressed limestone would appear to be later. All the mills are built of local stone and now have roofs of imported slate. Of the corn mills Creg, Abbey and Meadow belong to Jones's *town* type, while Grenaby is typical of the *upland* group. Other known uses of water power along the Silverburn are churning butter, the grinding of bark, powder, earth colours, polishing agents and snuff, fulling, scutching, carding and cotton spinning, paper-

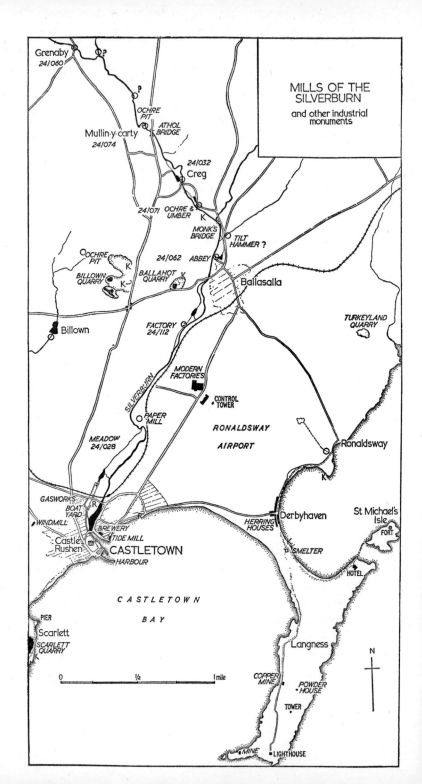

MILLS OF THE
SILVERBURN
and other industrial
monuments

Grenaby
24/060

Mullin-y-carty
24/074

OCHRE
PIT

ATHOL
BRIDGE

24/032
Creg

24/071

OCHRE &
UMBER

MONK'S
BRIDGE

TILT
HAMMER ?

OCHRE
PIT

BILLOWN
QUARRY

BALLAHOT
QUARRY

24/062   ABBEY

Ballasalla

Billown

FACTORY
24/112

TURKEYLAND
QUARRY

MODERN
FACTORIES

CONTROL
TOWER

SILVERBURN

PAPER
MILL

RONALDSWAY

AIRPORT

Ronaldsway

MEADOW
24/028

GASWORKS

BOAT
YARD

WINDMILL

BREWERY

Castle
Rushen

TIDE MILL

CASTLETOWN

HARBOUR

HERRING
HOUSES

Derbyhaven

St Michael's
Isle

FORT

SMELTER

HOTEL

CASTLETOWN

BAY

PIER

Scarlett

SCARLETT
QUARRY

Langness

N

COPPER
MINE

POWDER
HOUSE

TOWER

0   ½   1 mile

MINE   LIGHTHOUSE

making, spade production and, at the present time, driving a round-about. By a fortunate series of coincidences many documents have survived relating to most of the mills, which will be described here from north to south, ie, from the headwaters of the river to its mouth.

In Glion Cam, SC 267741, GBM 24/163, the stream was har-nessed for the first time to drive the paddles of a butter churn housed in a little lean-to at one end of the farmhouse. The wheel must have been about 4m in diameter. Only the wheel trough, drive shaft and a few metal parts survive but an account has been pub-lished.

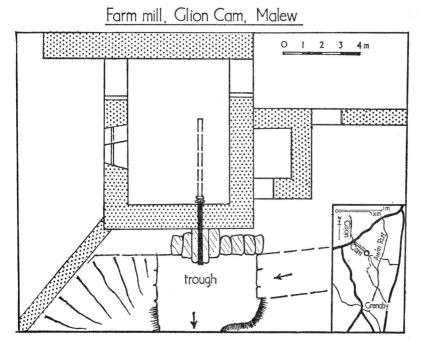

Farm mill, Glion Cam, Malew

Glion Cam churn mill, Malew (sketch plan from IA record card)

Opposite: The valley of the Silverburn: (K) limekiln; (R) ropewalk; Langness lighthouse is on southern tip of peninsula, with further mine trails on the shore to the north west

The most important mill on the upper reaches of the river was at Grenaby, SC 265724, GBM 24/060. Its miller's house has been modernised but the mill itself is a roofless shell with only the remains of one stone to show that it once ground grain for the whole of the north of the parish of Malew. There seem to have been at least two more mills in the Grenaby area but their precise sites have not been located, though one of them, Mullin y Kelly, is well documented.

On the right bank of the Silverburn just upstream of the Atholl bridge stands the remains of Mullin y Carty, SC 272716, GBM 24/074 (see section on Fulling, p 165). Its roofless walls have recently been lowered for safety since the whole glen is used by the Boy Scouts. The original course of the leat is obscure. The wheel was on the end wall furthest from the stream and a few fragments survive to show that the last used wheel was very similar to that at the Factory.

The monks of Rushen Abbey, a Cistercian foundation and a dependency of Furness Abbey, had two mills on the Silverburn, which is not surprising, as monks were responsible for much improvement to British milling. The Creg Mill, SC 276710, GBM 24/032, has a sizeable dam, now used as a boating lake, and elaborate watercourses: its wheel has been persuaded to turn again as a 'tourist attraction' and a second wheel has been brought from the Foxdale mines to power what is believed to be a unique roundabout. Patterns used to produce the larger gear wheels of many of the Manx mills, salvaged by the Field Section of the Isle of Man Natural History and Antiquarian Society from a local foundry, are preserved here. The next mill downstream is the Ochre and Umber mill, SC 278707, GBM 24/071 (see p 137), which is now a private house, though its dam and millpond are well preserved by the Manx National Trust. This area is freely open to visitors, as is the attractive glen lying between Mullin y Carty and the Creg mill.

The Abbey mill, SC 279703 GBM 24/062, the next mill downstream, is placed at right-angles to the river just opposite Rushen Abbey, to which it belonged. A brick-built kiln whose floor is supported on a 'fan vault' of immense slate beams has been added.

Grenaby, Malew

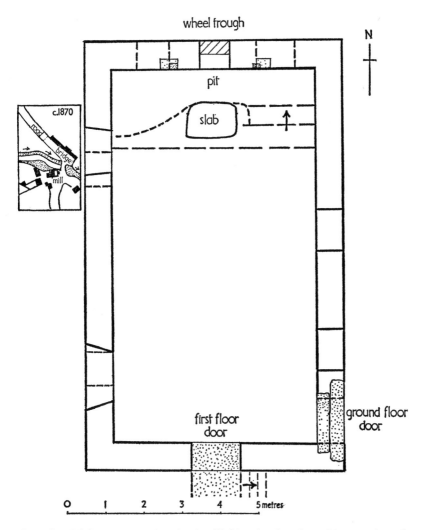

Grenaby, Malew, a typical upland mill (sketch plan from IA record card)

Unusually for the Isle of Man the wheel is completely enclosed and made largely of metal. The other fittings have gone and the building is used as a store. In many ways its structure and fittings are reminiscent of Mullin y Quinney, SC 302712 GBM 24/065. The dam of dressed limestone was destroyed by floods, so draining the millpond behind the mill.

There may have been one or more farm mills on the tributary that drains the Fildraw area and during the nineteenth century advertisements appeared for the bark mill at Ballasalla; this may have been housed in the side of the Abbey mill away from the stream or at the Creg mill. The main use for the ground bark would have been in the tan pits of the net factories, though there were a few tanneries. According to a number of documents, one John Stole, 'Iron smith of Ballasalley', erected 'a Tilting Mill or Plating Forge' about 1760–3. It is likely that this mill was on the smaller tributary just upstream from the Abbey mill, though no trace of a wheel survives in the appropriately situated building, SC 281705. The chief product would be spades.

Below Ballasalla is the Factory, SC 275696 GBM 24/112, whose history will be found under Cotton (p 169). The buildings surround a courtyard that, since it serves to shelter cattle, is usually ankle deep in mud. The cracked walls of the downstream house splay outwards, so that there is a difference of more than a metre between ground- and first-floor measurements. Decay has accelerated since 1965. The paper mill (see p 159) stood on the left bank of the Silverburn about half-way between this mill and the next, Meadow mill.

The imposing limestone buildings of Meadow mill, SC 266681 GBM 24/028, stand some way from the river and are served by a leat and embanked millpond. The wheel is no longer working, the still-operational machinery, mainly used for feed, being powered by electricity. The threshing mill, and a large storehouse on the downstream side of the courtyard, are now partly derelict. It is probable that here was situated the snuff mill mentioned in a legal opinion concerning the right of millowners to change the use of their mills.

The river between the Factory and Meadow mill has been extensively canalised; as there were many early disputes about its correct course, erosion and the building and repairs to dams, it is possible that the original Castletown mills were both further upstream and nearer the river, though this site has a well-documented history. Only the wheel-pit and the position of the sack-hoist remain of the early tide mill in Castle Rushen—in the 'dungeon' in which Bishop Wilson was imprisoned—but they serve to indicate how well the Lord of Mann's stronghold was prepared for a siege.

Smaller Mills. Several of the large and prosperous farms of Rushen sheading had their own mills for threshing, preparing feed and other barn work. Since water power was free and required little attention, it was used where practicable even if this meant the construction of large dams and elaborate watercourses. Where water was not available horse power was used. The handsome limestone buildings of Balladoole, SC 249687, on the seaward side of the main Castletown–Port St Mary road, include a circular horse-walk as well as an open-fronted shed whose roof is supported on cast-iron columns salvaged from the verandah of Balladoole mansion house. Ballavarvane, SC 302746, also had a horse-powered threshing mill, which has been destroyed.

Among the better-preserved farm mill buildings is that at Scholaby, SC 224707 GBM 24/110, which has been gutted and is now used as a machinery store. It is noteworthy for its very large double dam, which may possibly have supplied water to the washing floor of one of the adjacent mines, and the skilful way in which the building has been fitted to the difference in ground levels.

Small mills now gutted or totally destroyed existed at Surby, SC 205702 GBM 24/064; Ballachurry, SC 208697 GBM 24/139; north of Ballabeg, SC 243709 GBM 24/113; Ballamaddrell, SC 252705 GBM 24/138; Ronaldsway, SC 290683 GBM 24/136; Billown, SC 261695 GBM 24/137; Ballaglonney, SC 304721 GBM 24/141; and Ballastrang, SC 302713 GBM 24/142. In addition to the

Scholaby, Rushen

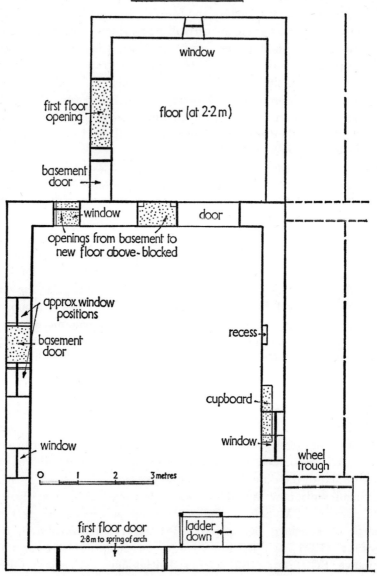

first floor opening

floor (at 2·2 m)

window

basement door

window

door

openings from basement to new floor above - blocked

approx. window positions

basement door

recess

cupboard

window

wheel trough

window

0   1   2   3 metres

first floor door
2·8 m to spring of arch

ladder down

Scholaby, Rushen, a typical farm mill (sketch plan from IA record card) main mill at Kentraugh (see p 245) there was a small mill at the house, SC225692 GBM 24/068, and a saw mill on the shore, SC 222689 GBM 24/090. The line of the leat to the last is conspicuous and the building itself is well preserved. Remains of an ice house—another has been found at Bishop's Court—are in the same area.

Colby mill, SC 231705 GBM 24/061, stands on the left bank of the Colby river a little way up the 'Glen road' from the village. The small slated building of whitewashed local stone is typical of the upland group of Manx mills. There was a mill here in 1511 but there seems never to have been a substantial dam. It was last worked by Thomas Cubbon, who died in 1927 after having held it for fifty-four years.

The Colby river also powered the group of mills, already mentioned, at Kentraugh. The oldest of these, also listed in the earliest manorial roll, SC 225691 GBM 24/090, was then held by Robert McWhaltragh, whose descendants, the Qualtrough family, continued to work it until the nineteenth century. The little stone building is in a fairly good state of repair, since the present owner is interested in its preservation.

The Town of Castletown

The harbour has already been described (p 29). Among the buildings of interest are the remains of the gasworks (p 47); the station, which is unusual for the Isle of Man railway in being built of local limestone and not red brick; and the windmill. The latter, known as the Witches' Mill from the museum it now houses, was built in 1828. '. . . It will be a most beneficial addition to the conveniences of that neighbourhood: many watermills, from occasional drought, being incapable of supplying the inhabitants with grinding . . .' The opening was celebrated by 'the spirited proprietors' giving 'an excellent dinner . . . to the mechanics etc', but was marred by the sail arms being blown off. A similar incident occurred in 1829 and the mill never seems to have worked profitably; it closed before the end of the century and only the shell of the tower survives.

M

Mines in the Baldwin Valley

A ring wall enclosing a fine rubbish deposit and some spoil are all that mark the site of the Injebreck trial, SC 359850, which reached to some 22 fathoms about 1874 without producing any appreciable traces of ore. The Isle of Man (Foxdale) Mining Co made trials further down the Baldwin valley, on the east bank of the Glass, which were also unproductive and although attempts were made during 1850–5 to sink a shaft it was not until some ten years later that the Baldwin Mining Co Ltd really started work in this area. Two flooded adits, one to the south of the village and the other in the south bank of Awin ny Darragh about a quarter of a mile away, and two shafts with spoil heaps indicate its approximate position, SC 354812. Slight masonry traces on the left bank of the stream probably indicate the position of the 24ft waterwheel that dewatered the workings. This wheel was fed from the race of Baldwin mill and the lade, probably made entirely of wood, crossed both the watermeadows and the stream. There are traces of copper, lead and zinc in the spoil but the total output was small.

The Ohio or East Baldwin mine was similarly unproductive. Spoil heaps and remains of building mark its site on the left bank of the Baldwin river, SC 360823. Initially it was worked by a trial company, the Ohio Lead Mining Co, 1866–7. This was succeeded, 1868–74, by the Ohio Crown Lead and Silver Mining Co Ltd—capital £12,000—which in turn was superseded, 1875–9, by Manx Silver Lead Minerals Ltd. A 30ft wheel, the *Elizabeth Loch*, was completed in 1868; it was hauled on a sledge by the Douglas Volunteers over the hill from Onchan, where it had been built by Cain, the joiner, at a cost of £90. Despite this expenditure of time, money and effort the total output seems to have been 24½ tons of lead and 39 tons of zinc.

Mills

On the Santon River. The Santon river had fewer mills than the Silverburn and they were less important. The manorial roll, c 1511, records small mills only. Of the mills whose sites are definitely known, that at Ballacorris, SC 311741 GBM 24/096, was a tuck mill; unfortunately it was gutted about 1950 and converted into a farm store, but a photograph taken about 1951 (see plate, p 125) shows a wheel roughly 4m in diameter. The dam, now filled in, lies partly in a quarry that was presumably the source of building stone for the adjacent buildings, which include an early-looking single-storey cottage, now used for agricultural purposes. From inspection it appears likely that the stone used to build the mill was in part robbed from some earlier structure.

Mullenaragher, SC 308733 GBM 24/057, is of interest because though basically a farm mill, it dates from at least as early as 1541. Unfortunately its solid little L-shaped stone building, on the right bank of the stream, is now empty of all machinery, though Thomas Kinnish was listed as miller here as late as 1857. The only sizeable mill building on the Santon river is Mullin y Quinney, SC 302712 GBM 24/065, which was the parish mill; the existing building and internal wheel probably date from 1868–9, but surprisingly, it seems to have only worked intermittently from this date and grinding ceased completely in 1922. Its watercourses now supply a fish hatchery. The fittings of the three stones were about to be removed in September 1970.

Other Mills in Santon Parish and on the Crogga River. It has proved impossible to locate the fulling mill mentioned in the early manorial rolls but it is likely that it was on the stream reaching the sea at Port Grenaugh, though it may have been on the Santon river where there are scanty remains of a flax-breaking mill downstream from Mullin y Quinney. In Glen Grenaugh there is the shell of a

Ballacorris, Santon

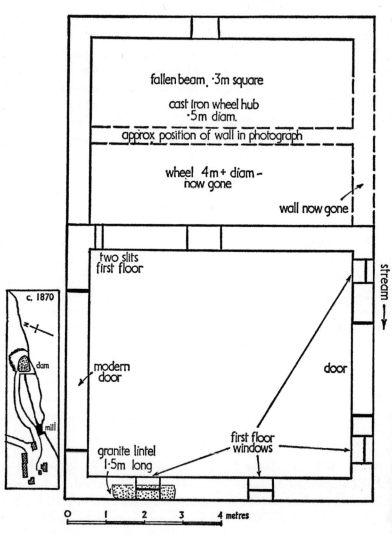

fallen beam, ·3m square

cast iron wheel hub
·5m diam.

approx position of wall in photograph

wheel 4m + diam -
now gone

wall now gone

stream →

two slits
first floor

c. 1870

z

dam

mill

modern
door

door

granite lintel
1·5m long

first floor
windows

0   1   2   3   4 metres

Ballacorris tuck mill, Santon (sketch plan from IA record card) corn mill, SC 315710 GBM 24/070, some 7m by 12m, which is now used for agricultural purposes. It had a fall of some 5m and is likely to have been the successor to the water rights of John Wode's tuck mill. Some way upstream is a two-storey mill, SC 315717 GBM 24/102, about 11½m by 7m, which was probably used for threshing but may also have served for heckling. Ballavale, SC 316722 GBM 24/143, appears to have had a farm mill and buildings survive of two on the Crogga river—Mount Murray, SC 330742, and Crogga, SC 336728 GBM 24/097—and another, less certainly, at Arragon, SC 302704. According to *Mona's Herald* of 3 January 1865 there was a water-powered threshing mill at Meary Vooar and a mill is indicated on older maps (SC 324705 GBM 24/140), but the present owners maintained there was now no trace. It is, however, possible that the newspaper report relates to the substantial building, SC 332708 GBM 24/103, gutted by fire fairly recently. The stone-built structure is very similar to GBM 24/102, about 8½m by 5½m, and is probably of a similar nineteenth-century date.

The Mills of the Dhoo and the Glass and their Tributaries including those in Glenfaba Sheading. The headwaters of the tributaries of the Dhoo were harnessed to drive farm mills. A gutted shell survives at Cooilslieu, SC 309822 GBM 24/127. Other mills existed at Rock, SC 319804 GBM 24/128, and Bawshen, SC 330812, on the north, and at Ballaquinnea, SC 334771 GBM 24/135, Coolingel, SC 315795 GBM 24/130, and Ellerslie, SC 329783 GBM 24/059 (shell and wheel surviving), to the south. There are more substantial remains of the corn mill building at Greeba, SC 301814 GBM 24/054, which is presumably on the site of the mill 'in the tenure of Cristian Ine Caly and her [son]' at the time of the first manorial roll. A flax mill was recorded on the Ballaquinnea Mooar farm in 1828 but further research is needed to determine its location. The substantial buildings of the combined woollen and corn mills at Union Mills, SC 354778 GBM 24/073, have been much altered and are now used as a factory (see p 167).

Ballaughton, SC 367760 GBM 24/036, a town mill rebuilt in 1842, took over the water rights of Mullin Aspick, the Bishop's mill. In 1804 it was bought by the Duke of Atholl from W. Leece for less than £500 but was not then run at a profit. It was equipped with a patent turbine, however, by 1843 and seems to have been very successful in the late nineteenth century by reason of its efficient machinery. There were a number of smaller mills on the tributaries that enter below Ballaughton, including another manorial mill, Middle, which is likely to have originally been a horizontal mill, since its rent was only 5s. It probably stood on the site of the corn mill, SC 361748 GBM 24/058, where in 1871 William Collister, the miller, employed four men and a boy, though it may have been nearer Ballaughton. The building was of the upland type and has since been destroyed. There was a second mill, SC 361747 GBM 24/080, in the area. These two mills were variously spade mills, breweries, thrashing mills and dye works. Some of the buildings survive on the south side of the road.

The now-destroyed Pulrose mill, SC 367756 GBM 24/035, was just downstream of Ballaughton. In 1840 some of its fittings were sold including '. . . A pair of MILLSTONES for grinding Wheat, made from French Burrs, a Machine for Dressing Flour, A Sack Tackle and Chain, Dressing Sieves, Coolers, Tumbling Shaft and other Machinery . . .' The undershot wheel then in use was 15ft in diameter and worked on a fall of 7ft. Later it was re-equipped with a pair of wheels (see plate, p 125) but nevertheless became a steam laundry and was finally demolished. The Nunnery mill, SC 375753 GBM 24/069, stands on a site occupied by a mill at least as early as 1643, when 'a water corn miln called the Nunnery Miln' was compounded for by Robert Calcott. The present buildings of local stone with roofs of imported slate probably date from just after a fire in 1796. By 1857 the mill was operated by Henry Whiteside & Co and by the end of the nineteenth century it had become William & Thomas Quine's roller mills. The buildings are now used as a store but much of the machinery, including the internal wheel, survives.

The history of several of the Baldwin valley mills appears under Paper (see p 161). There was also a saw mill, SC 354813 GBM 24/089, now destroyed—a photograph in the Manx Museum shows a rectangular building of local stone with the wheel on the gable end— which was already roofless at the end of the nineteenth century. Also in the West Baldwin valley was a manorial roll corn mill, SC 360800 GBM 24/087, and a now-vanished paper mill. The surviving ex-paper mill is now a fertiliser works, Litt's, SC 365796 GBM 24/088, standing just downstream of the junction of the two Baldwin streams; it probably took over the water rights of Ballaoates Flax mill, also called Woodside mill. The site of the third paper mill, SC 372778, is now occupied by Clucas's laundry. The large mill dam belonged to the period of use as a sailcloth works, GBM 24/085, whose workers' houses, Cronkbourne village, survive. There was a manorial roll corn mill somewhere in this area as well and the precise history of the mills on this stretch is a little confused. The only other sur-viving mill above the junction of the Dhoo and the Glass is the little farm mill at Port e Chee, SC 372772 GBM 24/100, (see plate, p 144), though the owner of the adjacent nursery has attempted to harness the stream to a modern wheel just upstream.

Mills in Onchan. There were many farm mills and several important corn mills in Onchan parish. Among those now vanished was the Burnt mill, SC 393773, at the north end of Douglas Bay, whose '. . . Dam & remaining walls . . .' were sold in 1812; it is likely that this occupied the site of a horizontal mill for which Patrick Clerke paid mill rent in the earliest manorial roll. The Groudle mill, SC 420784 GBM 24/066, was pulled down when the Douglas water-works was built but a fine datestone, 'J.B. 1854', on the gable indicates the probable date of the present building. Patrick McCray paid mill rent of 4s 2d on it in the manorial roll, suggesting that it was also a horizontal mill at this date; but the rent was still the same in 1865 when 'Samuel S. Callow & James Kewley's Trustees' held it. The stream, which reaches the sea at Groudle, also powered Wellington

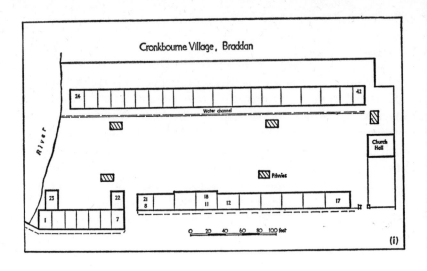

Cronkbourne Village, Braddan

Water channel

River

Privies

Church Hall

0 20 40 60 80 100 feet

(i)

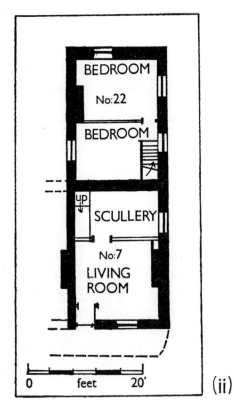

BEDROOM

No: 22

BEDROOM

SCULLERY

UP

No: 7

LIVING ROOM

0   feet   20'

(ii)

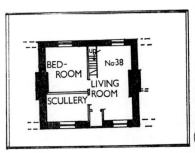

BED-ROOM

No: 38

LIVING ROOM

SCULLERY

UP

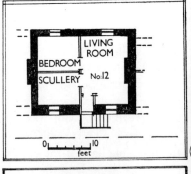

LIVING ROOM

BEDROOM

SCULLERY

No: 12

0   10
feet

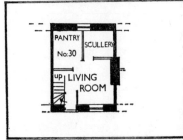

PANTRY

SCULLERY

No: 30

UP LIVING ROOM

mill, SC 399789 GBM 24/154, a sizeable corn mill with a long history. There was a threshing mill, SC 400779 GBM 24/159, and also, apparently a windmill owned by Philip Moore. This was, according to *Liber Assed*, erected in the 1780s but has not yet been located. The Bowring Mills, SC 396796 GBM 24/075, processed wool; their buildings are now ruinous.

Douglas harbour is described earlier (p 30), also the breweries (p 147), the theatres, cinemas and other places of entertainment (p 114). The railway stations are described under Transport (p 42).

Cronkbourne Village Industrial Housing

This is almost the only example in the Isle of Man, apart from the mining areas, of housing erected by a firm for its workers. The dwellings have recently been bought by the Braddan Parish Commissioners and this note has been prepared with their permission and that of S. F. O'Hanlon, FRICS, their architect, and with the help

Cronkbourne village: (i) ground plan; (ii), (iii), (iv), (v) types of houses found in the village

Front terrace
(ii) 1–7, and 22, 23 at rear: two-up, two-down, c 16 × 28ft deep internally
(iii) 18–21, below and behind 8–11, two-up, three-down, c 21 × 18ft deep
(iv) 8–17, single storey, three rooms, c 26 × 15ft deep internally

Rear terrace	*Internal measurements*
(v) 24 & 25, 26 & 27, 28 & 30, two-up, two-down, stairs at front, living room not full depth	Living room: c 8ft × 10ft 10in Scullery: 7ft 6in × 9ft Pantry: 7ft 6in × 6ft 2in
(ii) 28, 31, 36, 41 and 42, two-up, two-down	Living room: 14ft 2in × 10ft 5in Scullery: 6ft 8in
(iii) 32–5, 37–40, two-up, three-down	Living room: 10ft 7in × 17ft 5in Scullery: 10ft × 6ft 5in Bedroom/sitting room: 10ft × 10ft 7in

of the plans made before modernisation. The forty-two houses were arranged in two parallel rows at right-angles to the river (see Plan i).

The rear terrace had a runnel, down which freshwater flowed, along its front and failing to keep this clear was one of the offences for which tenants were fined (see Appendix Three). The dwellings were fitted to variations in the ground level. The roofs are hung with imported slates, as they probably always were, and the walls are now rendered and colour-washed deep pink. It is obvious from an early photograph (see plate, p 126) that the rough-coursed walling of local slate was originally exposed. Despite varied dimensions and arrangements there were only two basic ground-floor plans, consisting of two (living room and rear scullery) or three rooms. Except for numbers 8–17 they are two-storey. The single-storey houses, whose total internal measurements are 18ft × 21ft or 15ft × 26ft, were divided longitudinally into a living room the full depth of the building and a scullery with bedroom behind. The larger three-roomed houses have a similar plan, with access to the centrally placed stairs from the living room (see Plan iii). In the two up, two down front terrace the stairs along the party wall are reached from the scullery (see Plan ii), while in the smaller rear terrace houses, where the third room was a mere pantry sharing a window with the scullery, they start from beside the front door (see Plan v). With the exceptions mentioned the window pattern is of one per room in the outside walls. The main alterations have been the addition of kitchens and bathrooms and the demolition of 8 (20) and 9 (21) to improve access. It is pleasant to be able to record preservation instead of demolition.

SHEADING OF GLENFABA

Glen Maye Mines

The earliest mining in Glen Maye probably dates from the seventeenth century and the Company of Mine Adventurers of England also made trials about 1740–1. In 1823 the Duke of Atholl granted

Michael Knott of Chester a lease of all the mines in the Isle of Man except those in the parish of Lonan, but Knott soon sold his lease to a company in which he had an interest, the Isle of Man Mining Co. This company concentrated its efforts at Foxdale but made trials in many places. By 1826 these had revealed in Glen Maye two north/south 'main veins' and three north-west/south-east 'cross veins', with feeders. 'The whole of these veins, laders and feeders bear lead ore to the surface, and are in every way promising to be productive in that metal.' Throughout 1832 a level was driven into the hill on the south side of the glen but no discovery of importance was made. It was eleven years before work restarted on 'the western side of the hill' but this proved equally unrewarding. Although a local farmer was promised £20 a ton for the first 5 tons of ore he could produce on the opposite side of the valley and a shaft was sunk (probably that marked on Gordon farm on the 25in plan), the Glen Maye workings still failed to live up to their promise.

Nevertheless, when the area was again available for lease there was some competition for it and a number of people had interests in the area, including the Isle of Man Peel Castle Mining Company, which was replaced by the Peel Castle and Glenmay Mining Company (Limited). One of the first actions of the latter was to erect a water-wheel about 20ft in diameter by 4ft breast 'with Pumping Apparatus, and power sufficient to drive Crushing Mills, &c.' on the left bank of the stream just before it passes under the road to the shore, SC 228799; portions of its stone case survive. A dam head 20ft high and 20yd long, formed by two walls 2ft apart with an infilling of earth and sods from the stream bank, was also erected, but later this was replaced by another, upstream. Although the local newspaper thought that this construction enhanced the beauty of the glen, such a view was apparently not shared by all, and on the night of Sunday 1 September 1861 the wheel was seriously damaged by 'the malicious insertion of a wedge within the cogs'. Further troubles of about the same date included the destruction of the lower dam by flood, and litigation.

Work continued in a desultory fashion and by the beginning of 1864 the mine had one shaft to 8 fathoms, an engine shaft to 15 fathoms and about 200 fathoms of levels, but the company's capital was nearly exhausted. A new lease of life was given by an issue of a further 500 £5 shares. (Of the company's nominal capital of £10,000 in £10 shares only half had previously been issued.) Public confidence was also augmented by Captain Edward Bawden (senior), who had accepted the post of manager on his retirement from the Isle of Man Mining Co (his career is dealt with more fully on p 92). Even his reputation served to sell only about twenty of the new shares but when work was started on this meagre capital lead was found and sales prospered. Although Captain Bawden recommended sinking a shaft to 50 fathoms—Manx miners seem generally to have believed that the better ore was at depth—this was not done and money again became short. A further strike brought more hope and yet another new company was formed in 1866, the North Foxdale Mining Company (Limited). Captain Rowe of the Laxey Mining Company was brought in to offer advice and Captain Bawden was finally allowed to sink his deep shaft.

This required improved pumping arrangements and the directors '. . . engaged Mr Thomas Cain, of Douglas, to erect a new wheel 34 feet by 4, and they expect to have it finished within four months of this date'. As a compliment to both the Manx and Irish shareholders this new wheel was called *Mona-Erin*; and to celebrate its starting all concerned were treated to a dinner in a barn that still stands on the north of the shore road.

William Watterson, owner of an adjoining farm, Ballakirkey, had returned from Australia to find his property extensively damaged by mining; not unnaturally he applied for compensation. While his action was being heard, the property of the company was arrested. This gives an opportunity to discover what was required to work a fairly small mine—compare with the liquidation sale (p 206) and Rhennie Laxey (p 211). The property was listed as follows:

One four wheel slide
Two large shear legs and chains and two gins connected with the shaft
One large wooden Airbox called a Duck
One wooden rail about twenty-six feet long
One large ladder connected with the shaft
Four pieces of timber
One piece of wooden Air pipe
One large water wheel and apparatus connecting wheel to shaft
One large chain box, connecting chain to wheel
One wooden hand barrow, One plank. Two Iron Bars. One piece of wooden air pipe
Smithy & Smiths Apparatus. One draw Bucket
Five Iron pipes, twenty pieces of old Timber. One wooden shed attached to Water Wheel. One wheel barrow
One coal Tar Cask. A Bucket.
One mine house and contents
One square log of Timber about 5 feet long. One wooden Step Ladder
One lot of Mortar.
One large wooden water sluice and channel which conveys the water to wheel
One wooden House used as offices.
Four pieces of wooden Scantling, each piece about 20 feet long
One Trespass Sign Board
One Wooden House used as a stable, with contents

The jury's verdict was in favour of Watterson, the damages due being assessed at £60.

The remains of the case of the *Mona-Erin* are conspicuous just downstream of the gate from the wooded part of the glen on to the shore road, SC 231798, and the line of its lades can be traced from the lip of the waterfall almost to the wheel.

Captain Bawden was succeeded by one of his sons, another Edward, but their persistence was not rewarded and the company was liquidated. The *Manx Sun* of August 1870 contains the following:

SALE OF NORTH FOXDALE MINE,
Lease and Plant &c.

Mr. Raby respectfully announces that he is instructed by Silas Evans, Esq., the Liquidator, to SELL by AUCTION, on THURSDAY, Sept. 8th 1870, all and singular the North Foxdale Mine and PLANT, situate at Glenmay, Isle of Man.

The lease is dated 13th March, 1860 from the Woods and Forests Commissioners, comprising an extensive piece of Mining Ground in the parish of Patrick, adjoining Glenmay Village, at a royalty of 1–12th for ores obtained without steam power and 1–14th for same with steam power, with a dead rent of £1 per annum.

The goodwill of the lease and everything appertaining thereto, with all plant &c. &c. will be offered in 1 lot so as to enable any speculators to continue the prosecution of the works; if not so sold the Plant will at once be sold separately in lots, which comprise—

A 20ft. Water Wheel, Winding Gear complete
About 50fms. of 6 and 7"—Pumps, with clack doors and boxes &c.,
2 6" Plunger Poles,
About 50 fms of 6¼" Main Rods, with Strapping Plates &c.,
2 Bobs, with Brasses, Pedestals, &c.,
40 fms. of 1¾" round Iron Rods, with Shieves &c.,
About 100 fms. of Tram Iron 2½" × ½",
Iron Skip and 2 tram wagons,
100 fms. galvanised Wire Rope, 2" circ.,
About 14 fms. of a small Plunger-in Pole,
1 Smith's Bellow, Vice & Smith's Tools,
Good Die, for screwing different size bolts,
Office Furniture, with different other articles.

Auction to take place on the Ground, at 12 o'clock, Noon.

Auctioneer's Rooms & Offices—Drumgold St. Douglas;
Residence—21 Prospect-hill, do.

The lease was not disposed of and mining ceased.

Mills

Glen Maye Mills. The waters of the Glen Maye river also powered at least two corn mills, GBM 24/050, 051. The shell of one survives just below the main road and one of its stones provides an ornamental feature in a garden on the opposite side. There were extensive slate quarries on the left (south) bank in the area more generally known as Glen Mooar. Traces of terracing left by the quarrymen are conspicuous and part of the quarry has been converted into a small reservoir, SC 248782; there is a water-board control point higher up the stream, which is now flowing through Glen Rushen. The mines in this area are described with those of Foxdale, which were worked by the same company. Glen Maye itself, with its walks and planted trees, large hotel and café, and secluded atmosphere is typical of the pleasure grounds developed in the nineteenth century. It is now a Manx National Glen, preserved for the future by the insular government.

Small West Coast Mills. Most of the streams running to the west coast have very steep courses and many end in an abrupt plunge over the cliffs. So precipitous is the little stream at Eary Cushlin, SC 224758, that it was found worthwhile to harness it to provide power for barn work. The mill building of local stone with a slated roof is tolerably well preserved but only fragments remain of the wheel and nothing to indicate precisely what operations were carried out. The farm and mill are now the property of the Manx National Trust and the latter has been reroofed.

There are appropriately situated buildings on several of the small streams north of Peel, Lynague, SC 281868, for example, but little real evidence that they were indeed mills.

The Mills of the Neb. As with the Dhoo and the Glass the upper reaches and smaller tributaries were harnessed for farm mills, though the farms on the left (south) bank of Glen Helen are noteworthy for their horse-powered threshing mills. The Foxdale corn mill, SC 276795 GBM 24/049, has well-preserved buildings and must be of fairly early date. The Forestry Board has greatly altered Mullin y Clie, SC 278813 GBM 24/048, but traces of both the building and the dam survive; from the low rent, 7s 4d, payable at the time of the first manorial roll, this site may then have been occupied by a horizontal mill of Norse type. The farm mill at Kennaa, SC 287808 GBM 24/122, has also been destroyed but its dam survives.

There were several textile mills downstream of St John's, including Ballabrooie, SC 279824 GBM 24/083, but their history has not yet been unravelled. The group round the still-operating Tynwald mills is of greater interest and, not unnaturally, better preserved. Upstream, in Glen Helen is a corn mill, SC 288837 GBM 24/053, where a turbine was once used to generate electricity; its millstones now ornament the front of the building, now only a shell. Below the Tynwald mills the site of the Abbey brickworks, SC 265822, has very slight remains, though it is of considerable historical interest. The last waterwheel here, GBM 24/072, was used to power a pug mill and was finally moved to the Kella mill, Sulby, GBM 24/026. It apparently stood on the site of the mill for which the Monastery of Rushen paid mill rent in 1511, presumably a corn mill at this date.

The large farm of Ballamooar, Patrick, SC 250821, had a threshing mill, GBM 24/125. Downstream, the handsome stone buildings of Glenfaba mill, SC 244831 GBM 24/038, built about 1850, are now partly occupied by a store. When first built it had four pairs of stones, a kiln and a threshing mill powered by the same wheel. The stones were two French Burrs, one for oats and one for barley-meal; the wheel was 19½ft in diameter and 'the supply of water unfailing, as the whole of the Peel river may be made available if required'. A year later, in 1851, Cooper's or Peel mill was also described as having 'three pairs of stones, Shell Barley Stone, Wheat Dressing Machine &c. and has always a plentiful supply of water as the whole Peel River can be turned in if necessary . . .' This mill, SC 240837 GBM 24/034, paid only 11s 8d rent in the manorial roll and was shared between Nicholas Alcar, Reginald Cross, Thomas McKye and Huan Worthyngton. Their rather non-Manx surnames suggest the importance of Peel as a port while the low rent may indicate that the mill was small. This mill was that bought by the Duke of Atholl in 1795 and subsequently let at £2, with an additional 12s 3d for the house. Its sale price was twenty-five years' tithes. It is likely that the existing building, now a shell of local stone, is mid-nineteenth century in date. Although the structurally sound mill is now used for other purposes, its dam—sometimes used for testing boats— and watercourses are quite well preserved.

The City of Peel

The harbour works have already been described (p 32). There are a number of interesting buildings surviving in the 'sunset city'. It is still a herring port and several processers are still working, notably Moore's kipper factory just upstream of the station. The latter, an undistinguished building, is now a soft furnishers. In the same area are the remains of the gasworks, the Glenfaba Brick Company, a handsome corn mill building (see p 246) complete with dam and, furthest upstream, the power station.

Graves's shipyard occupied the site of the Viking garage and adjacent coalyards. The speed and efficiency of the yards may be judged by the following announcements from the *Manx Sun* of 15 and 22 November 1848:

> Sat 11th launched from the Quay yards of Mr Henry Greaves, timber merchant, 'King Olafe' . . .
> A splendid schooner called the Rod-dan Ushteg (Water Rat) was launched from the yard of Mr Graves of Peel.

Graves's rivals included Watson's, upstream of the harbour bridge, and Corris's, who somehow contrived to launch their vessels down the street. Little trace now remains of any of these yards but one net factory still dominates Factory Lane and investigation of the town centre will still reveal many other traces of its seafaring past.

SHEADING OF GARFF

Mines

Glen Roy. Like North Laxey, this mine was an offshoot of the Great Laxey mine. There are considerable surface remains, including the cases of two waterwheels; that nearest the stream, SC 409836 GBM 24/152b, is 8½m long and its 1m thick walls are preserved to a height of over 4m. Its water supply was probably carried in wooden

N

troughing from the same source as that used by the larger wheel, GBM 24/152a. The smaller wheelcase is embedded in the tailings from the shaft, which is about 30m upstream. The larger case is about 18½m long and only 3½m wide and its water supply was carried in troughs on the square-sectioned stone pillars that survive. An adjoining building probably housed a crushing plant. In addition to crushing, this wheel may have pumped water from a shaft on the opposite bank, the pump rods running in the channel between the building and the wheelcase.

The small quarry just behind the upper wheel probably supplied building stone for all the surviving structures, including the small house upstream of the upper wheel. There are substantial traces of the long leat that carried the water from well up the valley. The mine worked approximately from 1864 to 1882. The main shaft reached some 122 fathoms with levels at 10, 25, 40, 55, 65 and 108 fathoms. There may also have been 100 and 122 fathom levels. But only the 25 fathom level was really productive and most of the total yield of 9 tons 9cwt of lead ore and 136 tons 9cwt of zinc must have been derived from it. It is not known whether any later attempts were made to reopen the workings but the age of the trees growing among the ruins suggest that there were none.

Snaefell Mine. Originally this mine, at the head of the Laxey valley, was run by the same company as Great Laxey. It worked from 1856 into the early twentieth century under the Snaefell and Great Snaefell companies. Most of the surface remains were left by Metalliferous Holdings Ltd, which installed a ball crushing-mill and modern flotation tanks when it was reworking the deads in the 1950s. The main adit, leading to a shaft to 171 fathoms, is on the right bank of the stream just above the remains of the wheelcase. This wheel (see plate, p 143) was fed by the wide leat that can easily be traced round the contour of the hill to the head of the branch stream, SC 404872. The roofless stone powder-house stands a little above the wheel. On the other bank are a number of stone-built subsidiary buildings, including a smithy and a substantial house. The mining company was also responsible for building the road to Agneash, which required several bridges, and its office was some distance away down this road. The 1870–1900 output was 4,567 tons of lead —averaging 14–16oz of silver per ton—and 8,926 tons of zinc. There are a number of minor workings elsewhere in the valley.

The Dhoon or Rhennie Laxey Mine and the Dhoon Valley. The most noteworthy surviving feature at this mine is the case of the 50ft waterwheel, which is built of local stone and has an attractive arch upstream, apparently to provide access for servicing the wheel (see plate, p 144). Water for the wheel was carried by a leat from just below the modern road bridge; most of its length can still be traced but the wooden troughs which bridged the gap from the hillside to the top of the supporting tower have, like the wheel, long since gone. The wheel apparently pumped water and lifted spoil from the shaft immediately beside it; the projection nearest the stream on the upstream side probably served to support the counterweight. The mine worked from about 1859 to 1869 in search of lead and zinc with an almost total lack of success. Its final sale notice in the *Manx Sun* of 20 August 1870 gives an interesting picture of the equipment needed for even a small mine (compare it with Glen Maye, p 205):

> Liquidation of the Rhennie Laxey Mining Co. Water-wheel 50 feet diameter, 2ft 8in breast, Spur Wheel Crab Whinch and 14 fathoms of Chain, drawing lift 30 fathoms, 8 inch 50 fathoms of chain in shaft Ladders Girders Stays Timber-work Timber Tools Dial Tramway Iron etc. etc.

There were a number of other trials in the area, including a small adit, still open, just west of the road before it crosses the MER, SC 455869. The large Dhoon quarry, SC 458871,was one of the reasons for the extension of the Manx Electric Railway in this direction and was provided with its own goods station. It had a tram track into the main quarry area—rails now removed—and substantial traces remain, though even the most recent buildings are now ruinous.

The Cornaa Valley. In the upper part of the valley, between the mountain road and the coast road, there are a number of mining areas. The East Snaefell, North Laxey or Great North Laxey mine, SC 427890, has the best preserved surface structures. On the left bank of the stream are the mine office, a wheelcase (wheel, GBM 24/147) with particularly fine stone piers to support the lade, and various other associated structures, including the supports for the pump-rods. An adjoining building probably housed crushing machinery powered from the same wheel as the pumps, and must belong to a late period in the history of the mine as it does not appear on the 25in plan. The powder house is higher up the valley on the same side. On the right bank are paved and ducted washing floors and the main adit entrance. There were two shafts, North and South, which reached 174 and 110 fathoms, respectively. The large spoil heaps contain abundant traces of lead, though the mine's output from 1856 to 1897 was only 1,763 tons of ore.

The Glen Cherry mine, SC 431890, lies slightly further down the valley. It was little more than a trial, with a South shaft to a mere 15 fathoms but laddering, pump piping and level flooring survives. The deeper 35 fathom North shaft is obscured. Like the East Snaefell mine it was operated by the East Snaefell Mining Co, the Great North Laxey Mining Co and the Glen Cherry Consols Silver Lead Mining Co. The East Laxey mine, SC 454897, was much nearer Corrany bridge and little trace remains. It worked from 1866 to 1869 in search of copper but little was found. It had a fine wheel, *Ellan Vannin*, GBM 24/146, but its case, illustrated in P. G. Ralfe's *Birds of the Isle of Man*, was destroyed about 1910. Either this wheel or that from the Dhoon may have been the wheel moved to Blisland in Cornwall, where it is now to be preserved as the largest waterwheel in England. The Welsh maker's name is correct for the *Ellan Vannin* but as there were several wheels of about 50ft diameter in the Laxey area, and no contemporary account of the move has yet been found, it is impossible to be certain where the Blisland wheel originated.

There are 'old levels' marked on the maps at SC 423885, 424888, 428889, 451898 and in Glion Barrule, SC 439898. There are remains of spoil heaps at the first four but little trace in Glion Barrule. Some trials in the area seeking to extend the Maughold haematite deposits were also made.

The Ballaglass stream continues parallel to the MER track for a short distance and a former power station for this railway may be seen. Soon after the stream passed under the line its waters were used by the Ballaglass mine to turn a wheel, GBM 24/145. This lead mine, operated by the Great Mona Mining Co, worked from 1854 to 1857 and 1866 to 1867 but produced little ore, though its shaft, now obscured, reached to 50 fathoms. In addition to the wheel-case, with the curiously positioned office against it, there are traces of cuttings in the stone of the river channel for the dam head. The mines buildings of local stone are well preserved.

The Maughold Iron Mines. Traces of mining activity may be found in many places on the cliffs of Maughold and on both sides of the valley running north-west from Port Mooar to Port e Vullen. It is likely that some iron ore was obtained here at an early date but unfortunately analysis of material from the Dark Age site at Kiondroghad, NX 397001, and the medieval site at Braddan, SC 364769, did not prove conclusively that the ore being smelted came from Maughold. As with the identification of any ancient ore source, there was the problem that surface exposures would be worked but the samples available for comparison came from deeper levels and might thus be of a different composition. The small workings on Maughold Head operated in the eighteenth century. Drynane was the more important and also yielded large quantities of haematite, 1857–74. Some masonry traces and a level, with sumps, connected to a shaft may be traced. Another working was the Glebe, with two levels on a lode. At Ballajora, to the south of the valley, there were two shafts to 18 and 30 fathoms respectively on the School House lode. This operated mainly from 1858 to 1874. The ore was exported for processing: Slater's *Directory* of 1852 connects 'William Dixon, proprietor, Maughold Iron Ore Mines' and 'the Govan Iron Works, Lanarkshire, Scotland. Andrew Kerr, Manager'. The mines were the subject of a lawsuit and therefore extensive plans and documents survive for consultation in the library of the Manx Museum by anyone wanting to locate all the numerous shafts and adits. Other minerals were obtained in the area: copper was alleged to exist in the Maughold Head mine which worked 1866–7 and the Hope Copper Mine, near Port Mooar, apparently operated in 1846; but the most important was the stained slate that was processed into umber, which was also exported in some quantity.

The Laxey Valley

The MER approach from Douglas is over an interesting bridge, SC 437844, during whose construction the line terminated at the sheds, SC 434842, where much of the rolling stock is still stored. The MER station is in the middle of the upper village and still retains its original booking office, SC 433845. The nearby road bridge, SC 432844, was built as part of the New Road and ready just in time for the opening of the Laxey wheel in 1854.

The Laxey Glen flour mills nestle in the valley beyond the road bridge. They were built by Richard Rowe, the best known of the Mines Captains, and bear his family crest. Behind the flour mills are the Laxey Glen Gardens—with a boating pool, sports area, pavilions, bandstand, open-air dance floor, croquet and bowling lawns, and a fine variety of trees and shrubs, including a eucalyptus over 100ft tall. These gardens were already a popular resort, 'Beauty Spot of Mona' in 1900.

The former Laxey Co-op, SC 432844, now a café, stands on the corner of the station entrance from the New Road; its stable and coalyard have been opened up and developed as a small shopping precinct. Alma House, SC 431846, now called Hillcrest (up the Baldoon road opposite the old Co-op), was reputedly built by the mines company for Casement after he had designed the *Lady Isabella* for them. Just inside the station is Christ Church, SC 433844, built on land given by the mines company, which also contributed to its cost. At the other end of the station, the Station Hotel, SC 433846, was originally the Mines Captain's house; about a third of it was demolished to make way for the MER and what remains has been much altered. The adjoining MER goods shed was the stable for the horses used on the mines tramway to the harbour.

Captain's Hill is the original extension of the Glen road to the upper valley and the mine workings. Below Captain's Hill the Laxey river runs past the washing floors, SC 434846 (see p 18). These have been turned into ornamental gardens but still identifiable are the remains of the walling for races, wheelcases, and the supports for the associated water troughs, settling areas and (under the bridge) the lower part of the Haaman lift, SC 433847. On the far side of the floors can be seen the teams (ore storage bunkers). The tunnel under the Ramsey road, which now houses a transformer, originally carried the mines railway, the track of which can be followed from above the bridge to the vicinity of the adit, SC 433850; the location of the latter is now marked by a substantial spring. Nearby was one of the early trials for copper.

Most of the valley bottom was once occupied by the spoil heaps, 'deads', which towered some 50ft or so above the Mines Road, completely dwarfing Dumbell's Terrace, SC 432847, the long row of miners' cottages. Mines House, SC 432850, is the only house on the right (north) of Mines Road. In the left river bank can be seen the walled-up entrance of the Cross Cut adit with the changing house alongside.

Beyond the mines yard, at the foot of the hill, are the works of Manx Engineers—housed in a former flour mill. The small dam behind provided water for the washing floors and not for this flour mill. The bridge opposite gives access to the Wheel car-park which covers about half the area used by the Switchback, or Browside tramway. At the lower end of the car-park is Cronk e Chule farm, SC 432851, which has the remains of a horse walk. The building nearest the Wheel is not part of the farm but a machine house for the Corner Shaft—now marked only by a depression in the upper corner of the field.

The *Lady Isabella* can hardly be overlooked at this point. The viaduct carrying the pump-rods leads up the valley to the pump head and engine shaft, SC 432854, passing on the way the Mooar Tunnel and the cistern which stored water for the wheel. Both the tunnel and the lade—the latter recently repaired—lead from the cistern to the machine house, SC 432855. The older engine house is high on the hillside above this. On the opposite (right) side of the valley the supply pipe and the cistern feeding the machine house (situated close to the Agneash road) are clearly visible. The Welsh shaft is a little further up the valley and the compressor house is higher still—with its cistern in the field above.

A track from Agneash village leads to Snaefell mines (see p 143) and Dumbell's shaft (with machine house, SC 432860) can be seen opposite it. The Agneash shaft, with remains of a wheelcase, may be

Engine House, Machine House and Cistern, Laxey.

The turbine house, Laxey

located easily in the valley bottom. Still higher up the valley are the remains of a reservoir, SC 433866, and an uncompleted turbine house. Tracks from this area lead 'over the tops' to the Cornaa valley mines.

In the lower valley the lower end of the washing floors was known as Little Egypt, and the large mill on the left bank is the St George's woollen mills, founded to further the ideas of Ruskin and now using hand equipment again. The remains of an automatic weir can clearly be seen in the river just below it. On the right bank of the river, behind Victoria Terrace, is an old mining trial, SC 435841. Lower down on the same bank a small engineering works, SC 435841, was in turn a carpet factory, a power house, a woollen mill and a paper mill. The same race complex also served a turbine house, now a carpenter's shop, and there was another paper mill in this area.

Further down the Glen road is the Methodist Sunday School, SC 438840, and former chapel, SC 439839, now a store for the pipe factory; Methodism had a strong influence on the miners. The remains of Richard Rowe's brewery may also be seen on the left. The old Laxey Co-op, SC 441837, at the junction with Minorca hill, still retains some of its original fittings. The bridge here marks the older crossing-point and beyond it is the harbour. The group of workshops and warehouses near the latter is dominated by the 'Erskine' works, now used as a tobacco pipe factory. The car-park in front of this building occupies the site of the ore compound, where the ore was stored while awaiting shipment.

On the Cairn, SC 443838, out on the cliffs to the south can be seen signs of further mine trials and in the distance the main dynamite store of the mines is visible on Clay Head, SC 440807. The whole Laxey valley is worth a leisurely visit, armed with a large-scale map.

Port Cornaa Limekiln

Near Port Cornaa shore are the remains of a large and convenient limekiln, SC 474877, where limestone imported by sea could be

burned. Port Cornaa is typical of the little sheltered bays used by
local vessels when road transport was difficult and costly. There were
considerable difficulties in carrying unslaked lime but if the stone
was carried costs could be reduced, since a local fuel could be used
for burning—there is peat on the Barony, SC 464877, and timber
does well in the sheltered valley. When local fuel became harder to
find, imported coals would be landed at the same 'port' as the limestone. There are traces of mining trials in the cliffs.

Mills

The history of the manorial Cornaa mill, SC 465898 GBM 24/145,
has already been given (see p 153). In addition to the corn mill,
which had a kiln and a threshing machine, there was a smaller mill
(presumably for breaking flax) just upstream. In 1970 the two mills
and the Cornaa mill house were being converted into modern dwellings. The curious roofless concrete building in the lower Ballaglass
glen was intended to be used as an explosives factory; its history is
obscure but it is alleged to have some connection with Nobel and
bellite production, and work was stopped by a public outcry. Since
there are fittings for a sluice it would appear that the little building
nearly on the shore at Port Cornaa may have housed water-powered
machinery, perhaps a saw mill.

There were several mills near the Corrany bridge, and the right
to operate a mill here may once have belonged to the holder of the
manorial mill for Maughold parish, but the early wheels on this site
were much affected by flood damage. On the left bank, just above
the main road bridge, was a flax mill, SC 453897 GBM 24/029, of
which building remains survive. Its water came from the covered
reservoir just above Glion Barrule. There was also a corn mill,
since destroyed. Both mills were occupied by the Kennish family in
the nineteenth century.

The most substantial mill in Lonan outside the Laxey valley is
Garwick, SC 428817 GBM 24/031. Its whitewashed stone building

is well preserved and its wheel is in a fairly good state, the rather large millstones ornamenting the yard. It is conceivable that this mill will be preserved but rather more probable that it will be converted for use as a dwelling or café. Planning permission has already been sought for the former but the owner intends to preserve the wheel as long as is possible.

SHEADING OF MICHAEL

Mills

The remains of the farm mill in Glen Dhoo, SC 351908 GBM 24/157, indicate the nineteenth-century prosperity of the farm, which is now uninhabited, its fields used only for grazing. The little rectangular building is about 6m by 7m, with walls of local stone and a roof of imported slate. A large depression upstream marks the site of its dam. The Ordnance Survey called it a tuck mill but the few surviving iron cogs suggest a threshing mill. The manorial mill for the parish of Ballaugh, held by the 'Wife of Hugh McCurry' for 15s, was Scrondal, SC 351923 GBM 24/041; it is merely a roofless shell with only slight traces of its leat in the field called *Faaie Wyllin*. On the opposite side of the road a much better preserved threshing mill is used as a store; its wheel trough is lined with fine slate slabs but all its fittings have gone. The mill at Ballaterson, SC 343940, has also been converted into a barn, not having been used as a mill in living memory, possibly because of the inadequacy of its water supply, for the river bed was dry when it was visited for the Survey.

Better preserved until very recently was the Squeen corn mill, SC 345937 GBM 24/033, which has a date stone 1736, though this may merely indicate rebuilding. Most of the machinery was present in 1969 but disintegration was progressing. Curiously enough, though the fittings are moderately well preserved the mill is said to have gone out of use about 1900–10. The stone of the walls has obviously been obtained from an earlier building and includes red sandstone from the Peel area. The fast-crumbling roof is of imported slate. One point to note is the presence of brick-built pigeonholes in the gable over the wheel, a reminder that apparently there were no restrictions on the keeping of pigeons in the Isle of Man, whereas in England this right might be reserved by the Lord of the Manor. Across the yard from the corn mill was a typical threshing mill, destroyed in 1967, which seems normally to have been worked by a horse; there were indications, however, that the power of the wheel might have been used when water was plentiful.

Three stones on top of a sandy hill west of the farm buildings at Ballacooiley, SC 336944, mark the site of a horse-powered mill, where gorse was prepared as feed, and last used at the end of the nineteenth century. Local tradition asserts that this feed gave animals particularly fine coats and rough land was deliberately sown with imported seed to ensure a good supply. The metal-framed wheel, similar to that at Port e Chee, remains at Bishopscourt, SC 331925 GBM 24/114. There was a corn mill in Glen Mooar, SC 305894 GBM 24/160, and some of its millstones survive at the site. Remains are more substantial at Glen Wyllin: originally there was a mill, with lineshaft drive according to T. Brew, near the shore, SC 311907 GBM 24/067, and another, longer established, above the road, SC 316901 GBM 24/027. The latter is sufficiently well preserved for Mr D. H. Jones to have been able to record a full description.

The Killane mill, SC 340969 GBM 24/039, was the manorial corn mill for Jurby: 'From Patrick McBrew for the mill of Carlane, with the freshwater fishing there, by the year, demised to him, 17s'. It collected its water by way of a complicated series of drains from a large area of marsh curragh land; in the seventeenth and eighteenth centuries it was held by members of the Christian family (MMMs 5608–19c). Like most other Manx mills its most recent buildings are of local stone and its roof of imported slate; it has recently been renovated as a dwelling.

SHEADING OF AYRE

Mills

In the Sulby Valley. The site of a Norse-type horizontal corn mill
was excavated in Druidale on the headwaters of the Sulby river.
Such mills were apparently common in the Isle of Man but, unlike
Faeroe, they did not survive into the twentieth century. The
presence of a mill suggests that the pattern of farming and settlement
in the area has changed considerably, a view reinforced by the finding
of a corn-drying kiln of apparently medieval date at the Forester's
Lodge and the positioning of the line of farms, again probably
medieval on the evidence of pottery finds, on the 750ft contour above
the valley. That called Killabrega, SC 375908, has interesting buildings including a horse walk for driving a threshing machine.

Miss M. Quilleash wrote an account of the Sulby mills, which we
are glad to summarise. There was a manorial mill of which all trace
has been lost on the right bank below the Starch mill, SC 381934
GBM 24/094, and the latter is now used as a filter station (for its
history see p 149). The next mill downstream is Southward's woollen
mill, SC 282928 GBM 24/077 (see p 166). There were also mills on
the monastic farm of Ballamanagh, and at least three flour mills—
Staward, SC 385942 GBM 24/042; the Claddagh, SC 395948 GBM
24/043; and the important Kella mill, SC 388947 GBM 24/026. It
would appear that the Sulby river once reached the sea on the west
coast by way of the depression now occupied by the Lhen, though
it now turns east at Sulby and flows to the east coast at Ramsey.
The streams running down from the hills along the first three miles
of its easterly course have short steep beds and at least two farms—
Glenduff, SC 413942 GBM 24/118, and Glentramman East, SC
417940 GBM 24/117—have harnessed their flow to drive farm
machinery. At the latter the shell of the mill building, and the wheel,

are preserved. There was a water-powered bark-mill serving a tannery here in 1837 but the surviving wheel probably belonged to a threshing mill.

Glen Auldyn. The main tributary of the Sulby flows down Glen Auldyn. There was a farm mill near its head, SC 424917 GBM 24/095, but this is now a ruin. There were also two corn mills, SC 433933 GBM 24/045 and SC 437943 GBM 24/030; the latter, Milntown, housed a threshing machine and though it is no longer functional its wheel has been restored. The 'chemical works', SC 432931 GBM 24/091, is a ruin. After the junction with the Glen Auldyn stream the Sulby river reaches the sea by way of Ramsey harbour, but its original mouth lay some distance to the north, about SC 454954.

The Lhen Mill, Andreas. The Lhen mill, NX 379012 GBM 25/001, is listed in the manorial roll, 'From Gilbert McHelly for the mill of Lanmore, with the freshwater fishing there, demised to him 20s'; and like the Killane mill its water was collected from a very large area with very little fall. In 1809 it was bought by the Duke of Atholl from J. Corlett for £600 for each half-share but by 1823 it was estimated that £200 were required for improvements. Thirty-five years later an advertisement for its sale in the *Manx Sun* suggested that farms in the area would be improved if the mill was demolished, so that the drainage could be altered; but the substantial stone building still stands, in fairly good repair, since it has recently been used agriculturally. The dam has been filled in and almost all indications of the original use have disappeared, apart from traces of the wheelpit.

Mines and Quarries

The most imposing relic in the upper Sulby valley is the fine stone-built wheelcase of the 50ft wheel *Fanny*, SC 389869 GBM

24/155, marking the site of an unsuccessful mine operated in 1866–7 by the Sulby River Mining Co. There are other trials visible further down the valley, mainly on the left bank between the valleys leading to Bloc Eary and the Rhenass falls. There are also imposing quarries in the Bloc Eary valley on the north of its entrance and just below the reservoir, SC 389900, and smaller workings in a number of places in the main valley.

Ballacoarey Brickworks

The site consists of a 10 acre field, SC 433988, from about half of which clay has been extracted to a considerable depth. There are remains of three kilns (the 25in plan shows another, now destroyed, nearer the road), a main building and a chimney—all in a fair state of preservation. Local tradition asserts that the works were in operation at least as early as 1825 and a brick and tile manufacturer is listed as working here in the 1851 census. Most of the structures now standing belong to the 1925 re–equipping, when Jones & Sons of Buckley built a 'fourteen-chamber Hoffman continuous kiln' from which waste heat and fumes were led to the brick chimney about 100ft high, tapering from a 24ft base, built by a single bricklayer with assistant labourers in seventeen days. Despite its apparent efficiency the new works only operated one full year. The two twelve-chambered kilns must date from an earlier period of operation, as do the hand moulds lying on the site. The products, samples of which have been deposited in the Manx Museum, were mainly bricks and drainage tiles. The main building has now been adapted for agricultural use.

Mine Outputs

A. TOTAL ANNUAL OUTPUT OF IRON ORE, MAINLY FROM MAUGHOLD (TONS)

Haematite		Spathose iron ore [1] Spathose [2] Haematite	
1855	2,240	1872	[1]122
1858	566		[2]872
1859	1,282	1873	[1]512
1860	1,671		[2]2,256
1861	967	1874	[1]718
1862	647		[2]425
1863	339	1878	100
1865	120	1879	230
1868	220	1880	9
1869	1,291	1881	120
1871	75		

Note: c 1836–40 annual shipment from Glebe Mine was stated to be c 500 tons a month; 1857–84 Drynane Mine working but its ore was in discontinuous 'bunches'; 1858–74 Ballajora was also working and there were other mines and trials in the area.

B. TOTAL ANNUAL OUTPUT OF UMBER, OCHRE, ETC (TONS)

1854	164	1870	142	1878	232
1856	151	1871	172	1879	156
1858	120	1872	148	1880	166
1861	116	1873	248	1881	207
1866	130	1874	156	1882	171
1868	149	1875	183	1883	188
1869	139	1877	170		

The ochre deposits may have been in Bradda or Ballacorkish mines or somewhere in Malew. Umber was also mined in Malew and the Baldroma mine, Maughold. Rotten-stone and Fuller's earth are included in these figures.

C. TOTAL OUTPUT OF LEAD WITH ESTIMATED QUANTITY OF SILVER AND ZINC IN LEAD ORE, 1845–1919

Year	Lead (Tons)	Zinc (Tons)	Silver (Oz)
1845	2,259		
1846	2,316		
1847	2,575		
1848	2,521		
1849	2,826		
1850	2,175		
1851	2,560		33,980
1852	2,415		36,700
1853	2,460		47,105
1854	2,800	1,435	52,262
1855	3,573	3,990	52,203
1856	3,218	3,000	60,382
1857	2,656	2,917	48,016
1858	2,457	2,777	46,985
1859	2,464	—	56,974
1860	2,810	3,181	60,170
1861	2,718	3,255	67,282
1862	2,508	691	70,592
1863	2,561	2,298	74,289
1864	3,118	5,363	125,020
1865	3,143	5,488	147,516
1866	3,494	4,960	178,718
1867	3,799	5,361	172,528
1868	4,290	3,278	176,631
1869	4,302	7,219	145,433
1870	4,604	4,177	163,058
1871	4,645	5,768	161,612
1872	3,529	3,123	183,524
1873	4,371	5,520	170,105
1874	4,204	7,010	186,019
1875	4,429	1,898	110,496
1876	4,353	8,669	100,476
1877	4,464	9,043	59,667
1878	3,920	9,569	84,865
1879	4,358	7,427	129,769
1880	5,119	7,507	125,940
1881	5,675	7,567	123,251
1882	5,494	7,756	132,315
1883	5,828	4,820	135,456
1884	6,007	4,820	134,353
1885	6,868	5,685	138,033
1886	6,257	5,510	139,304
1887	6,560	4,795	129,124
1888	6,356	4,994	125,350
1889	6,433	4,596	124,949
1890	6,141	4,388	122,010
1891	6,682	3,561	111,325
1892	6,698	3,380	120,302
1893	6,427	3,628	107,643
1894	5,624	2,579	91,710
1895	5,287	1,535	76,419
1896	4,953	1,489	72,131
1897	4,273	2,009	66,067
1898	3,948	2,135	
1899	3,924	2,602	
1900	3,843	2,124	
1901	3,774	1,897	
1902	4,192	1,924	
1903	3,604	1,697	
1904	3,274	1,883	
1905	3,070	1,960	
1906	2,511	2,423	
1907	2,103	2,859	
1908	2,699	2,412	
1909	2,520	1,876	
1910	2,014	2,025	
1911	930	1,860	
1912	300	2,050	
1913	300	953	
1914	323	1,621	
1915	229	1,401	
1916	208	865	
1917	165	897	
1918	208	957	
1919	129	787	

No statistics available until 1851

No estimates available for silver for years 1897–1919

o

D. OUTPUT OF GREAT LAXEY MINE BETWEEN 1845 AND 1900

	Copper tons	Zinc-blende tons	Lead tons	Silver contained in lead ore (oz)	Total estimated value (£)
1845	79		327	—	—
1846	92		220	—	—
1847	60		375	—	—
1848			695	—	—
1849	—		815	—	—
1850	—		810	—	—
1851	—		900	—	—
1852	—		800	32,400	—
1853	—		689	28,130	—
1854	64	1,435	900	32,336	—
1855		3,990	800	24,400	—
1856	94	3,000	700	24,675	—
1857	169	2,909	500	17,625	—
1858	403	2,777	600	21,068	—
1859	354	—	800	19,826	—
1860	333	3,181	800	16,936	—
1861	731	3,255	600	11,184	—
1862	942	691	700	16,380	—
1863	1,263	2,298	800	19,440	—
1864	127	5,356	1,250	59,000	—
1865	1,317	5,488	1,500	65,293	—
1866	294	4,960	1,800	81,054	—
1867	400	5,362	2,100	93,365	—
1868	412	3,278	2,300	105,020	—
1869	400	7,208	2,200	101,244	—
1870	300	4,067	2,130	87,760	—
1871	100	5,718	2,300	98,221	—
1872	300	2,973	1,300	52,316	—
1873	—	5,370	2,355	94,870	—
1874	—	6,925	2,100	86,268	58,246
1875	—	11,753	2,400	107,420	90,915
1876	75	8,582	2,500	57,460	85,046[1]
1877	8	8,645	2,222	94,749	77,835
1878	30	9,411	1,395	49,898	52,947
1879	—	7,200	1,200	40,500	46,792
1880	35	7,425	1,300	24,745	53,474

[1] Plus Cu.

	Copper tons	Zinc-blende tons	Lead tons	Silver contained in lead ore (oz)	Total estimated value (£)
1881	—	7,568	1,700	52,500[2]	59,188
1882	—	7,750	1,755	70,200	19,950[2]
1883	200	4,720	1,540	61,600	45,176
1884	—	5,625	1,537	61,188	43,408
1885	236	5,340	1,588	63,219	42,700
1886	—	4,715	1,765	72,030	47,622
1887	—	4,540	1,545	63,052	42,207
1888	46	4,600	1,535	62,643	42,158
1889	—	3,900	1,615	65,908	43,880
1890	—	3,844	1,430	58,359	48,328
1891	—	2,825	1,120	45,708	32,763
1892	—	2,390	943	39,427	24,763
1893	—	2,145	902	36,811	18,701
1894	—	2,040	527	21,507	13,042
1895	—	1,417	403	16,447	8,917
1896	—	1,180	399	15,884	8,762
1897	—	1,610	247	10,080	8,894
1898	—	1,575	138	5,632	9,404
1899	—	1,390	158	6,448	11,831
1900	—	1,216	95	3,877	7,471

[2] Figure uncertain.

E. ANNUAL OUTPUT OF SILVER-LEAD ORE, FOXDALE MINES, 1845–1900

Year	Lead (tons)	Silver (oz)
1845	1,902	
1846	2,071	
1847	2,040	No
1848	1,566	data
1849	1,527	
1850	1,340	
1851	1,660	
1852	1,600	12,224
1853	1,750	18,800
1854	1,900	19,926
1855	2,535	26,756
1856	2,500	35,512
1857	2,125	30,136
1858	1,820	25,807
1859	1,650	37,028

Year	Lead (tons)	Silver (oz)	Estimated value (£)
1860	1,950	43,100	
1861	2,082	56,098	
1862	1,739	53,900	
1863	1,715	54,480	
1864	1,792	65,173	
1865	1,590	57,236	
1866	1,615	65,808	
1867	1,579	70,675	
1868	1,774	72,427	
1869	1,700	69,959	
1870	1,800	81,880	
1871	1,670	75,032	
1872	1,734	86,050	
1873	1,433	57,727	
1874	1,673	67,868	31,563
1875	1,722	73,564	37,804
1876	1,607	65,183	33,284
1877	1,727	87,700	32,314
1878	1,959	53,453	29,753
1879	2,766	55,319	37,363
1880	3,486	49,799	42,993
1881	3,419	69,080	39,145
1882	3,211	48,807	36,356
1883	3,700	48,100	35,100
1884	4,020	51,525	33,500
1885	4,670	59,851	42,400
1886	4,013	51,435	43,000
1887	4,322	55,396	41,500
1888	4,009	59,397	44,600
1889	4,185	62,010	44,400
1890	4,160	61,640	44,500
1891	4,700	69,641	45,200
1892	4,650	73,550	40,250
1893	4,650	73,550	35,400
1894	4,800	85,522	34,430
1895	4,600	359[1]	39,200
1896	4,250	188,473	36,700
1897	3,775	76,697	34,100
1898	3,610	66,125	34,000
1899	3,610	62,515[1]	39,800
1900	3,610	58,905	43,100

[1] Figure doubtful.

F. OUTPUTS OF THE GREAT LAXEY, SNAEFELL AND FOXDALE MINES—
LEAD AND ZINC (TONS), 1900–19

	LEAD			ZINC	
Year	*Laxey*	*Foxdale*	*Snaefell*	*Laxey*	*Snaefell*
1900	95	3,610	138	1,216	908
1901	112	3,550	112	862	1,035
1902	108	3,930	154	963	961
1903	98	3,400	106	1,180	517
1904	129	3,050	95	1,538	345
1905	176	2,850	44	1,685	275
1906	119	2,300	92	2,017	406
1907	213	1,800	90	2,388	471
1908	218	2,408	73[1]	2,103	309[1]
1909	280	2,240		1,876	
1910	294	1,720		2,025	
1911	300	630		1,860	
1912	300			2,050	
1913	300			953	
1914	323—(13,566oz silver)			1,621	
1915	229			1,401	
1916	208			865	
1917	165			897	
1918	208			957	
1919	129			787	

[1] Shaft blocked by fall—not re-opened.

More complete statistics are not readily available, particularly for the 1920s when Laxey was working on a much-reduced scale after a prolonged strike had closed down the old company. The silver values were still quite high at Laxey and were probably enhanced by improved recovery rates. The Laxey ores in 1914 at the mine were worth: Lead £5,007, Zinc £8,593. A mine in the Island produced 74 tons of copper in 1913. This may have been Laxey but could possibly have been Langness, which produced on a small scale. In the 1950s there was some reworking of the deads at Snaefell and Foxdale but mining has not otherwise been resumed.

G. OUTPUT OF LEAD ORE FROM EAST, OR CENTRAL, FOXDALE MINE

Year	Lead (tons)	Silver (oz)	Year	Lead (tons)	Silver (oz)
1872	50	819	1881	400	5,362
1873	135	2,200	1882	450	10,440
1874	58	968	1883	530	15,900
1875	20	280	1884	330	9,839
1876	70	591	1885	325	6,447
1877	198	1,184	1886	319	10,149
1878	360	6,074	1887	418	11,625
1879	360	4,337	1888	250	6,953
1880	250	5,032	1889	92	2,559

Milling Costs 1709–1875

DETAILED extracts from the accounts of a number of mills have been given to provide some indication of costs. It would seem that it took about £500 to erect a new mill and some £20 a year to keep it in repair and fully equipped. Until the mid-nineteenth century wages were fairly static. A labourer received about 1s (5p) a day and a tradesman about twice as much, or his food and a lower daily sum. Building stone was fairly cheap—selected limestone 2s 6d (12½p) a cartload or 12s (60p) a boatload, at the quarry. Cartage was a considerable item and it is noteworthy that a boat, which presumably could hold about four times as much as a cart, was used even for the short journey from Poyllvaish to Rhenwyllin during the building of the smelt mill. Timber, all imported, was expensive: 2s 6d (12½p) a foot for that in the smelt mill wheel or 1s 6d (7½p) a foot for Dantzig baulks (1834). Dressing it was also dear ('Sawing 8 cuts 18 feet long 12 inches wide @ 6d . . . 4 shillings'), since sawing large baulks by hand required two men who were each paid about 2s 6d (12½p) a day. Early Manx mills were thatched but most were subsequently slated. Iron fittings were usually made locally at Douglas foundries, but it is possible that those for the smelt mill were made on the spot, since the mine already had a forge and there is an entry for the freight of coals and iron. Specialist milling equipment was imported, particularly in the later period. Regrettably no early records of the return which might be expected from investment in a mill have come to light but many of them seem to have failed to work profitably despite heavy expenditure on repairs and modernisation.

ACCOUNTS FOR BUILDING THE SMELT MILL, RHENWYLLIN, 1793

AP X50/29

Smelting Mill Accompt

	£	s	d
Mr. Maughen 141 Feet of Timber to the Wheel @ 2s/6d	17	12	6
Mr Taubman 13 Cwt. of Iron @ £1/1s	13	13	0
Messrs. Wm. & Edwd Perry per Bill joined with the Mine	24	18	6
Henry French 30½ Weeks @ £1/1s	32	–	6
Thos. Turnbull Blacksmith 18 Weeks @ 11s/	9	18	–
Speding Hicks & Co. Cast Iron for Bills	68	11	9
Patrick Mulacreast 13200 Slates @ 17/	11	4	4
Wm. Quirk 12500 Do. @ 15/	9	7	6
Edwd. Allison Carting the above Slates from Baruel	12	3	9
Jacob Place 3500 Slates @ 17/	2	19	6
Do. Large Slates	–	5	–
Patrick Tobin for Timber Deals &c per Bill	108	5	–
Thos. Holmes 4 Boat load of Stones from Pulvash	2	8	–
Thomas Cargean Lintles 6 Dozn @ 7/ pr. Dozn.	2	2	–
Thomas Qualtrough Mason 99½ Days @ 2/	9	19	0
Thos. Crystal　　　　　6½ Do. @ 2/	–	13	–
Freight of Coals Bricks as Bill	26	8	–
Thomas Robinson 6 Days @ 1/6 & 5 Days @ 1/4	–	15	8
Wm. Thompson 6 Do. & Do do		15	8
John Richardson 50 Do. @ 1/4 & 21 Do. @ 1/6	4	18	2
Henry Martin 3 Do. @ 1/6 & 4½ Do. @ 1/4	–	10	6
John Gill Mason 26 Days @ 2/–	2	12	–
Thomas Clucas 18 Do. @ 1/4	1	4	–
Willm. Shimmin 12½ Do. @ 1/8 & 11 Do. @ 1/	1	11	10
Robt. Cargean 50 Do. @ 2/–	5	–	–
Richd. Sansome 4 Do. @ 1/–	–	4	–
John Moore Fleshick 21 Do. @ 1/–	1	1	–
John Greasey 16 Do. @ 1/–	–	16	–
Thos. Quirk 6 Do. @ 2/–	–	12	–
Henry Skilley 5 Do. @ 1/–	–	5	–
John Shimmin 38½ Do. @ 1/–	1	18	6
John Walton 40 Do. @ 1/5 & 1 Day @ 1/7	2	18	3

Carried Over　　£377　11　11

	£	s	d
Brought Forward	377	11	11
Peter Woodwoorth	–	1	–
Thos. Holmes Mason 88 Days @ 2/–	8	16	–
Matt^w. Haven Do. 96 Do.	9	12	–
Robt. Davey 50½ Do. @ 1/4	3	7	4
Pat. Kegg 143½ @ 1/1	7	15	5
John Cargean 22 Do. @ 2/–	2	4	0
Thos. Curtis 112½ Do. @ 1s	5	12	6
John Harrison 5 Do.	–	5	–
John Moore Ballacregin 8 Do.	–	8	–
Thos. Nixon 16 Do. @ 1/6	1	4	–
John Taylor 32 Do. @ 1/–	1	12	–
John Dawson 10 Do. @ 1/6	–	15	–
Thos. Dawson 5 Do. @ 1/–	–	5	–
John Carrin 83½ Do. @ 1/4	5	11	4
Pat. Clark 77 Do. @ 1/4	5	2	8
Hen: Morrison 17 Do. @ 1/4½	1	3	–
John Cubin joiner 28 Do. @ 1/2	1	12	8
James Kelly Mason 21 Do. @ 2/–	2	2	–
W^m. Jinrad Do. 55 Do. @ 2/–	5	10	–
Step^n. Longlands Do.86 Do. @ 2/–	8	12	–
Thos. Moore Do. 61 Do. @ 2/–	6	2	–
John Southard 42 Do. @ 1/–	2	2	0
John McGray 7 Do. @ 1/–	–	7	–
John Baxter 43 Do. @ 1/–	2	3	–
John Moore Crossakelly 18 Do. @ –/8	–	12	–
Richd Casteen Mason 16 Do. @ 2/–	1	12	–
Thos. Stokoe Do. 122 Do. @ 2/10	17	5	8
Rich^d. Stokoe — 104 Do. @ 1/–	5	4	–
Silvester Fargher Mason 52 Do. @ 2/–	5	4	–
Phil. Fargher Do. 66½ Do. @ 2/–	6	13	–
Thos. Kannan 36 Do. @ /6		18	–
W^m. Hugon 30 Do. @ /7		17	6
Benj^m. Rowling 6 Do. @ /10	–	5	–

Carried forward £498 8 –

			£	s	d
Brought forward			498	8	0
Ceasor Quirk Mason	18 Days @ 2/–		1	16	–
Robt. Waterson joiner	47½ Do. @ 1/6		3	11	3
John Harrison	11½ Do. @ /10^d		–	9	7
John Morehead	90 Do. @ /8		2	5	–
John Craig	17 Do. @ /8		–	11	4
W^m. Kegg	38 Do. @ /8		1	5	4
Robt. Gelling joiner	34 Do. @ 1/6		2	11	–
John Cubin do.	23 Do. @ 1/8		1	18	4
W^m. Cain do.	41 Do. @ 1/8		3	8	4
Rich^d. Gilbert	14 Do. @ 1/–		–	14	–
John Dawson Cart pr. Bill			54	10	6
Sundries paid to Mill for Bill			20	4	11

			591	13	7
To deduct for Deals Iron &c. sold to miners pr Bill			5	14	2
			585	19	5
To Add to Mr Taubman's Bill	0″ 13″ 0				
To Add to Mr. Tobin's Bill	0″ 11″ 8½				
To Add to Pat. Clarck's acct.	0″ 8″ 8		1	13	4
			587	12	9
To Deduct an over Charge in Mr Perry's Bill			1	18	6
			585	14	3

ACCOUNTS FOR THE DAM AT MULLIN Y CARTY
Ms 90c/3

The Rhenwyllin mill seems to have shared the water supply of the corn mill, so the accounts for the Mullin y Carty fulling mill dam are included to indicate how much it cost to erect a complete mill.

The 16 June 1808
Expences for a Dam head made between/John Shimmin and John Kewn both of the/parish of Kk Malew made for the purpose of/A Cloth mill

		£	s	d
First the said John Shimmin being one day/at the Smithy		0	1	6
Ditto being 3 Days at the Dam head		0	6	0
John Shimmin Junior being 3 Days at Do		0	6	0
Henry Kermod	7 Do	0	14	0
John Quaggin	4 Days Do	0	8	0
Robt. Shimmin	2½ Do	0	5	0
John Shimmin Senior 2 Days		0	4	0
John Shimmin Junior 4 Do.		0	8	0
Thos. Bridson—3 Days at 1^s and 6^d per Day		0	4	6
John Shimmin senior 1 Day		0	2	0
Ditto got (Iron) for the Mill 17^{lb} and ½ at/ 6 pence pr. pound		0	8	6
To repairing 2 Boults and 2 plates		0	0	8
To 6 scrow Boults for the mill		0	3	0
To Repairing the Damhead – – – – – – – –		–	–	–
John Quaggin 3 Days at 2^s pr. Day		0	6	0
John Shimmin Do at Do		0	6	0
John Shimmin junior 3 Days at 2^{s.} pr Day		0	6	0
Thos. Shimmin	3 Do Do at Do	0	6	0
Henry Kermod	1 Do Do at Do	0	2	0
Wm. Shimmin	5 Do Do at Do	0	10	0

British £5 7 2

REPAIRS

Once built mills required constant running repairs which were even more costly after a period of neglect, or a sudden flood.

An Acct. of the Expences towards repairing		£	s	d
1795 the Tuck Mill at Silverburn				
Oct 26th	To 4 Screw pins and Nuts @ 4^d per	0	1	4
	To two pins repaired and new Nuts	0	0	6
	To two pins and two plates repaired	0	0	8
	To an Iron Swingletree wt. 13lbs @ 5^d per	0	5	5
1796				
March 30th	To an Iron Stroke plate wt. 13^{lbs} @ Do	0	5	5
May 15th	To a new bolt wt. 2^{lbs} @ 5^d per	0	0	10
	To a small plate & two wedges	0	0	4
	To two bolts and two repaired	0	0	8
	To a new door for the Mill	0	3	0
	To two new head stocks put in	0	4	0
	To Seven Men to repair the dam head	0	7	0

		£	s	d
Novr. 5th	To two plates for the Swingle tree wt. 1¾lbs	o	o	11½
	To a bolt repaired and a forelock	o	o	7
Decr	To two new hoops for the swingle tree	o	o	6
	To repairing the swingle tree	o	o	7
	To two new wedges wt 1½lbs @ 6d per	o	o	9
	To a new plate for the Stroke wt. 13lbs @ 6d pr.	o	6	6
	To thatching and roping the Mill	o	8	o
1797				
May 5th	To two new hoops for the Efsletree ⎫ wt 26lbs @ 5½d per ⎬	o	11	11
	To two old hoops repaired	o	o	8
	To a pound of nails	o	o	6
	To a Journey to Douglas to speak for ⎫ Gudgeons from (Engineers) ⎬	o	2	o
	To a Journey for myself & horse to get Do	o	2	o
	To attending the Carpenter three days	o	3	o
	To Victuals to three Carpenters three days	o	6	o
		3	13	1½
	To the amount of Jon. Crosss Bill	1	10	o
	Britt	£5	3	1½

ROOFING AT MULLIN Y CARTY, 1796

		£	s	d
December				
13	to thack for the mill	o	4	o
	to Straw ropes maker and thacker	o	2	o
	to the mill repaired with thack	o	2	o

The straw ropes were required because the mill was thatched 'Manx style' with the thatch secured by a network of ropes secured to stone pegs projecting from the walls, and not by wooden pins. Parish mills were supposed to be kept in repair by their bound tenants but Mullin y Carty was a private venture. From the mid-eighteenth century on, slates began to replace thatch in order to reduce the ever-present risk of fire. Between 1753 and 1757 it cost the executors of John Brew £5 1s 2d to slate the house and mill at Mullin y Quinney, Santon, plus £9 6s 11d 'to rebuild the mill' (this probably meant altering the walls to take the slate roof) and £1 0s 9d for repairs to the dam. Manx slates were 15s to 17s a thousand as compared with the following for the Ochre mill, 1834:

April 21	£	s	d
1 hund Doubles slates 4/4 4 hund ladys 28/–	1	12	4

where the sizes indicate the use of imported, probably Welsh, slates and the prices show the penalty of living on an island.

MILLING EQUIPMENT

Early Manx mills probably used local millstones but subsequently the stones were imported, the only indication of their cost being a valuation in the will of John Brew of 'half [a share of] a mill stone 12s 6d'. The stones were dressed with special picks, which, like the sieves for the flour sifters, were imported. Compare the charges for 1834 (A) and 1871 (B):

(A)
Jas Grellier Esq$^{r.}$
            for Ballasalla Mill (Douglas)
                  To Thomas Gelling   –   –   – (Dr.)

	s	d
1834		
April 5 ...		
QUERY[1] Turning 2 large gudgeons	7	0
...		
Augt. 16		
QUERY[1] 4 Steel'd picks 9¼lbs (@) 1/–	9	3

(B)
Cornaa mill [unregistered mss]
John Staniar & Co.   27th February, 1871
Manchester Wire Works

---

[1] The items marked QUERY probably appear in error in Grellier's bill and should have been charged to Moore for his Ballasalla, ie Abbey, mill.

2 Mill chisels 3½lbs	6lb 10oz 1/4	8	10
2 Pointed Picks 4lbs	7lb 10oz	10	2
1 Iron Mill Pick Handle		4	6
Per steamer with best thanks			

Feb. 4, 1875			£	s
	1 Clothing Round Bar for Cyl. 3ft long 16″ diam		1	1
100	oNails for do			2
1	8 Brass Sieve	22 dim.		7
1	10 ,, ,, ,,			7
1	12 ,, ,, ,,			7
	Per Steamer from Liverpool to Ramsey to care of		2	4
	Jno Kneale Miller Ramsey			

MILLWRIGHTS

Not surprisingly, in view of the large number of mills, there were a number of firms that described themselves as millwrights. As yet it has not been proved possible to produce an exhaustive list but the following extracts give some indication of their number and distribution.

1851 census, Lonan parish

		Age	
John Casement	Laxey village	30	—lodger with a miner
William Casement		26 ⎫	
John Casement		25 ⎬	born in Lonan
Edward Cubbon	apprentice m.	13	—unusually young?
Edward Kewley	apprentice m.	19	

Thwaite's Directory, 1863

William Radcliffe	Greenhill, Ayre sheading
James Gill	Ballakeighan, Onchan
James Caine	Onchan—*particularly notable for mine work*
John Killip	(& joiner) Cronk na mona
Thomas Maddrell	Grenaby (the miller)
Cain & Nicklin	Peel Road, Douglas—*also noted for mine work*
Milburn & Dixon	7, Fort Street, Douglas

1871 census, Bride

John Dawson	Regaby
Thomas Cormode	(& joiner) Keeiltushag House
Daniel Lace	Ballayonague
John Tyson	Ballasalla

APPENDIX THREE

RULES AND REGULATIONS for the government of Tromode flax-spinning, bleaching, and sail-cloth manufactory, near Douglas, Isle of Man.

1.—All Persons employed in this Concern are expected to attend on the Public Worship of Almighty God, at least once on every Sabbath Day, and the Parents are earnestly requested to take their Children along with them.

2.—The hours of working are from 6 o'clock in the morning until 7 o'clock in the evening, (except on Saturdays when the Works stop at 5) allowing there-out each day 35 minutes for breakfast, and 45 minutes for dinner.

3.—All the workpeople to be at their work by the time the bell ceases to ring. The bell to ring three times in the morning, once at breakfast and once at dinner-time; if five minutes late $\frac{1}{2}$d, if ten minutes and not exceeding fifteen minutes 1d., if thirty minutes 1$\frac{1}{2}$d. Boys and girls earning less than 4s. weekly to be fined half the same for offences against the rules.

4.—Any Person or Persons absenting themselves from the Works until breakfast-time forfeit quarter of a day's wages.

5.—Any Person or Persons absenting themselves from the Works for a longer period without giving previous notice forfeit one day's wages.

6.—Persons wishing to leave their situations are required to give the Manager notice in the Counting House a week previously (on Thursday night); and prior to any of the Hands being discharged they may expect a similar notice; except in case of misbehaviour, when they subject themselves to be discharged without any notice.

7.—For trespassing on the grounds at the Works, or on the grounds
of any neighbour, bathing in the river or reservoir, or playing at
any game or games on the Sabbath will be fined 1d or
not more than ..   ..

8.—For going to or returning from their work by any
other way than the appointed entrance, ...

9.—All Hands in the Spinning Mill are allowed to go
to the Water Closet five times daily; if they exceed
three minutes each time, fine ..   ..
The Foreman to decide the time.

10.—Any Person or Persons going out of the Mill or to the
Water Closet without pass or permission from the
Foreman, ½d; for losing the pass, ...

11.—Any of the Hands found talking together, and
neglecting their work,

12.—Any Person or Persons employed at the Works
guilty of theft forfeit all wages due, and are discharged
forthwith.

13.—Reelers making unnecessary waste, for each offence

14.—Carelessly breaking or injuring any part of the
machinery or utensils, pay for the damage done.

15.—For profane swearing, using indecent or abusive
language, lifting hands to strike, or striking each other,
not less than 2d., or more than

16.—Any person found reading, or sewing, during working hours, ...

17.—For smoking, or drinking spirits or fermented
liquors at the Works, ...

18.—For bringing, or sending for any spirits or fermented
liquors, or being intoxicated on the premises during
working hours, not less than 1s., or more than 2s. 6d.,
each; if repeated, will be discharged.

19.—For being drunk, or fighting, at any time or place,

20.—Persons practising that obnoxious habit of chewing

P

tobacco in the Shops, are to provide themselves with   S.   D.
spittoons, of a proper size; the sand in which is to be
renewed daily: if neglecting this, or spitting or squirt-
ing tobacco juice on the floor, for each offence,   ..   o   ½

21.—Any Person breaking, or injuring a window, either
at the Works, Cottages, or School-house, shall, in the
course of the week, or sooner, if necessary, have the
same repaired by the Glazier usually employed (if not
put in accordingly, to be done and deducted off their
wages); and if it cannot be proved who broke or injured the window, the expense of repairing it shall be
paid out of the funds arising from the fines; except in
the Dwelling-houses and Hand-weaving Shops,
whose tenants must always be accountable for their
own; and also if it cannot be proved who broke or injured any window or windows in the School-house,
untenanted Cottage, or opposite unoccupied Looms;
the damage must be paid in equal proportions by
the children who are in the habit of throwing
stones.

22.—Neglecting to clean the Road and Gutter weekly,
opposite the door of their Cottages ..   ..   ..   o   3

23.—For introducing any stranger into the Manufactory
without leave from the Master or Manager   2   6

24.—For enlarging holes in the Gas-burners   1   o

25.—For leaving a gas light burning unnecessarily, or
neglecting to extinguish the light on leaving the
premises   ..   ..   o   6

26.—For soliciting a gratuity under any circumstances,
which, if obtained, will also be forefeited to the fund
arising from the fines   1   o

27.—Any Person allowing a discharged power-loom
weaver to work at his hand-loom without permission,   1   o

28.—Reelers for every thread short count under twelve,

		S.	D.
and for every thread over count exceeding twelve in each six cut slipping of yarn, ...		o	½
29.—Preparers for small places in rovings, arising from neglect in not keeping up the ends, for each roving, ..		o	½

30.—Warpers for blunders in warping, to pay the loss occasioned to the Weaver.

31.—The Workers to be supplied with water for drinking in the several rooms by order of the Foreman; and any persons going out themselves for water.. .. ..   o   ½

32.—Any Person leaving the Weaving Shop and going into the Mills or Heckling Room, or any of the Hands leaving their work and going into any other part of the Works, without a necessary errand, not less than 3d., or exceeding .. ..   o   6

33.—For tearing or otherwise defacing these Rules and Regulations.   2   6

34.—Any gratuities or rewards left in the Counting House will be added to the fund arising from the fines.

35.—The fines will be deducted from the Wages and applied to the relief of any of the indigent workpeople when ill, and fines for all offences committed by children, not employed at the Works, will be deducted from the Wages of their parents, or those with whom they live.

36.—All Hands employed at these Works are expected to be Members of the Sick Fund Society for supplying medical aid.

37.—The workpeople are to quit their houses at any time should they be required to do so, on receiving a month's notice.

38.—The same Rules and Regulations apply to piece as well as day-workers.

39.—The Foremen in each room are required to see the lights extinguished before quitting their work. They are also held accountable for the good behaviour of the workpeople placed under them, and for the work being properly executed; due attention and civility are therefore expected to be rendered to persons appointed to such situations, as well as to the other Foreman, and the Manager.

N.B.—The above Rules and Regulations are intended solely for the purpose of maintaining proper order in this establishment, and preventing wasteful and unnecessary expense, and notice is hereby given that they will be strictly enforced.—Moreover, I rely upon the assistance and hearty co-operation of my Work People in detecting all Offenders, and in the carrying out of these measures, always remembering that their own interests are bound up with the interest of their Employer.

W. F. MOORE

Tromode Works, 1st Jan., 1850

R. H. Johnson, Printer, 2, Great Nelson-Street, Douglas.

APPENDIX FOUR

MILLS LISTED IN THE EARLIEST COMPLETE MANORIAL ROLL 1511–1515

Parish	Tenant(s) of Mill	Rent	Mill	Grid Reference and International Mill Survey Number (prefixed 24/25) probable site	
Rushen	Robert McWhaltragh	15s	Kentragh (*Kentraugh*)	225691	090
(Note: Renmolyn (*Rhenwyllin*) is so listed, suggesting that there had already been a mill in the area, though no mill rent was then being paid)				213687	063
Arbory	Gibbon McClement	20s	Colby	231704	061
Malew	John Gretehede	20s	Grenby (*Grenaby*)	265724	060
	William Hubart	30s 8d	'two grain mills near the Castle' (Meadow Mill)	266681	028
Santon	John Wode	⎰ 23s 4d	'for a fulling mill' possibly Glen Grenaugh	314710	070
		⎱ 20s	'for a grain mill'	302712	065
Marown	1. James McTere 2. Gibbon McHelly 3. Fynlo Clerke	6s	'for three small mills'[1]		
			1. also held Ballayemmany now *Eyreton*	3279	
			2. also held Ballanicholas	3075	
			3. also held 'Saurebreck' which was probably near Ballacorris, Santon	3174	
Onchan	John More	7s 4d	Tremote (*Tromode*)	372778	085
	Gibbon McCorkell	4s	'Horaldre', site unknown?	396796	075
	Patric McCray	4s 2d	Crawdle (*Groudle*)	420784	066
	Patric Clerke	12d[2]	'A small mill'—also held Howstrake. Mill possibly on site of 'Burnt Mill'	394773	

[1] Evidence has been produced to show that 'little mill' in the manorial roll can be equated with a Norse-type horizontal mill (*JMM*, Vol IV, no 63, p 199).

[2] There were fourteen pence, Manx, to the shilling.

Parish	Tenant(s) of Mill	Rent	Mill	Grid Reference and International Mill Survey Number (both prefixed 24) of probable site	
Braddan	Donald Abelson & the widow of Mold McKewley	11s	Baldall (*Baldwin*)		
	Otes McTagart	9s 8d	Doway (*Union Mills*)	354778	073
	Thomas McPerson	5s	Medall (*Middle*)	361748	058
Lonan	Gibbon McFaile	16s 4d	Laxay (*Laxey*)	432844	056
	(+ freshwater fishing at 2s)				
Maughold	John McCristen	28s	Cornay (*Cornaa*)	468897	047
Patrick	Nicholas Alcar Reginald Crosse Thomlyn McKye Huan Worthyngton	11s 8d	Holmtoun (*Peel*)	240837	034
	Jenken McCaly & Thomas Kerdar	12s 8d	Glen Moy (*Glen Maye*)	235795	051
	Patric Bane Gilbert More	7s 4d	Balyhig (*Mullin y Cleigh*)	278813	048
	Monastery of Rushen	3s 4d	'water to the Abbot's mill' (*Abbey brickworks* near site)	265822	072
Michael	Richard McFayle	22s	Bordall (*Glen Wyllin*)	316901	027
Ballaugh	Wife of Hugh McCurry	15s	Scrondall (*Scrondal*)	351924	041
Jurby	Patric McBrew	17s	Carlan (*Killane*)	340969	039
	(+ freshwater fishing)				
Lezayre	John McCaly	26s	Soulby (*Sulby*)		
	John McCristen	7s 5s	Breryk Altadale (*Glen Auldyn*)	?433933	045
	(+ freshwater fishing)				
	Wife of Murghad McCowle	7s	Alia Altadale		
Andreas	Gilbert McHelly	20s	Lanmore (*Lhen Mooar*)	25/379012	001
	(+ freshwater fishing)				

APPENDIX FIVE

PROVISIONAL LIST OF MANX BREWERS AND BREWERIES—IN ROUGHLY
CHRONOLOGICAL ORDER

As far as possible, but without exhaustive checking of deeds, successive occupants of a brewery have been listed. Most of the list has
been taken from directories where the fact that more than one
brewer was working at a given brewery may be obscured. However,
it seemed worthwhile to compile this list to give an indication of a
possible area of research.

Ref No	Town	Brewer's name(s)	Location, etc	Date(s)
1	DOUGLAS	(a) unknown	The Howe, SC 382752	1793
		(b) Gelling, Robert		1807–9
		(c) Cosnahan & Forbes	possibly not brew-ing	1817
			—probably empty	1820–30
		(d) Thomson, S.		1831
		(e) Young, J. & C. (Charles Young, 1837–8, licence)		1831
			from Kewaigue	1833
			becomes preserved potato works	1846
2		Mullen	unknown	1793
3			The Hills—sold up	1794
			—offered for sale, etc	1820–36
4		Kelly, Paul	'far end of the Sand Side'	1794
5			Lake brewery, SC 379753	1779
		(a) Critchley, John		1820
		(b) Cochrane & Co (ie, with P. Quirk)		1821

Ref No	Town	Brewer's name(s)	Location, etc	Date(s)
		(c) R. Cochrane & Co		1825
		(d) Curphey, Ed & Co		1837
		(e) Hogg, John		1843
		(f) Hogg & Co		1846–63
		(g) Clinch, J. W. (Dissolved Company files 204 Clinch's Brewery Co Ltd 29.8.1948)		1868
6		Cubbin, Thos	Cattle Market St/ Sand St (tannery/ brewery)	180?–2?
7		Moore, Mr (later Mrs)	Duke St	1804–25
8		Cosnahan, Mark		1809–18
9		Curphey, Thos	Bigwell St	1823
			—for sale	1826–9
10		Maddrell, Wm	Factory Lane to	1820
11		(a) Robinson, James	Hanover (Princes) St	1810–12
		(b) Hastings, Robert		1816–24
		(c) Whittingham, R.—from Nunnery	? All at	1825
		(d) Nelson, John—licence 1837–8	same site	1837
		(e) Kelly, William		1843–6
12		(a) Merryweather, R.	Society Lane	1813
		(b) Maddrell—as 10?		1817
		(c) Radcliffe, John		1829
13			King St	1820–3
14	BALLAUGH	(a) Taubman, Moore & Quayle —issued card money from this address		1809–20
		(b) Taubman, James (Ballacrosha) (both licensed 1837–8—? two breweries)		1837–46
		Taubman, Thomas (Ballaugh)		1837–43
		(c) Taubman, Robt		1852
		(d) Taubman, James		1857
15	BALLACREGGAN		near Ramsey	1823
16	BALLAQUANE		near Peel	1831
17	CASTLETOWN	(a) Faulder, J.—correspondence with Ed Gawne, Atholl Papers X/41–23, etc		1823
		(b) Faulder, Thos	Market Place	1824

Ref No	Town	Brewer's name(s)	Location, etc	Date(s)
		(c) Faulder & Primrose—licence		
		1837–8	Arbory St	1837
		(d) Faulder, Henry	Arbory St	1843
18	GLEN WYLLIN	(a) unknown	possibly two	1820
	Michael	(b) Giles	sites in use	1830
		(c) Gell, Evan—licence 1837–8		1837
		(d) Cannell, Susan		1843
		(e) Cannell, Susannah		1846
		(f) Cannell, Louisa		1857
19	LAXEY		British brewery	1808–27
20		Taubman	'near the shore'	1814–34
21		Dobree	Laxey Gill	1818
22	MOUNT GAWNE,	(a) Gawne family, owners	SC 215687	by 1793–1826
	Gansey	(b) Gawne & Connal—licence		
		1837–8		1837
		(c) Connal, Michael		1843
		(d) Connal & Co		1852
23	PEEL	Crane		1802
24	POOLDHOOIE		near Ramsey	1827
			SC 442949	
25	RAMSEY	Christian, John		1809
26	SULBY		Kella c SC 390948	1824
27	DOUGLAS	Curphey, Thos		
		? moved from 9	Atholl St	1824
28		(a) Davidson, Cochrane	Fort St	1823
		(b) Davidson & Garrett	(Union brewery)	
		(c) Garrett, Thos		1824
		(d) Garrett, Thos & Son	Cattle Market St	1839–52
		(e) Garforth, Samuel		1863
29		(a) Kayll, John James—Atholl		
		Papers III [2nd] 36		1822
		(b) Kayll, James	Castle St, possibly	
			c SC 382759	sold 1840
30		Kewin, Douglas	Duke St	1824
31		(a) Killey, Wm—& Tanner	Castle St	1824
		(b) Killey, Philip—licence 1837–8	possibly as 30	1837–52
			c SC 382759	
32		White, Thomas	Parade St	1824
33		(a) Whittingham, Richd	Nunnery mill	1824
		(b) Cain, James—no licence		
		1837–8	SC 374752	1825–36
34	CASTLETOWN	Quayle, John	(i) The Parade	1824

Ref No	Town	Brewer's name(s)	Location, etc	Date(s)
		(a) Quayle, John—licence 1837–8	(ii) Douglas St	1837–52
		(b) Quayle, Robert & Co	SC 265675	1857
		(c) Bell, John	SC 265675	1882
		(d) Boddington (IOM) Ltd		
		(Dissolved Company file 132)		6.4.1900
		(e) C'town Brewery Ltd,		29.8.1948
		258 C'town Brewery (1906) Ltd		(still working)
35	LAXEY	Simpson, Mathew		1824
36	PEEL	Carren, Thos		1824
37	RAMSEY	Cowley, Daniel		1824
38		Kneen, Wm		1824
39		Mylrea, Daniel		1824
40	DOUGLAS	(a) Young, J. & C. (to Nunnery)	Kewaigue	to 1833
		(b) Cain, Shimmon & Co		1837
		(c) Cain, Nelson & Co—licence 1837–8		
41		Kelly, William—licence 1837–8, possibly moves to 11	Shaw's Brow	1837
42		Radcliffe, John—licence 1837–8	Strand St	1837–43
43	BALLAKILLEY	Bell, Thomas, jnr ⎱ No licence	near Castletown	1837–52
44	BALLASALLA	Kermode, John ⎰ 1837–8	near Castletown	1837
45	LAXEY	Lace, John—licence 1837–8	Laxey Glen	1837
46		Kelly, William—? as 41		1843–6
47		Kermode & Co		1852
48		Thompson, Samuel—no 1837–8 licence, ? from Howe brewery, Douglas		1837
49	PEEL	(a) Clark, Philip—1837–8 licence	Custom House St	1837
		(b) Clark & Quayle	Harbour	1843
		(c) Clark, Robert	Custom House St	1852–7
50		Oates, Michael—1837–8 licence	Quay	1837–46
51	MAUGHOLD	Matheson, Dugald—1837–8 licence		1838
52	ONCHAN	Alexander & Best—1837–8 licence		1838
53	RAMSEY	(a) Moore, Thomas—1837–8 licence	(i) Lezayre St	1837
			(ii) Albert Row	1843
			(iii) Tower St	1852
		(b) Dobson, Francis	Royal Albert brewery	1857
		(c) Ware, John		1863
		(Dissolved Company files 145)	Royal Albert brewery	13.10.1923

Ref No	Town	Brewer's name(s)	Location, etc	Date(s)
54		Paton, William—1837–8 licence	Milntown, SC 436942	1837
55	DOUGLAS	(a) Alexander, Henry—possibly as 52	Castle Hill brewery	1843
		(b) Dutton, Lionel Courtier	SC 380763	1846
		(c) Dutton, Jane & Courtier		1852
		(d) Atkins, George & Co		1857–63
		(e) Brown, John		1882
56	BALLAUGH	Dougherty, Robert		1846
57	RAMSEY	M'Dowell, William	Lezayre Rd	1852
58	DOUGLAS	Garforth & Castle (Samuel Garforth at 28, by 1863)	Cattle Market St	1857
59		(a) Okell, William	Falcon Patent brewery	1857
		(b) Okell, Wm & Son	SC 382764	1882 (still working)
60		Allen, Wm, Mona Brewery— possibly as 28	1 Cattle Market St	1882
61		Roberts, Thomas	Back Strand St	1882
62		Woolf's (& mineral waters) (Dissolved Company files 108)	Ballaughton	1882 22.8.1923
63	RAMSEY	(a) Finn, James	West St	1863
		(b) Radley, William	4 West St	1882

APPENDIX SIX

Glass bottle* and stoneware bottle† indicated thus are preserved in Manx Museum. *Italics* indicate name of bottle maker and brackets ( ) date of directory entries.

Allen & Taubman:† stone ginger beer, Ramsey (as grocers, 1882)

Boddington IOM Ltd:* product unknown, bottle corked (Castle Rushen brewery)

Castletown Mineral Water Co: Geo Dodd secretary, John Dowis manager, 1889—castellated entrance to works survives

Chrystal Bros: Bowring Road, Ramsey (1889)

Corlett, J. J.:* Sulby Glen Mineral Waters—carpenter's square as trademark. Works near Kella mill (1889)

Dixon, J. C.: Back Berkeley Street, Douglas (1894)

Dodd, I. M.: see Castletown Mineral Water Co (1894)

Downward's, Aldcroft Ltd: various name changes, firm still operates †'Stone Ginger Beer/Lake Works/Douglas & Ramsey IOM, six-pointed star round AD monogram, also *

Dury Evans:* Douglas Road. *Eclipse Reg. Trade Mark 41859*

Harris, W.:* 'Mineral Water Manufacturer/Douglas'

Heron & Brearley Ltd:* still survives, primarily as a bottler and shipper for the licensed trade.

Irving, J.:† Special Brewed Ginger Beer, Peel. *Pearson & Co Whittington* (1894). Firm still survives in Peel

Joyce Joseph: St Peter's Lane, Peel (1889)

Kelly's Minerals, Hill Top, Braddan—still operating

Manx Mineral Water Co: (1894) presumably Douglas

Marsden, John: St Peter's Lane, Peel (1894)—possibly succeeded Joyce

Marsden & Co:* Drumgold Street, Douglas (1894)

Meyer IOM: bottle known—probably Douglas

Mona Aerated Water:* JC monogram

Mona Aerated Mineral Water Co: P. T. Screetch, Secretary, Rope Walk Road, Woodbourne Works (1882 and 1889)

Mona's Pride Mineral Water Co:* *Dan Ryland, Barnsley*

Moore, Thomas:* The Douglas Mineral Water Works—with a tower as trademark (1889 8 Castle Street; 1894 Brunswick Road)

Pritchard, T. M.: 5 West Quay, Ramsey (1882)

Qualtrough & Co:* established 1854 and still operating. Main works on left bank at Stone bridge, Douglas, but also at the Shipyard, Ramsey, in 1894

Sidebotham, William: ginger-beer maker, 17 Church Street, Douglas (1846)

Silverburn Glen Aerated Water:* *Cannington Shaw & Co Ltd, St Helens*. This works was in the small building upstream of the Creg mill dam, SC 274711. (1889) John Davies, proprietor

Sulby Glen: see Corlett, J. J.

Swindley & Co:* 1 Market Street, Douglas. † Stone brewed ginger beer (1889)

Thompson, Taylor & Rhodes: Fort Street, Douglas (1882)

Union Mills Aerated Water Works*

Williamson, Robert:* Laxey Glen, with the Great Laxey Wheel as trademark. Works near the present Commissioners' Office, SC 434841 (1882, 1889, 1894)

Woolf's Brewery Co Ltd:* Spring Valley, Douglas (1889–94)

Wylde, Thomas P.:* Christian Street, Ramsey (1894)

This list gives all firms identified before May 1970 but as there are no local directories for the period 1900–69 other early twentieth-century firms may well have existed. Some of these may have used paper labels on standard bottles and thus be difficult to trace until all the local newspapers have been indexed. Almost all the named glass bottles preserved are of the 'marble in a pinched neck' type but plain egg-shaped bottles are quite frequent.

Bibliography and Sources

ABBREVIATIONS

An asterisk indicates works of major importance, such as:
*Cubbon, William. *A bibliographical account of works relating to the Isle of Man*, 2 vols (1933 and 1936)
This is an invaluable guide to works relating to the Island and in most cases it has been thought unnecessary to duplicate its entries.

MANUSCRIPT SOURCES IN THE MANX MUSEUM LIBRARY

AP   Atholl Papers   —records relating to the connection of the Dukes of Atholl with the Isle of Man and mainly concerned with payments in connection with the 'manorial' rights of the Lordship.

BHP Bridge House Papers—records of the Quayle family of Bridge House, Castletown, particularly those concerned with mills.

NSS Northside sales and
SSS Southside sales   —official records of the transfer of land and properties.

NEWSPAPERS

The Manx Museum has fairly complete files, the earliest of which have been indexed. The more important as sources for industrial history are:

Manks Mercury (& Briscoe's Douglas Advertiser)	1793–?1801
Manks Advertiser	1801–42
The Rising Sun or Mona's Herald	1821–4
becoming *The Manx Rising Sun*	1824–6
and *The Manx Sun*	1826–1906
Mona's Herald	1833 ⎫
Isle of Man Times	1861 ⎪
Isle of Man Examiner	1880 ⎬ to present
Peel City Guardian (still hand set)	1882 ⎪
Ramsey Courier (now *Isle of Man Courier*)	1884 ⎭

DIRECTORIES

During the nineteenth century the Isle of Man was included in several national directories and after 1863 directories were issued for the Island only. Regrettably there is no full directory 1900–60, although *Mercantile Manxland* (1900) gives some information and Barrett's Publications of Blackpool produced a *Douglas, IOM Directory* in 1955.

pages covering
IOM

1824 ⎱ *Pigot & Co's National Commercial Directory, Ireland, Scotland*   ⎰ 16
1837 ⎰   *& important English towns*   ⎱ 32
1843   *Pigot & Slater's General & Classified Directories of Liverpool,*
            Manchester, etc   26
1846 ⎫ *Slater's National & Commercial Directory of Ireland, im-*   ⎧ 32
1852 ⎬   *portant English & Scottish towns etc*   ⎨ 24
1857 ⎭   ⎩ 36
1863   *Thwaite's History & Directory of the Isle of Man*
1882 ⎱   ⎰ (1881 on
1894 ⎰ *Brown's Directory of the Isle of Man*   ⎱ title page)
1889   *Porter's Directory of the Isle of Man*

GENERAL HISTORIES, GEOGRAPHIES, ETC

*Birch, J. W. *The Isle of Man: a study in economic geography* (1964). Particularly
    valuable for the tourist trade.

Craine, D. *Manannan's Isle*, Manx Museum (1955)

Freeman, T. W., Rodgers, H. B., & Kinvig, R. H. *Lancashire, Cheshire & the Isle
    of Man* (1966)

*Kinvig, R. H. *A history of the Isle of Man* (1950)

*Lamplugh, G. W. *The Isle of Man. Memoirs of the Geological Survey of the United
    Kingdom* (1905). A vital source for the mines

*Moore, A. W. *A History of the Isle of Man* (1900)

MANX LEARNED PERIODICALS

The Isle of Man Natural History and Antiquarian Society was founded in 1879.
It publishes papers read to it, with some additional matter. The titles have been:

Transactions, vol I (1879–84)—a manuscript index exists (in Manx Museum) to
    earlier numbers

Yn Lioar Manninagh (YLM), vol I (1880–92), II (1892–5), III (1895–1900), IV
    (1901–5)

Proceedings and Transactions (1906 to present)

The Manx Museum was founded under an Act of Tynwald in 1886. It publishes
a variety of guidebooks and, since 1924, *The Journal of the Manx Museum*, which
normally appears annually (*JMM*).

Some of the more relevant papers in the above periodicals have been cited under
the appropriate chapter headings.

CHAPTER TWO (*The Sea*. Page 21)

SHIPS AND SHIPBUILDING

Bersu, G., & Wilson, D. M. *Three Viking graves in the Isle of Man*, The Society for
    Medieval Archaeology Monograph series, no 1 (1966)

Corlett, E. C. B. 'The iron tank ship "Ramsey" 1863–1883', *JMM*, vol VI, no 81,
    p 233

Craine, D. 'A Manx merchant of the 18th century', *Proc NHAS*, vol IV, p 640

Greenhill, Basil. 'The Schooner, "Peggy", unique survival of the 18th century', *JMM*, vol VII, no 84 (1968). A number of other accounts have been written of this vessel and there is also a *Guide to the Nautical Museum, Castletown* in which she is housed
Kermode, P. M. C. 'Ship burial in the Isle of Man', *Antiquaries Journal*, vol X, no 2 (April 1930)
McMullen, Jerry. *'Star of India' the log of an iron ship*, Berkeley, USA (1961)
Megaw, B. R. S. 'The Development of Manx fishing craft', *Proc NHAS*, vol 5, and contemporary newspapers, BHP (Manx Museum), and other manuscript records
Serjeant, Ruth. 'The Graves family of Peel', *Proc NHAS*, vol VI, no 4, p 509
Teare, E. M. 'Old Peel', *Proc NHAS*, vol VI, no 3, p 295

THE ISLE OF MAN STEAM PACKET CO LTD
Many ephemeral publications and articles have appeared but the more valuable works are:
Duckworth, C. L. D. & Langmines, G. E. *West Coast Steamers* (1953), chap 1
Henry, F. *Ships of the Isle of Man Steam Packet Co* (Glasgow 1962)
Moore, A. W. (based on research by). *The centenary of the IOM Steam Packet Co Ltd 1830–1930* (Liverpool)

ANCILLARY TRADES
Official catalogue of the International Fisheries Exhibition (1883)
Mercantile Manxland (1900)
'William Knox's Net-hauling gear and windlass', *Marine Engineer* (1 Oct 1883)
Serjeant, Ruth, op cit
Teare, E. M., op cit
Also contemporary newspapers and directories, and AP (Manx Museum)

HARBOURS
Brown, J. C. *The Harbours of the Isle of Man* and *Radar for Harbour Control* (The Dock and Harbour Authority, May 1939 and April 1948)
'The Story of Douglas Harbour', *Proc NHAS*, vol V, p 350
Numerous reports of Commissioners, etc, and documents in the possession of the Isle of Man Harbours' Board, for whose co-operation thanks are due.

LIGHTHOUSES
'Lighting the Scottish & IOM Coasts', *Engineer* (4 Oct 1901)
Stevenson, D. Alan. *English lighthouse tours 1801, 1813, 1818—from the diaries of Robert Stevenson* (1946)
The World's lighthouses before 1820 (1959)
Reports, petitions and instructions to pilots, eg 1815 Enabling Act to allow the Commissioners for Northern Lights to erect lighthouses on the IOM and Calf, and 1853 *Returns of the numbers & situations of the lighthouses in or around the coasts of the IOM.*

CHAPTER THREE (*Service Industries*. Page 39)

RAILWAYS AND TRAMWAYS
One of the few areas of Manx industrial archaeology with many works in print.
Q

The more important include:
Boyd, J. I. C. *The Isle of Man Railway*, 2nd ed (1967)
Macnab, I. *A History and Description of the Isle of Man Railway*, 2nd ed (1968)
Pearson, F. K. *Isle of Man Tramways* (1970)
  Isle of Man Tramways Album (The Douglas Cable Car Group, 1968)
Wyse, W. J. & Joyce, J. *Isle of Man Album* (1968)

SERVICES
'Castletown first lit by gas', *Manx Sun* (5 August 1854)
History and description of the Corporation's waterworks (Douglas Corporation, 1958)
Russell, R. T. 'The West Baldwin reservoir railway', *JMM*, vol VI, no 80, pp 205–8
Stevenson, E. H. & Burstal, E. K. 'The sewage of Douglas', *Proc Inst of Civil Engineers* (date unknown)
Also *Douglas Waterworks Act* (1834), *Douglas Gas Act* (1836), and other enabling acts.

CHAPTER FOUR (*Extractive Industries*. Page 49)

*Jespersen, A. *The Lady Isabella Waterwheel of the Great Laxey Mining Co Isle of Man 1854–1954* (Copenhagen, published by the author). In addition to a complete description of the wheel, this contains plans, sections and descriptions of the mines
*Lamplugh. Memoirs of the Geological Survey, op cit
*Mackay & Schnellmann (consulting geologists and mining engineers). *The Mines and Minerals of the Isle of Man*—a report submitted to the Industrial Officer (duplicated copies in Manx Museum library). Largely a study of the possibility of reviving mining but with valuable sections on most major mines. It was clearly typed by someone unfamiliar with Manx placenames, which makes it confusing to use. Report on work 1953–7
For the medieval workshop on the Ronaldsway airport site, see B. R. S. Megaw, *JMM*, vol VI, no 77 (1960–1), p 105. The charter was apparently lost in the fire which damaged many Cotton mss but it is quoted in full from an early transcription in *Manx Society*, vol VII, pp 79–81.
The Manx Museum library has a considerable amount of manuscript material relating to the mines as well as printed items such as prospectuses, reports and share certificates. See Cubbon, W., *Bibliography*, pp 110–15.

CHAPTER FIVE (*The Tourist Industry*. Page 99)

This is almost entirely based on information found in guidebooks and newspapers and answers to the industrial archaeology questionnaires. Official statistics and reports have been consulted for the later period. Directories have also proved useful.

CHAPTER SIX (*Traditional Manufacturing Industries*. Page 127)

METALWORKING
AP X/10–28. John Stowell's plating mill at Ballasalla
AP 137–10, 11. Rhenwyllin mill. Also Mss 669A p 262 and SSS, Oct 1795–57, for the Duke of Atholl's purchase.

Bruce, J. R. 'John Murrey's smelthouse, Derbyhaven', *JMM*, vol VI, no 78, pp 152–4
Garrad, L. S. 'The Castle Rushen Mint', *JMM*, vol VII, no 82, pp 6–8
Killip, I. M. 'Spades in the Isle of Man' in *The Spade in Northern and Atlantic Europe* (Ulster Folk Museum, 1965)
Megaw, B. R. S. ' "Bakenaldwath" and the medieval lead mines', *JMM*, vol VI, no 77, pp 105–7
The Castle Rushen papers *Receipts & Disbursements* contain much information about the early working of the mines, smelting and the setting up the Castle Rushen Mint.

BRICKWORKS
Ballacoarey—*Isle of Man Examiner* (14 January 1927)
Castletown—the Castle Rushen inventory of c 1694 gives information about the Earl's attempt to promote brickmaking
Eames. E. 'A Tile Kiln site at North Grange, Meaux, Beverley, Yorks', *Medieval Archaeology*, vol V (1961)—covers Cistercian tile kilns.

PAPERMAKING
Cubbon's *Bibliography* has illustrations of watermarks, pp 1467–93
Williamson, K. 'Paper making in Man', *JMM*, vol IV, no 59, pp 126–9 and no 60, pp 147–51
Mercantile Manxland (1900) gives information about virtually all firms of importance at this time. It was probably a directory in which firms purchased entries.

MILLS—GRAIN AND FEED
Jones, D. H. 'Manx Water-mills', *JMM*, vol VII, no 82 (1966), p 11—and set of maps showing mill sites deposited in Manx Museum; also copy of list giving international mill numbers
Megaw, B. R. S. 'Mwyllin Beg: An account of the Horizontal mills', *JMM* vol IV, no 63 (Dec 1940), p 199
'More about the Little Watermills', *JMM*, vol V, p 147
Quine, Canon. 'A history of Manx milling', *Milling* (June 1925), p 9

TEXTILE MILLS
Cowley, J. W. 'The Manx woollen industry through ten centuries', *Proc NHAS*, vol VI, no i, p 39
Mathieson, Neil. 'A forgotten factory: Port-e-Chee Cotton mill 1772–80', *JMM*, vol VI, no 74 (1957), p 25, and no 75 (1958), p 62
Quilleash, Miss M. 'The last of the Sulby mills', *Proc NHAS*, vol VI, no iv, p 503
Rydings, Egbert. 'John Ruskin and the Laxey Woollen Mills', *The Young Man* (July 1895)

Acknowledgements

THE authors wish to thank all those people who completed Industrial Archaeology questionnaires and their fellow members of the Field Section of the Isle of Man Natural History & Antiquarian Society, without whose research this book could not have been written. Particular thanks are also due to the staff of the Library of the Manx Museum and the General Registry, Douglas. Special acknowledgement must be given to Mr Frank Cowin for material on the Great Laxey mines, Mr B. E. Crompton for information on railways and tramways, Mr M. C. P. Apps for research on Mullin y Quinney mill, Mr F. J. Radcliffe for investigating the mills of Ballaugh, and Mr D. H. Jones and Mr J. K. Major for encouragement in the study of mills and the plan of Squeen mill. Other illustrations are mainly by the courtesy of the Manx Museum and National Trust, and the Derbyshire Caving Club, or were commissioned from Manx Press Pictures. Maps and plans have otherwise been compiled by the authors.

Index